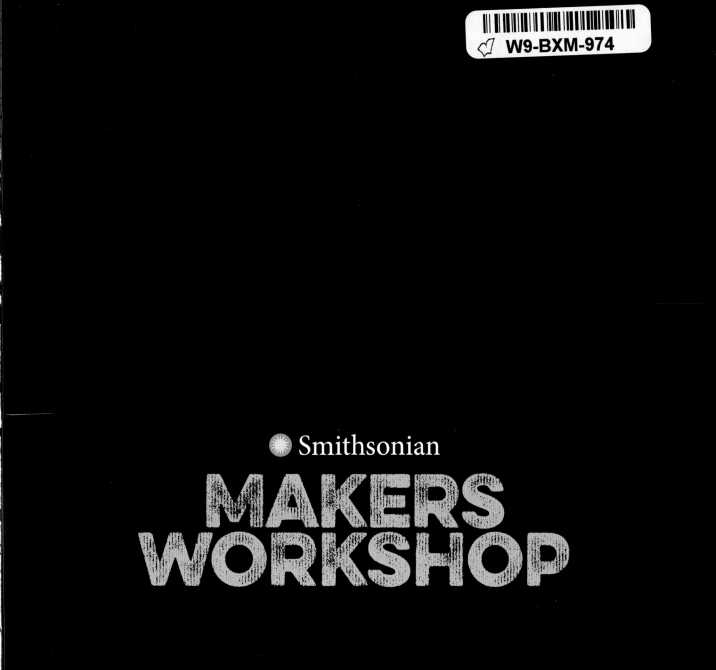

Smithsonian

MAKERS WORKSHOP

Smithsonian

MAKERS WORKSHOP

**FASCINATING HISTORY & ESSENTIAL HOW-TOS
GARDENING, CRAFTING, DECORATING & FOOD**

HOUGHTON MIFFLIN HARCOURT
BOSTON · NEW YORK · 2020

SMITHSONIAN® and the Smithsonian® logo are registered trademarks of the Smithsonian Institution. Used under license

For information about permission to reproduce selections from this book, write to trade.permissions@hmhco.com or to Permissions, Houghton Mifflin Harcourt Publishing Company, 3 Park Avenue, 19th Floor, New York, New York 10016

hmhbooks.com

Library of Congress Cataloging-in-Publication Data is available

ISBN 978-0-358-00864-4 (pbk)

Book produced by Waterbury Publications, Inc.

Printed in China

SCP 10 9 8 7 6 5 4 3 2 1

CONTENTS

Design & Decorating

Gardening

Introduction

The Smithsonian Institution is the keeper of American history and culture. *Makers Workshop* explores our history of a hands-on domestic life and inspires new generations to keep that tradition and grow it for generations to come.

THE STORY OF THE SMITHSONIAN

The Smithsonian Institution was established with funds from James Smithson (1765–1829), a British scientist who left his estate to the United States to found "at Washington, under the name of the Smithsonian Institution, an establishment for the increase and diffusion of knowledge."

Congress authorized acceptance of the Smithson bequest on July 1, 1836. After a decade of debating, on August 10, 1846, the U.S. Senate passed the act organizing the Smithsonian Institution, which was signed into law by President James K. Polk.

Once established, the Smithsonian became part of the process of developing an American national identity—an identity rooted in exploration, innovation, and a unique American style. That process continues today as the Smithsonian looks toward the future.

THE WORLD'S LARGEST MUSEUM COMPLEX

Smithson, the illegitimate child of a wealthy Englishman, traveled much during his life but never set foot on American soil. Why, then, would he decide to give the entirety of his sizable estate—which totaled half a million dollars, or 1.5% of the United States' entire federal budget at the time—to a country that was foreign to him?

Some speculate it was because he was denied his father's legacy. Others argue that he was inspired by the United States' experiment with democracy. Some attribute his philanthropy to ideals inspired by such organizations as the Royal Institution, which was dedicated to using scientific knowledge to improve human conditions. Smithson never wrote about or discussed his bequest with friends or colleagues, so we are left to speculate on the ideals and motivations of a gift that has had and continues to have such significant impact on the arts, humanities, and sciences in the United States. Visitors can pay homage to Smithson with a visit to his crypt, located on the first floor of the Smithsonian Castle.

A LEGACY DELIVERED

Smithson died in 1829, and six years later, President Andrew Jackson announced the bequest to Congress. On July 1, 1836, Congress accepted the legacy bequeathed to the nation and pledged the faith of the United States to the charitable trust. In September 1838, Smithson's legacy, which amounted to more than 100,000 gold sovereigns, was delivered to the mint at Philadelphia. Recoined in U.S. currency, the gift amounted to more than $500,000.

▶ The Smithsonian Institution Building, popularly known as the "Castle," is an iconic symbol of the museum. It served as the home and office of the first Secretary of the Smithsonian, Joseph Henry.

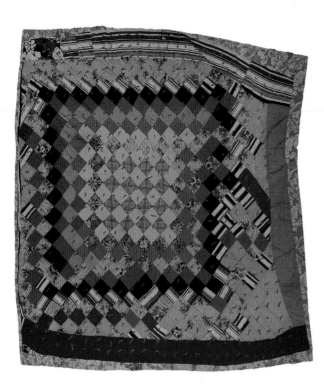

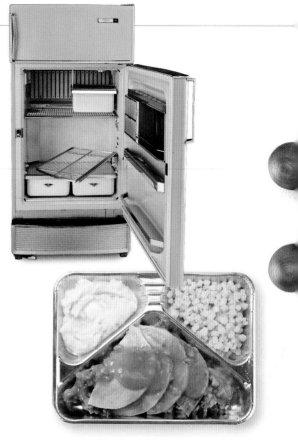

After eight years of sometimes heated debate, an Act of Congress signed by President James K. Polk on August 10, 1846, established the Smithsonian Institution as a trust to be administered by a Board of Regents and a Secretary of the Smithsonian.

Since its founding, more than 175 years ago, the Smithsonian has become the world's largest museum, education, and research complex, with 19 museums that contain more than 156 million objects, the National Zoo, and nine research facilities.

BRINGING HISTORY HOME

The Smithsonian has become the keeper of American history and culture, and it's in that spirit that this book was created. In particular, it's a look at history and culture through the lens of four areas of the domestic arts—crafts, design and decorating, gardening, and food and cooking.

Smithsonian Makers Workshop is a unique amalgam of how-to projects and stories of how American domestic life has changed and evolved from precolonial times to the present. It features instructions and recipes for creating things by hand for your home and also provides historical context—the prominent figures, events, and trends in each of these areas of domestic life over time. *Smithsonian Makers Workshop* is not a comprehensive examination of any one of these subjects (visit our museums for that!) but rather a fresh, lively look at them through the unique perspective of the Smithsonian and its curators. Its pages bring American history to life and—whether you're a curious beginner, a practiced expert, or somewhere in between— give you, the maker, satisfying ways to bring beauty to your home and life.

HOW THIS BOOK IS ORGANIZED

Smithsonian Makers Workshop highlights history in a number of recurring features.

An American Chronology is simply an historical overview of a particular category. It provides a quick, at-a-glance peek at the trajectory of events, people, and situations that created developments in American domestic life.

Who's Who highlights famous and influential figures who have had a profound effect on American craft, design and decorating, gardening, or food and cooking.

Hidden History brings attention to people or events that had a great influence on some aspect of everyday American life but are largely unknown.

A Moment in Time connects developments in American craft, design and decorating, gardening, or food and cooking with world events that became a part of history (and disappeared back into it) or that had a lasting impact we still feel today.

Everything Old Is New Again explores objects, movements, or trends that have historical context and that have reemerged in contemporary times.

Contemporaries introduces figures who are currently working in the fields of craft, design and decorating, gardening, or food and cooking who have returned to the roots of their passion and are redefining how it is approached in contemporary life or who are simply moving it forward to what's next.

Make It is the project feature of the book, whether it's instructions for stitching a needlework sampler, stenciling a dresser, planting a succulent terrarium, or baking a loaf of sourdough bread.

Crafts

Handcrafts have influenced America since the country's earliest days. Crafts help us express ourselves, provide comfort to loved ones, mark important milestones, pass the time, and keep traditions alive. From quilting a baby's first blanket to making and mending beloved garments, we use crafts to fill our lives with meaning and to create things that leave their own marks on history.

An American Chronology

The history of America is deeply entwined with the things we make. Craft helps us understand and preserve stories and traditions from the past.

▲ Spinning was generally seen as a woman's job. Women spun yarn at home, as well as with friends at "spinning bees," where food was served and prizes might be given to the person who produced the most or best yarn.

EARLY PEOPLES

For centuries, indigenous people of the Western hemisphere developed unique and beautiful craft traditions, including pottery, weaving, sewing, beading, basket making, doll making, painting, sand art, and more. For many indigenous populations, art and craft were deeply ingrained in everyday life and considered sacred traditions, which are carefully preserved and passed down over generations.

COLONIALISM AND THE AMERICAN REVOLUTION

When the first European settlers arrived in America, they brought their own craft traditions and imported textiles from England. Women managed domestic arts like spinning yarn, weaving, candle making, and soap making to provide for their households. During the Revolutionary War, women made clothing and mended uniforms for the military, and early flags like the flag that inspired the "The Star-Spangled Banner" were handmade by seamstresses.

THE TAPESTRY

As settlers expanded westward and immigrants came to America, craft traditions from many parts of the world spread throughout the country. New practices, designs, and techniques from makers from different cultures began to shape craft in America.

INDUSTRIAL REVOLUTION

Machines burst onto the scene in the late 1700s, leading to the mass production of craft materials. The cotton gin made processing raw materials more efficient, and factories and textile mills could now churn out fabric, yarn, and other materials. In 1855, the Singer sewing machine won first prize at the World's Fair in Paris and became one of the first machines to enter the home en masse. Women's magazines printed instructions for making garments, quilts, and home goods, and an increasing number of women from different economic

◀ Unidentified (Seneca/Iroquois) glass beads on velvet, cotton, and paper

backgrounds adopted crafting as a leisure activity rather than a necessity.

WOMEN'S MOVEMENT

During the mid-19th and early 20th centuries, women fought for their right to vote and for social and economic reform. During this time, handcrafts were seen by some women as old-fashioned and oppressive, and more women sought work outside the home. Between 1880 and 1910, the number of employed women jumped from 2.6 to 7.8 million.

ARTS AND CRAFTS MOVEMENT

As a response to the Industrial Revolution, the Arts and Crafts Movement worked to combat the perceived decline in American craftsmanship. Arts and Crafts groups advocated for economic and social reform with a call to return to artisan traditions.

WORLD WAR I

As American soldiers marched into their first winter of trench warfare, the U.S. government made a Call to Womanhood, asking women to knit cold-weather items for troops and reserve resources by making garments and housewares by hand. From 1917 to 1919, an estimated 370 million knitted items were produced by American Red Cross members alone. During World War I, Singer used its factories to produce munitions instead of sewing machines.

AMERICAN RED CROSS

OUR BOYS NEED SOX KNIT YOUR BIT

▲ Posters like this one from the American Red Cross encouraged women to aid U.S. troops through knitting.

"Creating is the most intense excitement one can come to know."

—*Anni Albers*

WOMEN HELPING WOMEN

During World War I, French women made embroidered work depicting soldiers, flags, and coats of arms and sold them to maintain their livelihoods and rebuild their communities. These items were sold in America through the Society for Employment of Women in France, and the profits went back to the women and their families in France.

◄ Inmates knitting at Sing Sing Correctional Facility in Ossining, New York, 1915

▲ A 2017 report by the Association for Creative Industries estimates that more than 28.8 million Americans participate in knitting and/or crochet.

THE GREAT DEPRESSION

During the Great Depression, garments were mended before being replaced, and many women returned to handcraft out of necessity. Making clothing and home goods from feed sacks became popular in rural and farming areas, and an ethos of thrifting, reusing, and making do was adopted by many Americans.

WORLD WAR II

In 1941, the U.S. was once again at war, and women picked up their knitting needles. Propaganda campaigns like Knitting for Victory and Make Do & Mend encouraged women to take up crafts to aid the Allies' war efforts.

HANDCRAFT RESURGENCE

After the war ended, many women continued to knit, but this time for personal use instead of for the war effort. Knitted sweaters and cardigans were staples of 1940s and 1950s fashion. Stores like JoAnn Fabrics and Crafts and Michaels opened in the 1960s and 1970s. Knitting and crochet were adopted by a new generation who made colorful garments and home decor that became emblematic of the times. In 1971, the first quilt exhibition was hung at the Whitney Museum of American Art, likening abstract quilts to fine art. In 1976, the Bicentennial sparked a resurgence in colonial arts and crafts.

In 2017, the total annual amount the U.S. market spent for crafting was nearly $43.9 billion.

TECHNOLOGY & CRAFTS

By the early 21st century, technology and the Internet were rapidly developing. Digital cameras made it easier to capture and upload images, and blogs became hubs for online craft communities. These new channels provided inspiration and education for a new generation of makers to modernize handcraft for the 21st century. When the financial crisis struck in 2008, the craft and hobby industry slowed temporarily, but a decade later, artisan culture continues to gain popularity. With innovative ideas, technological advances, and a nod to tradition, crafters today are entering a new era of craft and redefining what it means to be a maker in America.

"You can't sit around and wait for somebody to say who you are. You need to write it and paint it and do it."

—Faith Ringgold

▲ Smithsonian Kite Festival on the National Mall, Washington, D.C., circa 1974–1975

A MOMENT IN TIME

Cotton and Crafting

Many makers today use cotton for sewing, knitting, and needlework, but the history of cotton shaped the fabric of America. During the 19th and 20th centuries, cotton changed the U.S. economy and helped perpetuate slavery, making a mark not only on craft but also on American history.

THE AMERICAN SOUTH

The warm, humid climate in the southern United States is perfectly suited for growing cotton, and it is believed that cotton production began in the U.S. during the 1600s. Prior to the Industrial Revolution, most fibers were spun by hand before being woven into textiles, and production was laborious. In the late 18th century, textile producers in Europe invented time-saving machines like the spinning jenny, and demand for cotton was high. In 1793, the cotton gin made its debut, allowing cotton fibers to be quickly and easily separated from the seed. Cotton production was faster and more efficient than ever, and with machines at the ready, the time was ripe for a new economic power to take hold in America.

▲ The United States is the world's third-largest cotton producer behind China and India, producing more than 4,500 metric tons a year.

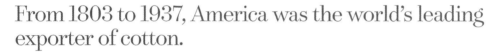

From 1803 to 1937, America was the world's leading exporter of cotton.

THE RISE OF COTTON

As with other labor-intensive crops grown in the South, plantation owners depended on slave labor to produce cotton. As demand for cotton increased, the Southern cotton industry expanded, and slavery became integral to the American economy.

Between 1830 and 1850, cotton production skyrocketed from 720,000 bales to 2.85 million. Around the world, mills were eager to transform American cotton into textiles for the home. Along with tobacco and

◀ African American slaves use a cotton gin. This image is a wood engraving after a drawing by William L. Sheppard from *Harper's Weekly* 1869, with modern watercolor.

sugar, cotton became a luxury commodity and was in high demand for nearly all textile goods—clothing, bedding, curtains, quilts, yarn, and more. The new glut of textile supplies was a gift to makers in America and abroad. Fabric was readily available, and producers were manufacturing new patterns and designs that were ready to be sewn into handmade items. Quilters began piecing bits of fabric together into quilt tops in new and more elaborate patterns, using many different fabrics in one quilt top. American patchwork—quilts pieced with blocks and patches—became prevalent in the late 19th century. Sewing machines were also entering the home, making it even faster and easier to sew. During the 19th century, this proliferation and innovation made its impact on sewing and craft. Though leisure sewing had been enjoyed by women for centuries, with the expansion of cotton and textiles more women across social and economic classes were now able to sew for fun.

THE END OF AN ERA

After the Civil War, cotton production was critical to restoring the nation's financial stability. Even after abolition, many "freed" slaves were kept in near-slavery conditions to maintain the economy and culture in the South. Decades of poverty and sharecropping ensued, and Southern plantations continued to produce cotton until the 1920s, when overproduction caused the price to collapse. Shortly thereafter, the boll weevil swept the nation and destroyed much of the cotton farmland. In Georgia alone, cotton acreage was reduced from 5.2 million acres in 1915 to 2.6 million acres in 1923. With the Great Depression right around the corner, cotton's reign in America was over.

Today the U.S. continues to produce cotton and is the world's third-largest cotton producer behind China and India, producing more than 4,500 metric tons a year. Today, cotton is grown mostly in Texas, Georgia, Arkansas, and California.

THE MANY USES OF COTTON

The craft and hobby industry is one of the largest consumers of cotton in the world. Makers across disciplines rely on 100%-cotton and cotton blends for fabric, yarn, batting, thread, and myriad other goods and materials. The Association For Creative Industries estimates the craft industry to be worth $36 billion globally each year. Next time you're browsing the fabric section looking for that just-right print, consider the history of cotton and how it shaped America.

◄ The Industrial Revolution allowed fabrics to be produced in a central location and on a mass scale.

HIDDEN HISTORY

Marie Webster

Marie Webster paved the way for generations of quilters by writing the first quilt history book, creating a line of quilting patterns and kits, and making quilting her business.

Marie Daugherty Webster was born in 1859 in Wabash, Indiana, and learned to sew as a young girl. Her mother was a fine seamstress, and she taught her daughters the art of sewing. Though Marie made a crazy quilt in her younger days, it wasn't until she was in her 40s that she started designing her own patterns. In 1905, the Arts and Crafts Movement was in full swing, and Marie, a proponent of the movement, wanted to make a quilt. However, none of the patterns of the day appealed to her, so she decided to design her own—a floral appliqué quilt inspired by her garden. She dusted off her sewing skills, began to appliqué, and the rest was history.

DESIGNING THE FUTURE

Marie submitted her newly finished quilt to the editors at

> *Quilts: Their Story and How to Make Them* by Marie D. Webster was first published in 1915. It is widely regarded as the first quilt book.

Ladies' Home Journal. They liked it so much, they invited her to submit three more designs to fill a full-page, color story in their January 1911 issue. The illustrated patterns instantly made Marie a star. With this newfound celebrity, she began designing and making even more quilts and began printing her own patterns. For 50 cents each, she sold pattern packets that included the pattern, a photo of the finished quilt, instructions, and blueprints for building and arranging the pieces. *Ladies' Home Journal* printed

▼ Marie Daugherty Webster (July 19, 1859–August 29, 1956) was a quilter and designer who went on to become the author of the first book dedicated to quilts and quilt history. She was a successful business-woman and inspired many women to quilt with her patterns and kits.

THE LADIES' HOME JOURNAL

THE NEW-YEAR NUMBER

JANUARY 1, 1911   10 CENTS

◄ Marie's quilt designs were first published in the January 1, 1911, issue of *Ladies' Home Journal.* The magazine later printed more than 20 of her quilt and pillow designs.

▲ Marie Webster's home in Marion, Indiana, was built in 1905 and declared a National Historic Landmark in 1993. The building now houses the Quilters Hall of Fame, honoring Marie and dozens of renowned quilters.

nearly two dozen more of her original quilt and pillow designs, and all around her, a quilting revolution was taking place.

QUILTS: THEIR STORY AND HOW TO MAKE THEM

Using her influence in the growing quilt industry, Marie began work on a quilt history book. In 1915, she published *Quilts: Their Story and How to Make Them*, widely regarded as the first book dedicated to quilts and quilt history. The book traced the history of quilts and their journey to America and featured images of Marie's own original designs. This book helped to legitimize the study of quilts and quilt history, laying the groundwork for more historians to follow in Marie's stead.

The book received great reviews, and Marie continued to inspire quilters the world over. As World War I came to an end, the quilt craze intensified as more materials became available and family life stabilized. Marie began speaking and lecturing, and in 1921, she created the Practical Patchwork Company with her sister Emma and two friends. Together, they sold patterns, quilt kits, and finished quilts. Marie continued working in the quilt industry until her retirement in 1942.

In 1991, Marie was inducted into the Quilters Hall of Fame, and her home in Marion, Indiana, was converted into the headquarters for the organization, honoring not only Marie's legacy but also other quilters who have made outstanding contributions to the world of quilting.

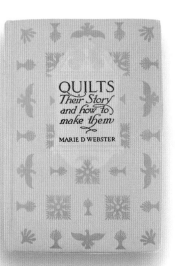

▲ *Quilts: Their Story and How to Make Them* was published in 1915 and is regarded as the first book dedicated to quilts and quilt history.

◀ A quilt by Marie D. Webster, made for *Ladies' Home Journal*, January 1911

The Quilters of Gee's Bend

FROM A SMALL, REMOTE AFRICAN AMERICAN COMMUNITY ON THE BANKS OF THE ALABAMA RIVER, A GROUP OF WOMEN MADE QUILTS TOGETHER AND CHANGED HISTORY. THEIR WORK CONTINUES TO INSPIRE QUILTERS, ARTISTS, AND HISTORIANS AROUND THE WORLD.

Gee's Bend quilts often feature bold colors, improvisational designs, and solid fabrics.

CHALLENGING PERCEPTIONS

The quilters of Gee's Bend have been inspiring quilters, artists, and historians for decades with their unique and stunning work. The quilters are recognized as master quilters and artists the world over.

The quilting tradition in Gee's Bend stretches back to the 19th century, passed down from mother to daughter for hundreds of years. In the past, quilters often sewed together in a community but now also create their own individual works.

Formerly a cotton plantation named for Joseph Gee, the community was later settled by freed slaves, and is home to about 700 residents. In 1962, the ferry connecting Gee's Bend to the other side of the Alabama River was destroyed, and the residents were almost completely cut off from the surrounding area. They continued to make quilts in isolation until their work was discovered in the late 1990s. Almost immediately, the work found its way from the bed to the wall, and the quilts began touring in a national exhibit in 2002.

The quilts of Gee's Bend feature bold geometric and improvisational designs and are often made from repurposed fabrics like clothes, bedding, and feed sacks. These fabric remnants are spontaneously pieced together to create stunning modern quilts with bright colors and unique designs. For those who make these quilts, art, community, collective history, and spirituality are closely intertwined.

EVERYTHING OLD IS NEW AGAIN

Patchwork Quilts

The patchwork quilt, featuring pieced, repeating block patterns, is considered by many to be an American icon of the craft world. In *Quilts Around the World*, Spike Gillespie writes, "The style of blocks sewn together—known as patchwork—is what Americans would become best known for. American quilters did not invent patchwork, but they certainly took the ball and ran with it."

Early American and European quilts were often wholecloth, appliqué, or medallion quilts, some of which featured patchwork, but sparingly. As American quilting evolved and printed cotton fabrics became more prevalent during the Industrial Revolution, quilters began piecing entire quilts out of pieced blocks, and American patchwork was born.

The Industrial Revolution also provided access to new technology. Sewing machines became the first machines to become a staple in the home, and making garments, quilts, and home goods was faster than ever. Quilters started to use these machines to create new and more-elaborate quilts, and quilters throughout the 20th century continued to innovate with the use of ever more convenient tools like rotary cutters, quilting rulers, and templates.

A NEW GENERATION

In the past several decades, new generations of quilters have taken up the craft. These new quilters are often inspired by traditional designs and motifs, but they put their own modern spin on them. Patchwork continues to inspire, and quilters today are pushing the boundaries of what can be created by simply sewing pieces of fabric together.

▲ This quilt comprises approximately 144 squares of challis wool (5×5 inches) stitched together to form a large square. These fabric "patches," when sewn together, create the patchwork style that is emblematic of American quilting.

▲ Friends of Mary Elizabeth Hitchcock Seamans created this quilt of fifty-six 9½-inch blocks, possibly on the occasion of her marriage to Stephen Harris Seamans in 1864. The blocks are made of printed and white cottons in the Friendship Chain or Album pattern.

Prism Quilt by textile designer Tara
Vaughnan, Oakland, California

"Quilts are not the domain of a
specific race or class, but can be
a part of anyone's heritage and
treasured as such."

—*Excerpt from the National Quilt Collection*

Crossroads Baby Quilt

Until the middle of the 19th century, most children slept in their parents' bed. The development of small beds for children and babies necessitated the creation of small quilts. This sweet and modern baby quilt is quick to sew and can be made by machine or by hand.

YOU WILL NEED

White Fabric: 1½ yards

Yellow Fabric: ½ yard

Backing: 3 yards

Binding: ½ yard
(5 strips 2½"×WOF)

Batting: at least 42"×52"

OPTIONAL

High-contrast thread like perle cotton or sashiko thread

Wide-eye needle for high-contrast hand quilting

Sturdy thread for hand piecing and binding

Long quilting ruler

CUT

From the White Fabric, cut:

2 strips 7½"×WOF
(G border)

6 strips 5½"×WOF, subcut:

- 8 rectangles 5½"×9" (C piece)

- 12 squares 5½"×5½" (A piece)

- Reserve 2 strips 5½"×WOF for the F border

From the Yellow Fabric, cut:

6 strips 2½"×WOF, subcut:

- 4 strips 2½"×26½" (E strip)

- 6 strips 2½"×9" (D piece)

1 Start by assembling the A/B row (Figure 1). Sew four A pieces to three B pieces as shown in Figure 1 and press seams to the side, toward the yellow strips. Your A/B rows should measure 26½"×5½". Make three A/B rows total.

2 Assemble the C/D row (Figure 2). Sew four C pieces to three D pieces as shown in Figure 2 and press seams to the side, toward the yellow strips. The C/D rows should measure 26½"×9". Make three C/D rows total.

3 Sew the E strips to the A/B strips to assemble the middle section (Figure 3). Press all seams to the side, toward the yellow strips. Your centerpiece should now be 26½"×23½" (Figure 4).

4 Add the C/D rows to your centerpiece (Figure 5). Your centerpiece should finish at 26½"×40½".

5 Add the borders. Start by adding the G borders to the sides of your quilt. Press seams to the side (Figure 6). Then add the F borders to the top and bottom, pressing seams to the side (Figure 7). Your quilt top should measure 40½"×50½".

6 Create your backing by cutting a piece of fabric about 54"×WOF. Press your backing flat. Baste your quilt back, batting, and quilt top together using your favorite method.

7 Quilt as desired. To add the secondary grid in your quilting motif, mark lines 1" away from all the yellow/white fabric seams using a pencil or fabric marker. Quilt along those lines by machine or with contrasting thread. Mark additional lines in the borders to add denser quilting.

8 Bind using your favorite method to finish the quilt.

▲ On the wrong side of each piece, mark ¼" away from the edge. This will be your seam line.

▲ Place two fabric pieces right sides together with marked lines facing out. Optional: Use pins to secure fabric in place.

◄ To hand-quilt, begin by tying a knot at one end of your quilting thread. Place two pieces right sides together and sew a running stitch along the marked line you drew in pencil. Backstitch every 2 to 3 stitches to secure.

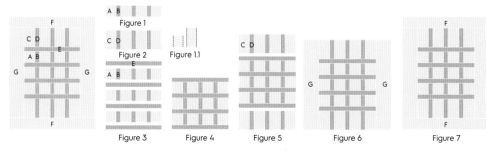

Figure 1   Figure 1.1   Figure 2   Figure 3   Figure 4   Figure 5   Figure 6   Figure 7

1830s Reticule

During the 19th and 20th centuries, small purses called reticules came into the height of fashion. Prior to this time, women would carry items in pockets sewn into their garments; however, as fashions changed and slimmer-fitting dresses replaced full skirts, women started carrying handbags. At the time, pockets were considered undergarments, and carrying a reticule was considered scandalous. Despite this, American women and girls loved reticules, to the point where they were called "indispensables." Publications like the *American Girl's Book* of 1831 printed reticule patterns for a variety of styles and skill levels, some of which have been reproduced here.

YOU WILL NEED

Fabric (size and material varies by pattern)

Ribbon

Cotton cord or string for drawstring

Needle

Thread

Transfer paper for embroidery

Marking tool such as pencil or iron-out pen

Embellishments such as tassels, beads, and embroidery floss for embroidering

Scissors

FOR A THREE-SIDED RETICULE

1 Cut a piece of silk into three pieces of equal size. Each must be about ¼ yard in depth and ⅛ yard wide. Cut each of the sides so they slope to a point about 3" from the bottom.

2 Sew the pieces of silk together (inserting a covered cord between the seams) so they meet in a point at the bottom.

3 Embellish each corner with a tassel or bow. Add one to the bottom as well.

4 Hem down the top and thread a ribbon through it to make a drawstring.

FOR AN EMBROIDERED RETICULE

1 Cut two pieces of muslin ¼ yard wide and just over ¼ yard in depth to allow for the case at the top.

2 Choose an embroidery pattern and trace it onto the fabric as desired. Use a piece of embroidery thread to embroider the design.

3 Sew together the two sides of the bag, hemming the top and threading it with a white cotton cord.

FOR A DIMITY RETICULE

1 Take ¼ yard of muslin or gingham and cut it in two equal shapes.

2 Cut the shape of a small scallop or point out of an old card or a bit of thick paper. Laying this on the fabric, draw a row of points or scallops all round the edges, taking care not to go too near the edge.

3 Baste or tack the two sides of the bag wrong sides together; following the outline of the scallops, sew on top of your marked lines with neat, short stitches, taking care to catch both layers.

4 Cut out the scallop shapes with a pair of sharp scissors, but avoid cutting too close to the stitch.

5 Turn the bag right side out and with a pen or chopstick, poke the scalloped edges into their proper shape. Hem the top and run a ribbon or cotton cord through it to make the drawstring.

Work Apron

This no-pattern tutorial makes for a versatile apron, and you can customize the fabric and shape to suit your craft, gardening, or kitchen needs.

YOU WILL NEED

A large piece of fabric big enough for your apron body, at least 24" wide by 26" tall

Strips of fabric or webbing for the apron straps

Single-fold bias tape for finishing seams

Tape measure

OPTIONAL

Scrap of fabric for the apron pocket or pockets, at least 10" wide by 8" tall

1 Decide what size you'd like your apron to be by measuring across your collarbones and around the front of your hips where the apron should cover. Write down these two measurements as Width 1 and Width 2. Measure the length of your torso between your collarbones and your hips where you'd like the tie to be. Write this measurement down as Length 1. Measure down from your hips to where you'd like the apron to end. (Often this is either just above or just below the knee.) Write this measurement as Length 2.

2 Fold your large fabric piece in half lengthwise and press the fabric to form a crease. This will be the center of your apron.

3 Mark your measurements on the fabric as shown in Diagram 1. Then connect the marked points by drawing lines to trace the outline of your apron.

4 Keeping the fabric folded, cut along the outline carefully with scissors. Open the fabric to reveal the full apron.

5 Finish the edges with bias tape. Using your sewing machine, stitch the unfinished edge of the bias tape to the raw edges of your apron on the front-facing side of the fabric. Stitch the finished edge of your bias tape to the back side.

6 Measure how long you'd like your neck strap to be and cut your webbing or fabric to length. If using fabric, cut the width of the strip to twice the width that you'd like your strap to be, then sew the fabric into a tube (right sides together). Turn the tube right side out and press.

7 Turn your neck strap under ½" and then another ½", pressing to keep it in place. Then attach the neck strap to the top corners of your apron on the back side with the unfinished edges tucked under so they aren't visible. (Skip this step if using webbing.)

8 Repeat Steps 6–7 for the waist ties, attaching to the corners at your Width 2 measurement.

9 Hem the top of your pocket piece by turning the edges under ¼" and ¼" again, pressing and then stitching in place. Then turn under the other edges of your pocket and sew it to the front of your apron where desired.

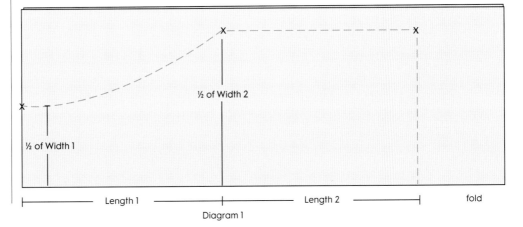

Diagram 1

A MOMENT IN TIME

Tools of the Trade

The right tools make crafting fun and easy and allow us to bring our creativity to life. We often take these simple supplies for granted, but the tools of the trade each have their own stories to tell.

SCISSORS

Scissors have been around since ancient times and have evolved throughout history. Early spring scissors date back to the Bronze Age and were often made of bronze and iron, later brass and steel. Many scissors were beautiful as well as functional, cast in unique and decorative shapes and adorned with engravings or precious metals. Scissors were designed for specific uses, like cutting hair, paper, cigars, or even eggs, before they were simplified for machine manufacturing in the late 19th century. Today, many crafters are first introduced to scissors through blunt-tip children's scissors or multipurpose scissors, but specialty scissors like dressmaker's shears and embroidery snips can be a maker's best friend.

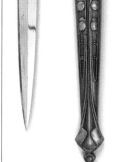

▲ Cast copper and brass scissors with forged steel blades and case

The sewing needle has been around for at least 20,000 years and has been made and used all over the world.

GLUE

Elmer's Glue first made its appearance in 1947 in a glass bottle, and the first convenient squeeze bottle made its way into the hands of crafters in 1951. In 1954, George Schultz invented the hot-glue gun (first called the Polygun) after seeing workers in a shoe factory get burned from dipping into pots of hot glue. Super Glue™ was discovered by Harry Coover, an American chemist working on military research during World War II.

◀ This hat box was used by milliner Mae Reeves to hold craft supplies. It was made from a pasteboard bottom printed in cream and gold stripes with clear plastic sides.

Coover discovered a compound that stuck to everything without the need for heat or pressure and later patented it as Super Glue™. In the late 1960s, the German company Henkel introduced the first glue stick under the Pritt brand. The glue stick was inspired by twist-action lipstick tubes and was marketed as small, convenient, and clean to use. As a nonliquid glue, the glue stick was unique at the time and is still a favorite tool of many crafters.

SEWING NEEDLE

The sewing needle has been around for at least 20,000 years and has been made and used all over the world. Primitive needles were made of bone with an eye drilled through one end. Some early metal needles didn't have an eye, but rather a hook to catch thread. In Europe, before needle making was refined, needles were often crudely made by blacksmiths, and fine needles were rare and hard to come by. With the rise of manufacturing, needles were mass produced and easy to obtain, becoming almost disposable for sewers. Today, needles come in various types and shapes and are sold in small sewing kits at virtually every grocery or drug store.

PAINT

Early artists made their own paints from natural pigments such as indigo or madder or purchased premade paints in liquid form. In 1780, William Reeves invented hard pigment cakes that could be rubbed in water to produce paint, a precursor to modern watercolors. Winsor & Newton, an English paint company founded in the 1830s, developed evermore convenient ways to store and package paint, like glass syringes and collapsible screwcap tubes that are still used today. Acrylic paints were developed in the 1940s and quickly became popular with artists and crafters. Today, a trip to the craft store presents dozens of opportunities to purchase paint for all uses and occasions.

▲ Sewing Machine Patent Model, Patent No. 8,294, issued August 12, 1851, to Isaac Merritt Singer of New York, New York. Hand-sewing needles were the precursors to the needles used in modern sewing machines.

ANCIENT STROKES

Early paintbrushes were made of bone, wood, animal hair, and plant fibers. Ancient peoples used paintbrushes to create art and communications, including ancient cave drawings that stretch back tens of thousands of years. Some of these works can still be seen today.

◄ Some craft tools change with the times. Others, like paintbrushes, differ very little from their historic counterparts.

EVERYTHING OLD IS NEW AGAIN

Macramé

The ancient art of knot tying has been around for thousands of years and is the precursor to modern macramé. Decorative knot tying is depicted in Babylonian and Assyrian carvings and was used in the Middle East for centuries to finish shawls and veils. In the 17th century, this tradition made its way from the Middle East to Europe, where England in particular caught macramé fever. For years, handmade macramé pieces adorned the clothing and walls of many Victorian women and their homes.

SETTING SAIL

Sailors throughout history have been adept at tying knots, and they created practical and decorative macramé items at sea. Macramé could be found adorning knife handles and in hammocks and belts. Polynesians were also master knot makers and users, and techniques like Maori Hei Toki lashing were both decorative and functional. Eventually, macramé made its way to North America, where it grew in popularity during the 20th century.

MODERN TIMES

During the 1970s, a macramé craze hit America, and it was found everywhere—including clothing, tablecloths, drapes, wall hangings, plant holders, and more. The fad quickly fell out of favor, but today, macramé is once again having a moment as a new generation of makers modernizes the ancient craft. Today, macramé can be seen in millennial homes and once again is making its way into clothing and fashion.

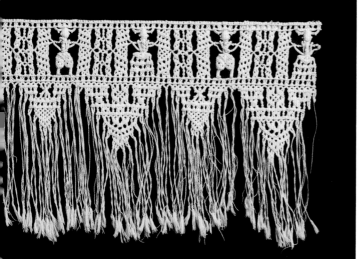

▼ Today's macramé artists, like Rianne Aarts-Zuijderduin of Teddy and Wool, incorporate geometric designs into their work.

▲ Border with highly stylized male and female figures, with pendant triangles below, finished with a long fringe

▶ Long, narrow macramé hanging in natural linen, with diagonal work, twisted bands, and long fringes at the bottom

Modern macramé can feature large-scale designs and abstract shapes, like this contemporary wall hanging by Rianne Aarts-Zuijderduin of Teddy and Wool.

A MOMENT IN TIME

Knitting for the War Effort

As far back as the Civil War, Americans knitted items for soldiers on the front as a way to connect those at home with those in the armed forces. During World War I and World War II, this effort continued. Women at home helped win the wars by knitting millions of items for soldiers.

In 1917, the American Red Cross received this note from Major Grayson M.P. Murphy, the American Red Cross Commissioner to Europe: "Begin shipping at once one and a half million each: knitted mufflers, sweaters, socks and wristlets. These are desperately needed before cold weather. In view of the shortage of fuel and other discomforts they will be of incredible value in both military and civilian work."

▲ World War I National Guard member wearing a knitted sweater and wool "leg longs"

CALL TO WOMANHOOD

The United States entered World War I on April 6, 1917, and only a few short months later, Europe was approaching winter. Women in America were serving as nurses, ambulance drivers, pilots, and more, but with an urgent need for cold-weather wear, the Red Cross put out a call for women to aid the war effort in another way—knitting. Knitted items provided warmth and comfort for soldiers fighting in the trenches, and women were able to send something handmade to their loved ones overseas. U.S. government officials put out a Call to Womanhood to serve the war effort from home, and a movement was about to begin.

KNIT YOUR BIT

Magazines began printing patterns for sweaters, scarves, socks, gloves, knitted helmets, wrist warmers, and more, with propaganda messages like "In war, more men die from cold and exposure and illness than from wounds. Every hour that you waste, you are throwing aside the life of one of our soldiers. Set aside a part of each day for your war work." Women responded in earnest. For many women, every hour of leisure was spent knitting. Knitting bees were held in public spaces to raise awareness,

◀ A Red Cross poster encouraging wartime knitting, 1918

funds, and donations. A grand jury in Seattle was even photographed knitting socks in 1918 (below). By the time World War I ended in 1919, it is estimated that 370 million knit items were produced by American Red Cross members alone.

KNITTING FOR VICTORY

Women put down their needles in the 1920s and 1930s, but when the U.S. entered World War II, women were once again ready to serve.

In 1941, *Life* magazine ran a cover article called "How to Knit," with instructions and patterns to knit items for U.S. troops. The article stated: "To the great American question 'What can I do to help the war effort?' the commonest answer yet found is 'Knit.'" One propaganda poster read, "Remember Pearl Harbor; Purl Harder."

Once again, women filled their free time with knitting, sending millions of items for soldiers fighting by land, air, and sea. Patterns were also developed for women in uniform to support the nurses, clerics, and technicians who were serving overseas in the newly formed Women's Army Auxiliary Corps.

The knitting frenzy continued until the end of World War II. Many women put down their needles after the need for war items had ended, but many continued to knit, now as a creative hobby, rather than as a call to arms.

▲ The comforts committee of the Army and Navy League held an Army and Navy knitting bee in Central Park Mall on July 31, 1918.

KNIT AND SING

Men and children also knitted for the war effort. A version of this song was printed in *School Education*, Volume 38 (1918) for Minnesota schoolchildren and the *Texas Department of Agriculture Bulletin (1919)* aimed at farmers: *Johnnie, get your yarn, get your yarn, get your yarn; Knitting has a charm, has a charm, has a charm. See us knitting two by two. Boys in Whittier like it too. Hurry every day, make it pay. Our laddies must be warm, not forlorn, 'mid the storm. Hear them call from o'er the sea, "Make a sweater please for me."*

> "There is one form of work that every woman can share. Don't say you are too busy to knit—it isn't true."
>
> —*The Delineator,* November 1917

◄ A U.S. Grand Jury in Seattle knits socks for soldiers during World War I.

Knitted Garments for Soldiers

During World War I and again during World War II, women were called upon to provide knitted items for their loved ones overseas. These patterns were published by the American Red Cross in *The Delineator* magazine's November 1917 edition.

THUMBLESS MITTENS OR WRISTLETS NO. 1

½ skein of worsted wool yarn (⅛ lb.)

1 pair needles size 7–9

WRISTLETS NO. 2

(Same as No. 1 but made in 1 piece)

½ skein of worsted wool yarn (⅛ lb.)

4 needles size 7–9

MUFFLER

2½ hanks of yarn (⅜ lb.)

1 pair needles size 7–9

THUMBLESS MITTENS OR WRISTLETS NO. 1

1 Cast on 48 stitches, knit 2 and purl 2 for 12".

2 Sew up, leaving 2" open space for thumb 2" from the edge.

WRISTLETS NO. 2 (SAME AS NO. 1 BUT MADE IN 1 PIECE)

1 Cast on 52 stitches on 3 needles: 16-16-20.

2 Knit 2, purl 2 for 8".

3 To make opening for thumb, knit 2 purl 2 to end of "Third" needle, turn; knit and purl back to end of "First" needle, always slipping first stitch, turn.

4 Continue knitting back and forth for 2 inches. From this point continue at first for 4 inches for the hand. Bind off loosely and buttonhole thumb opening.

MUFFLER

1 Cast on 50 stitches for 11". Plain knitting for 68".

KNIT STITCH

▲ To make a knit stitch, insert right needle through front of the first stitch on left needle, bringing right needle behind the left.

▲ Wrap the yarn over the top of your right needle to form a new stitch.

▲ Bring your right needle down and forward through the new stitch, pulling the yarn through.

▲ Lift the stitch off of the left needle and onto the right needle to finish.

PURL STITCH

▲ To make a purl stitch, insert right needle through back of the first stitch on left needle, bringing right needle in front of the left.

▲ Wrap the yarn over the top of your right needle to form a new stitch.

▲ Bring your right needle up and back through the new stitch, pulling the yarn through.

▲ Lift the stitch off of the left needle and onto the right needle to finish.

Crochet Granny Square

The granny square is the quintessential crochet pattern, beloved by beginners and aficionados alike. In the 1970s, the granny square was everywhere. Its ease and versatility make it the perfect pattern for everything—washcloths, clothing, throw blankets, and more. As a single unit, the granny square can be made into a pot holder, or you can join several together to make a scarf or blanket. Experiment with changing colors in each round to create concentric rings—the possibilities are endless.

YOU WILL NEED

1 skein of yarn. Any material will work, but we recommend 100% cotton in a worsted weight.

5.5–6.5 mm crochet hook (or a hook that is recommended for your yarn)

1 Make a slip knot and insert your crochet hook into the slip knot.

2 Chain 6.

3 Insert your crochet hook into the first chain you created and pull your yarn through to create a loop.

4 Chain 3.

5 Crochet 2 double-crochet (DC) stitches in the loop you've just created.

6 Chain 3.

7 Crochet 3 DC stitches in the loop.

8 Repeat Steps 6–7 two more times to create a total of four sets of 3 DC stitches in the loop (the first chain of 3 you created will be included in the first set).

9 Chain 3.

10 To finish round one, insert your hook into the third stitch in the first chain of 3 you created and pull the yarn through.

11 To begin round two, chain 1.

12 Crochet 3 DC stitches in the top left-hand corner loop.

13 Chain 3.

14 Crochet 3 DC stitches in the same top left-hand corner loop.

15 Chain 1.

16 Moving the crochet piece clockwise, crochet 3 DC stitches in the next corner loop.

17 Chain 3 and crochet 3 DC stitches in the same corner loop.

18 Repeat steps 15–17 two more times to complete the round.

19 To finish the round, insert your crochet hook into the first chain you created at the beginning of round two.

20 To begin round three, chain 3.

21 Crochet 2 DC stitches in the middle hole you've just created.

22 Chain 1.

23 Crochet a set of 3 DC, 3 chain, and 3 DC stitches in the corner hole, moving clockwise.

24 Chain 1.

25 Crochet 3 DC stitches in the next middle hole.

26 Repeat Steps 22–25 until you have completed the third round.

27 To finish, chain 1 and insert your crochet hook into the third stitch in the first chain of 3 from the beginning of the round.

28 You can continue crocheting additional rounds in the same way to create a granny square to whatever size you'd like. To finish your square, chain 1, snip the yarn, and pull it all the way through the chain, pulling tight. Weave the ends into your piece and trim to finish.

SLIP KNOT

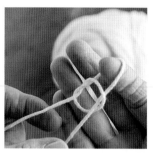

▲ To make a slip knot, make a loop as shown with the yarn end on the right and the tail end on the left. Leave a few inches for the tail.

▲ Grab the string from the yarn end and pull it through up and through the back of the loop you created in the last step.

▲ Pull the loop tight to finish the slip knot. Adjust the size of your loop by tugging on the yarn end.

CHAIN STITCH

▲ To chain stitch, insert your hook into the slip stitch as shown with the yarn end in your left hand and the tail end held out of the way to the right.

▲ Loop the yarn over the hook from the back side as shown, pulling the yarn end tight with your left hand.

▲ Slide the hook down and through the slip stitch, bringing the yarn through as well.

▲ Move your hook back into the first position to prepare for the next stitch.

DOUBLE CROCHET

▲ To make a double crochet stitch, begin by looping the yarn over the back of the hook.

▲ Insert your hook through the top of the next stitch in your work. You should have 3 loops over your hook at this point.

▲ Move your hook up to grab the yarn. Pull the yarn tight so you can pull it through the stitches in the next step.

▲ Pull the yarn through the first 2 loops on your hook, leaving 2 loops on the hook.

▼ Yarn over the needle once again, this time pulling the yarn through the last 2 loops on your hook. You will finish with 1 stitch on your hook.

Kaffe Fassett

ONE OF THE MOST PROLIFIC MULTIDISCIPLINARY MAKERS IN HISTORY, KAFFE FASSETT CONTINUES TO INSPIRE CRAFTERS EVERYWHERE WITH HIS COLORFUL FABRIC, KNITTING, NEEDLEPOINT, PATCHWORK, AND MOSAIC WORK.

Not one to shy away from color, Fassett makes items often defined by his bright, bold, and cheery color palettes.

50 YEARS OF CRAFT

Kaffe Fassett was born in 1937 in San Francisco and began his career as a fine artist in painting at age 19. In the 1960s, he moved to England and, during a trip to Scotland, fell in love with colorful yarns. Fassett bought 20 skeins of wool and some knitting needles and learned to knit from a fellow passenger on the way home. Soon after, he began designing his own garments and patterns, and his knitting quickly worked its way into the fashion world.

At the time, Fassett was collaborating on many projects with fashion designer Bill Gibb, and his knitwork became largely featured in Gibb's work. In 1970, one of Gibb's dresses featuring a knitted waistcoat made by Fassett was selected as Dress of the Year for the Fashion Museum, Bath, solidifying handcraft's position in the world of high fashion.

Fassett's work with the fiber arts eventually led him to other mediums—fabric design, patchwork, needlepoint, tapestries, and more, and with his talent and eye for color, Fassett became a leading designer for fiber and textile companies around the world.

Today, Fassett continues to push boundaries and inspire makers with his bold, bright, and colorful work. His fabric and patterns can be found at local craft stores, and his garments and artworks hang in museums around the world. Fassett has produced more than 30 books and publications, and he continues to work with fashion companies. In 2019, Fassett collaborated with Coach on a fall collection inspired by his work.

HIDDEN HISTORY

Art Versus Craft

In 1908, Elbert Hubbard wrote: "Art is not a thing—it is a way." The same could be said of not only art but also of craft, folk art, and many other creative endeavors. But while the questions of how to define art and craft have been ongoing for centuries, at their core, art and craft both celebrate the spirit of making and creative expression.

HISTORIC ARTS

In medieval times, artisan goods were made by a collective of makers, often working in communities. Groups of artisans would be commissioned to make something for a client—metalwork, wood carvings, glass, and also paintings and sculptures. Each commission would be purchased with a lump sum paid to the collective (not necessarily the maker), and the value was based on how well the work adhered to traditional design (not necessarily on skill or creativity).

During the Renaissance, skilled artisans like Michelangelo, Raphael, and Leonardo da Vinci began to emerge as master "artists," and their work was valued above work made by collectives. Over time, the term

Works in the Smithsonian American Art Museum's collection of Contemporary Craft and Decorative Arts blur the line between art and craft.

"art" became commonly used to describe painting and sculptures, while "minor arts" and "decorative arts" were used to describe things like wood carvings, pottery, weaving, and glass works.

ART AND CRAFT AT THE SMITHSONIAN

This distinction has persisted throughout time, and nearly 400 years later, we still debate the difference between art and craft. But the Smithsonian American Art Museum (SAAM) is home to collections of work from across the spectrum, celebrated for their own place in history and culture.

Art At the Smithsonian American Art Museum, art tells America's rich artistic and cultural history through its collection of pieces from the colonial period to today. The collection itself began in 1829, and SAAM was the nation's first collection of American art. Today it includes one of the largest collections of American art in the world.

Craft In 1972, the Renwick Gallery opened to the public as a branch of the SAAM featuring American crafts. SAAM's collection of Contemporary Craft and Decorative Arts features works by well-established craft masters, and works in this collection use traditional crafts like jewelry, studio furniture, and wood craft to create fine art pieces that are displayed alongside paintings and sculptures.

▲ Clarence Woolsey, Grace Woolsey, *Untitled* (Caparena Figure), ca. 1961–1972, wood, bottle-caps, and wire

Folk Art SAAM's collection of Folk and Self-Taught Art includes pieces that emanate from folk traditions such as quilting and woodcarving, as well as highly innovative works of great personal vision.

The Smithsonian also celebrates living traditions around the world with the Folklife Festival each year. The festival includes an artisan market where visitors can browse beautiful works made by skilled artisans from around the world.

◀ Fresco, *Expulsion of Heliodorus from the Temple* (1511–1513), Room of Heliodorus, by Raphael in Apostolic Palace Vatican Museums, Vatican

▼ Tlingit basket, donated to the Smithsonian by the U.S. Department of the Interior in 1910

◀ Charlie Willeto, *Untitled* (Mountain Lion Spirit Figure), ca. 1961–1964, painted wood

▲ Artisans crafted handmade wares in workshops. In this lithograph, coppersmiths are making cookware for a client.

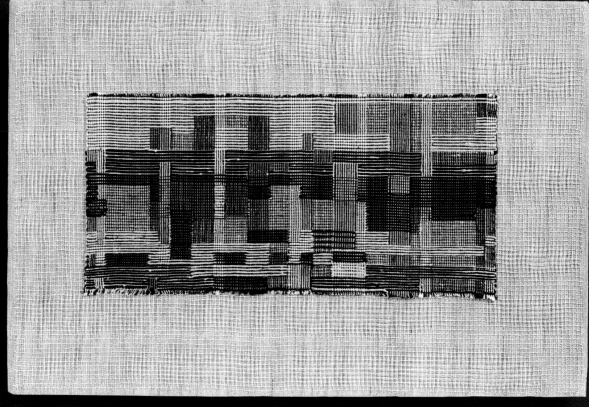

▲ *City,* 1949   Linen and cotton 17½×26½ in.

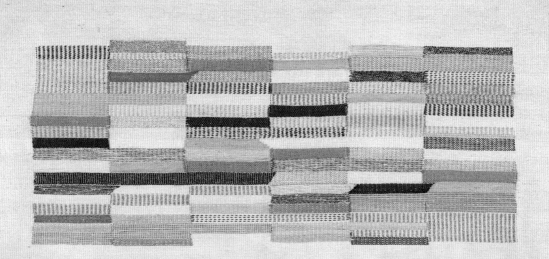

▲ *Untitled,* 1941   Rayon, linen, cotton, wool, jute 21×46 in.

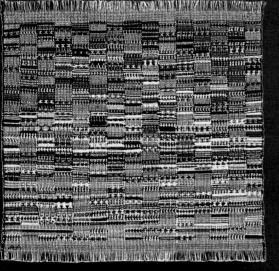

▲ *Open Letter*, 1958   Cotton 23×24 in.

Anni Albers

A WEAVER, ARTIST, AND DESIGNER, ANNI ALBERS BLURRED THE LINE BETWEEN CRAFT AND ART, CREATING STUNNING WORKS THAT EMBODIED BOTH FORM AND FUNCTION.

WEAVING FOR FORM AND FUNCTION

Anni Albers was born in Berlin in 1899 and attended the Bauhaus, an experimental college of art and design, when she was 23. She enrolled in the weaving department (one of the few open to women) and began experimenting with texture and color, creating works that were both beautiful and useful. She experimented with materials like horsehair and metallic thread in her textiles and created works that featured solid colors, straight lines, and an abstract aesthetic.

When the Bauhaus was shut down by the Nazis in 1933, Anni and her husband, Josef Albers (an artist and Bauhaus alum himself), moved to North Carolina and joined the faculty of Black Mountain College, another experimental art school. There, she taught her students to experiment with materials and play, which she believed would lead to work that was both beautiful and functional. In her book, *On Designing*, Anni Albers said on weaving: "Like any craft, it may end in producing useful objects, or it may rise to the level of art."

The Renwick Gallery honored Anni Albers with a retrospective exhibition of her woven and graphic art in 1985. Describing Albers' woven pieces, the catalog stated: "Creating work from fiber that is nonfunctional and beautiful, Albers opened the way for the development of contemporary fiber work."

▲ *Red and Blue Layers*, 1954   Cotton 24¼×14¾ in.

EVERYTHING OLD IS NEW AGAIN

Cross-Stitch

The simple and versatile cross-stitch was commonly used in American embroidery samplers and to embellish household goods in the 1600s to the 1800s. As its name implies, cross-stitch is made by crossing embroidery floss in an x-pattern to create letters, motifs, and images. Its simplicity has made it popular through the centuries.

STITCHING SAMPLERS
The Smithsonian's collection includes more than 130 American embroidery samplers, with the earliest made in 1735 by Lydia Dickman of Boston, Massachusetts. Cross-stitch is featured prominently in many of these samplers, depicting verses, flowers, houses, and religious and pastoral scenes. Because of its versatility, cross-stitch was used as the base stitch for many women to learn basic embroidery skills and to practice stitching their letters and numbers. Young girls stitched their name on their work, and parents often displayed it proudly in the home.

MODERN STITCHES
Today, modern makers are using cross-stitch to depict their own messages, images, and scenes that are relevant to today's world. The art of cross-stitch remains incredibly versatile, and patterns are readily available for a variety of designs, including pixelated motifs, flowers and plants, and political or feminist messages.

▲ Many early samplers featured cross-stitch letters and scenery. Young girls made samplers in part to practice their needlework.

▶ This sampler was made by Elizabeth Saggar in England around 1734. It features colorful silks on a natural linen background.

▼ This "spot" sampler was made in England between 1601 and 1650. Spot samplers feature motifs that are randomly scattered over the surface of the fabric—usually linen. This one features flowers, fragments of a repeating pattern, a snail, deer, fish, and falconer.

▲ A contemporary lemon motif cross-stitch pattern by Anne Mills at the Stitch Mill

Needlework Sampler

The earliest known American sampler was made by Loara Standish of the Plymouth Colony about 1645. The phrase in the center of this sampler was inspired by that early sampler, but it's updated with a 21st-century design.

YOU WILL NEED

12"×12" piece of canvas or linen cloth (white or off-white)

Carbon transfer paper

Stylus or ballpoint pen

8" embroidery hoop

Embroidery needle

Embroidery thread in several colors

Small scissors or thread snips

Felt for backing

1 Following the instructions on your transfer paper, trace the design onto the fabric, making sure all lines are visible.

2 Place your fabric in the embroidery hoop, centering the design so all lines are visible. Pull fabric taut.

3 Begin embroidering the lines of the sampler with various embroidery stitches. Use a backstitch or stem stitch for outlines; use a satin stitch or seed stitch for filling in areas. Use French knots for small dots and adding areas of interest. On the horizontal lines on the top and bottom of the design, you can embroider decorative stitches such as a split stitch, lazy daisy, chain stitch, or cross-stitch. When you are done with a color or section, tie a knot on the back of your work and trim your thread to finish.

4 When the sampler is complete, finish it with a felt backing. Cut a circle of felt just smaller than 8" so it fits on the back of your piece inside the hoop. Pull the fabric tight in the hoop, pull in the loose fabric ends, and place the felt over the back to cover the stitches. Stitch in place with a whip stitch to secure the felt. Hang your embroidery hoop on a wall to display.

A Satin Stitch

B Lazy Daisy Stitch

C Cross-Stitch

D Feather Stitch

E Chain Stitch

F Thread Running Stitch

G Fly Stitch

H French Knots

I Blanket Stitch

J Backstitch

K Couching

Enlarge 250%

Satin-Stitched Scarf

In 19th-century America, it was popular to embellish fabrics with hand embroidery. The Smithsonian collection includes more than 400 printing blocks that were used as embroidery designs. Makers would dip the metal portions in ink, stamp the design on their fabric, and then embroider the design. Here, we've re-created a popular design from *Godey's Ladies' Book* (1861), which you can trace and embroider onto a scarf.

YOU WILL NEED

At least ½ yard of 55"-wide 100% linen fabric for the scarf

Iron

Ironing mat

Sewing machine

Pen or stylus for tracing

Carbon tracing paper (gray for light fabrics, white for dark fabrics)

4 skeins of embroidery thread in the color of your choice

Embroidery needle

Small scissors

Awl or similar tool for creating eyelet holes

1 Hem the long sides of your scarf by turning the edge under ¼" and pressing with your iron. Turn it under another ¼" and press so the raw edges are hidden from view.
2 Using your sewing machine, stitch the hem in place, close to the edge.
3 On one short edge of your scarf, use a pencil, stylus, or needle to fray the edge. Carefully pull out cross threads from the end of your scarf until you have about a ½" fringe. Repeat on the other end.
4 Trace the embroidery design from the book onto a piece of paper or make a photocopy at 100% scale. Follow the directions on your transfer paper to transfer the design to the fabric in your desired pattern. (Note, some carbon transfer inks do not wash out, so we recommend doing a test and then carefully apply the design to your fabric.)
5 Use a stem stitch to embroider the solid line through the middle of the design.
6 The eyelets are created by first stabilizing the fabric, then poking a hole and finishing with embroidery. Use a running stitch or backstitch to embroider the edges of the eyelets. Then, using your awl, poke a hole in the fabric to the size of your eyelet. Satin-stitch closely around the edges of the hole, making sure not to leave any gaps in the embroidery.
7 Continue embroidering the designs on one edge, then the other, until your scarf is complete.

Stem Stitch

Satin Stitch

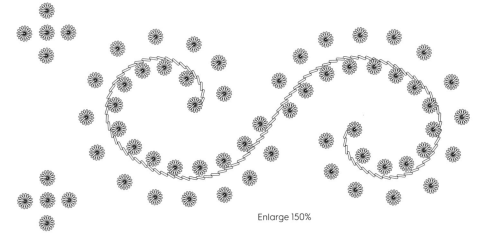

Enlarge 150%

HIDDEN HISTORY

Mark Twain

Mark Twain is most well-known for his contributions to American literature, including *The Adventures of Tom Sawyer* (1876) and *The Adventures of Huckleberry Finn* (1885), but the author was also an avid scrapbooker and created a patent for self-pasting scrapbook pages.

Mark Twain was born in 1835 and would grow up to be one of the most well-known names in American literature. Throughout his life, Twain was an avid scrapbooker and collected memorabilia from his travels. At the time, scrapbookers adhered clippings with mucilage, a finicky glue that was difficult to work with. Twain decided the scrapbook could be improved upon, and he set to work.

WHO IS SAMUEL L. CLEMENS?

In 1873, Twain registered his "Improvement in Scrap-Books" as a patent under his given name, Samuel L. Clemens. This was his second of three inventions—his first being an "Improvement in Adjustable and Detachable Straps for Garments" (elastic straps that could replace

> "Be it known that I, Samuel L. Clemens, of Hartford, in the county of Hartford and in the State of Connecticut, have invented certain new and useful Improvements in Scrap-Book."

suspenders) and the last being a memory game. But his most successful endeavor was the scrapbook. Twain's scrapbook pages came with an adhesive already present on the paper, which, when moistened, would become sticky. "It is only necessary to moisten so much of the leaf as will contain the piece to be pasted in, and place such piece thereon, when it will stick to the leaf," he wrote in the patent description.

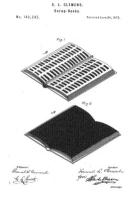

▶ Two pages from a four-page pamphlet Mark Twain designed to advertise different versions of his self-pasting scrapbook.

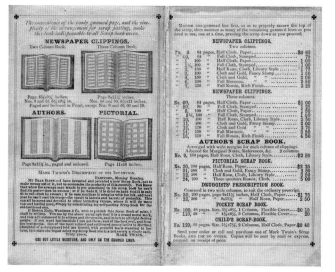

▼ Mark Twain (born Samuel Langhorne Clemens) was a writer, humorist, entrepreneur, and inventor, as well as an avid scrapbooker.

SELF-PASTING SCRAPBOOK

Twain's scrapbooks quickly caught on. An article from the *St. Louis Post-Dispatch* in 1885 reported that Twain's books earned him over $50,000 (about $1.3 million in today's dollars) over the course of his life, while his books earned around $200,000 (about $5.2 million in today's dollars). Twain used his humorous writing style to advertise his new invention—in one advertisement, Twain's description of the scrapbook reads as follows:

"I have invented and patented a new Scrap Book, not to make money out of it, but to economize the profanity of this country. You know that when the average man wants to put something in his scrap book he can't find his paste—then he swears; or if he finds it, it is dried so hard that it is only fit to eat—then he swears; if he uses mucilage it mingles with the ink, and next year he can't read his scrap—the result is barrels and barrels of profanity. This can all be saved and devoted to other irritating things, where it will do more real and lasting good, simply by substituting my self-pasting Scrap Book for the old-fashioned one."

A LASTING IMPACT

Twain's scrapbooks were in production for nearly 30 years, between 1877 and 1902, and likely made it easier and more popular for people to pick up the art of scrapbooking. Three of Twain's patented self-pasting scrapbooks are now housed in the collection of the West Virginia & Regional History Center.

> "I have invented and patented a new Scrap Book, not to make money out of it, but to economize the profanity of this country."
>
> —Mark Twain

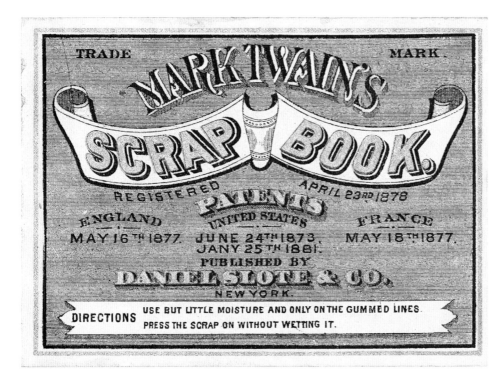

▲ According to the *St. Louis Post-Dispatch*, Mark Twain's scrapbooks earned him $50,000 over the course of his life.

◄ Twain patented a scrapbook whose pages were covered with the same type of adhesive that is on the back of postage stamps.

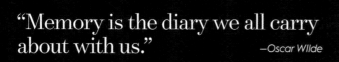

"Memory is the diary we all carry about with us."

—Oscar Wilde

THE FASTEST SEA-FIGHTER EVER BUILT
—U.S. NAVY VOUGHT-SIKORSKY—
A PRODUCT OF AMERICAN LABOR

Hollywood ★ Wednesday, January 7, 1942

"THUNDERBOLT"—As President Roosevelt called for 60,000 warplanes this year, interest turned particularly to the Republic P-47 Thunderbolt, which will cost be in quantity production, and which was described by the Army Air Corps as "the hottest thing in the air." It is said to be the world's fastest single-engined craft, powered by a 2000-horsepower engine driving a four-bladed propeller, with a diving speed of 680 miles an hour. At right, Alexander Kartvel, chief engineer of the Republic Aviation Corp., its designer.

1915
A.D.B.BABBETT
IDEA

ith cannon and guns of varying calibers / vering every angle of its smooth surface / s rising from its 132-foot fuselage, the B-19 / Corps. Largest and most powe...

plane in the world, this Douglas-built giant can ... / from inland United States to Europe and return ... as a troop transport it could / carry 125 fully armed soldiers ... At March Field, where the B-19 is being test flown by the / Air Corps, the huge ship dwarfs a primary training plane parked un... fuselage, above.

1972

PASTE

水題

八水ナリ
一自己ノ進路ヲ求メテ止ザルハ水ナリ
一障害ニ逢テ激シク其勢力ヲ百倍シ得ルハ水ナリ
一常ニ己ノ姿ヲ他ノ汚ヲ流シ清濁併セ容ルルノ量
一洋トシテ大洋ヲ充シ発シテ蒸気トナリ雲トナリ
一水ナリ
潔ヨキ冷ヲ帯上ニシ凝リテハ霊妙ナル鏡ト

名古屋市南區中町十三番地
合名山田紡機製作所
合資
電話南五二八番

SCRAP
BOOK

STEST WORKING
PEZE ACT
THE WORLD.
LY Act of its Kind
oing TEETH WORK.

STUBBLEFIELD TRIO

AMERICA'S FOREMOST

NOVELTY AERIALISTS

Chicago Oct 31   190

A MOMENT IN TIME

Scrapbooking

Humans have been keeping scrapbooks for centuries, but the craft reached its peak in 2004, when Americans were spending more than $2.5 billion on scrapbooking supplies.

The Italian "*zibaldone*," which literally means a "heap of things," was among the first scrapbooks kept by humans, found in 14th-century Italy. A century later, "commonplace books" were popular in Europe during the Renaissance and were used to contain recipes, poetry, letters, facts, tables, and more.

In the 19th century, the British coined the term "scrapbook" for these types of compendiums, and scrapbooks as we know them made their way to America, where they were popular among notable figures such as Mark Twain, F. Scott Fitzgerald, and Amelia Earhart. Scrapbooks remained popular throughout the 20th century, but at the dawn of the 21st century, America caught scrapbook fever.

▲ Modern scrapbooks often feature embellishments, while historic scrapbooks were made simply by pasting images and clippings to the page.

"Scrapbooks are as diverse as their makers."

—Eva H. Buchanan-Cates

◀ The Archives Center at the National Museum of American History acquires, preserves, and provides access to scrapbooks because they are careful, unique, and personal constructions of moments in time that contribute to the telling of America's story.

SCRAPBOOKS GO VIRAL

At the turn of the century, people flocked to scrapbooks. According to a 2004 report by the Craft & Hobby Association, sales from scrapbook materials more than doubled between 2001 and 2003 from $1 billion to $2.5 billion in the U.S. alone. A survey by *Creating Keepsakes* magazine estimated that people in a quarter of American households were participating in the craft.

Family photos were printed for every occasion, from weddings to Easter egg hunts. Scrapbook enthusiasts spanned all ages and styles—from traditional to punk rock. Tools and materials for scrapbooking were suddenly everywhere, and decorative paper, die cuts,

TOMB AND SHADE OF ELLSWOR
His Spirit still Lives.

Friend Thomas,—Oh! ho! so thee was a
to fight, friend Secede, was thee? I hope the
found out now that the Quakers are sound o
Union.

SECESSION WAGON.

Jeff Davis—My wagon is kind of caving in.
am afraid Uncle Abe will catch me before I g
far with these goods.

pinking shears, embossing tools, stickers, and stamps crowded the shelves at craft stores. Trade shows showcased new paper, tools, and trends for scrapbookers, and enthusiasts gathered for scrapbook conferences, workshops, retreats, and even competitions around the country. America couldn't get enough.

THE DAWN OF THE INTERNET

As the aughts pressed on, the Internet became more ingrained in daily life. Scrapbookers continued their craft, and many began supplementing their hard copies with online blogs, social media accounts, and websites. Some scrapbookers posted their scrapbook pages online to provide inspiration and tutorials for other scrappers. Others opted to start digital photo albums or blogs that would replace their hard-copy scrapbooks. Google Trends reports that the term "scrapbook" was searched for at its peak in 2004, but the term "digital scrapbook" was on the rise from 2005 to 2008.

RECESSION IN AMERICA

When the financial crisis hit America in 2008, one of the first casualties was the craft and hobby industry. Many scrapbookers boxed up their supplies (averaging more than $1,000 per household at its peak), opting for more-economical ways to preserve memories. The Internet was rapidly changing, and social media sites like Facebook offered new and exciting ways to record daily life. Today, the U.S. craft industry is once again on the rise, with the Association for Creative Industries reporting a $43.9 billion industry in 2017, but the golden age of the scrapbook may be one for the history books.

SCRAPBOOKS AT THE SMITHSONIAN

The National Museum of American History's Archives Center contains more than 1,400 collections documenting America's history—many of which are scrapbook pages from people who recorded their personal histories in a scrapbook. Archivists at the Smithsonian work to preserve scrapbook pages from deterioration and also digitize the information so it can be enjoyed for years to come. Hundreds of scrapbook pages can be found by searching the Smithsonian web archives at sova.si.edu.

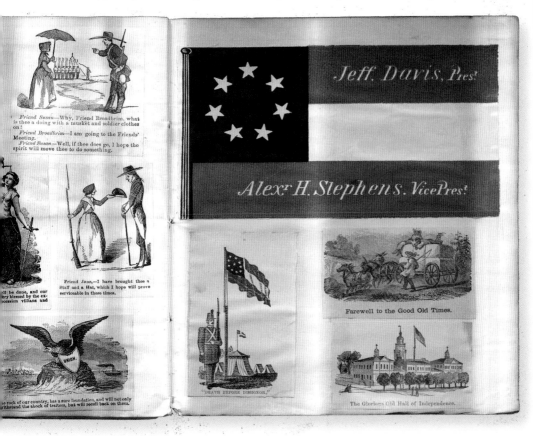

◀ Scrapbooks offer a glimpse into daily American life throughout history. The makers are often unknown, but you can see traces of their personal lives in the pages.

Crayola

CRAYOLA CRAYONS HAVE BEEN INSPIRING MAKERS SINCE THEIR DEBUT IN 1903. OFTEN A CHILD'S FIRST INTRODUCTION TO THE WORLD OF CRAFTS, THE COMPANY'S BELOVED CRAYONS, MARKERS, AND COLORED PENCILS STAND THE TEST OF TIME AND CONTINUE TO USHER IN A NEW GENERATION OF MAKERS.

▲ Cherished by generations of child artists, Crayola crayons were invented in 1903 by the Binney & Smith Company of Easton, Pennsylvania. Using paraffin wax and nontoxic pigments, the company produced a coloring stick that

A COLORFUL HISTORY

Crayola began as a pigment company in 1885, producing red pigments for barns and black for car tires. It wasn't until 1903 that the first box of eight crayons was introduced, which included the classic combination of black, brown, blue, red, violet, orange, yellow, and green (still sold today as Crayola's original eight-pack).

The name "Crayola" was coined by Alice Binney, wife of co-founder Edwin Binney, and is an amalgam of the words *"craie,"* the French word for "chalk," and "ola," for "oleaginous" or "oily." Alice Binney was a former schoolteacher, and the classic box of eight was released because the founders saw a need for safe and affordable crayons for schoolchildren. In 1903, it cost five cents.

Crayola's famous box of 64 crayons was released in 1958 and quickly became the company's most popular offering. Over the years, Crayola continued to offer more products that have become staples in craft rooms and classrooms around the country, including markers (first released in 1978), washable crayons, window chalk, and more.

For its 100th birthday in 2003, Crayola released four new crayon colors for the next century, including inchworm, mango tango, wild blue yonder, and jazzberry jam.

EVERYTHING OLD IS NEW AGAIN

Paper Cutting

Long before Johannes Gutenberg invented the printing press, people around the world were using paper for art and craft. Paper had many predecessors, including clay tablets, wood, and papyrus, but paper made from plant fibers was light, flexible, and easier to make than other parchments at the time. Early papers were created by the Chinese more than 2,000 years ago and were soon regularly produced for calligraphy, art, and crafts—including paper cuttings, which were used to decorate windows and screens. Women also adorned their hair with paper-cut designs. As paper was shared and adopted by other Asian countries, different styles of paper cutting were developed. Some of the oldest paper-cutting traditions come from China, Japan, and Korea.

Paper and paper cutting eventually made its way to Europe, where it was adopted for writing and art. In Germany, it is known as *scherenschnitte*, or "scissor cuts." Paper cutting has been used in Jewish traditions since the Middle Ages, commonly made for holidays and special ceremonies.

THE ART OF PAPER CUTTING

Traditionally, designs are traced onto a piece of paper, and sections are carefully removed with a sharp blade to create a silhouette. In some traditions, paper cuttings are pasted on top of a contrasting background; in others, they are hung in a window to allow light to shine through in the empty spaces.

MODERN PAPER CUTTING

Paper cutting remains popular for its versatility and simplicity—all you need is a sharp blade, a piece of paper, and a design, and you can create something beautiful. Makers today are creating contemporary designs ranging from the intricate to the simplistic, challenging and inspiring a new generation to try their hand at this ancient craft.

◀▲ Paper cuttings by artist Ira Blount, 2008 and 2007

▶ Paper cutting by artist Hiromi Mizugai, 2018

Martha Stewart attends the Michaels and Martha Stewart Experiential Craft Paint Launch Event at Hudson Studios on June 15, 2017 in New York City.

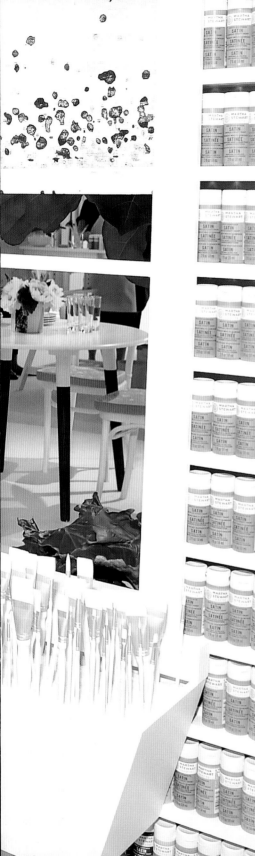

Martha Stewart

FOR MORE THAN 30 YEARS, MARTHA STEWART HAS BEEN A HOUSEHOLD NAME IN CRAFTING AND THE DOMESTIC ARTS. TODAY, THIS MULTITALENTED BUSINESSWOMAN CONTINUES TO LEAD THE WAY IN PUBLISHING CRAFT PROJECTS AND TUTORIALS FOR MAKERS OF ALL AGES.

QUEEN OF CRAFT

Martha Stewart was born in 1941 in New Jersey and learned several domestic arts from her mother, including sewing and crafting. In her book *Encyclopedia of Sewing & Fabric Crafts* (2010), Stewart describes learning how to sew from her mother, who always had a project, and taught Martha and her sisters to make clothes, scarves, aprons, and decorative household objects.

In the 1980s, Martha Stewart began writing articles on home-making for magazines and newspapers, and in 1990, *Martha Stewart Living* began as a quarterly magazine. Three years later, her TV show by the same name debuted, and Martha became the face of domestic arts and crafts in America and a household name around the world.

Martha's approach to do-it-yourself projects is fun, easy, and approachable, and she champions crafts for all ages and abilities (including children's crafts). Over the years, her personal brand burgeoned into a monthly magazine, several TV shows, and a lifestyle website, which today has tutorials for hundreds of crafts and techniques, including sewing, paper crafting, knitting and crochet, DIY home and furniture projects, and more.

Now, nearly 30 years after her first magazine was published, Martha Stewart continues to inspire as a figurehead for all things crafts and homemaking.

EVERYTHING OLD IS NEW AGAIN

Mending

Throughout history, people have mended clothes out of necessity. During World War II, the British government even ran a campaign encouraging people to "Make Do and Mend" so valuable materials could be used by troops. But from darning socks to repairing ripped jeans, mending has always been more than just fixing—it is also an art form.

THE ART OF THE MEND

Darning, the art of repairing holes in garments like socks, is one of the most well-known mending arts. Distressed areas are repaired by weaving individual strands of thread over a hole until the hole is completely covered. Cultures around the world have their own techniques for mending—like the Japanese mending techniques *boro* and *sashiko*, which involve using patchwork and a series of running stitch patterns with thick thread to cover and fortify a hole.

MODERN MENDING

Makers today are returning to mending as a craft and hobby, drawing on these traditional mending techniques. Modern mends are both functional and beautiful, and ripped-and-repaired garments are now displayed with pride on many social media accounts and websites.

SUSTAINABLE STITCHES

In the 21st century, mending clothes can also serve to combat wastefulness and promote sustainable fashion by repairing pieces that can still be used for years to come. Mending is part of the slow fashion movement, helping makers to connect with their clothing and infuse more meaning into the items that they wear every day. Because mending is easy, fun, and quick, many new makers are trying their hand at this simple craft and extending the life of their garments.

▼ A darning mushroom is a tool with a round top and a handle, usually made of wood. It is often used in sock mending, in which the sock is stretched over the top, pulled taut, secured in place, and mended with yarn.

▲ Modern makers still use darning mushrooms, needles, and colorful threads to mend holes in socks.

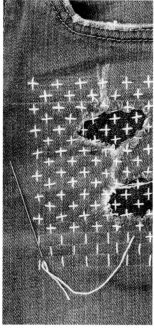

▶ Right and opposite page, Mending art by Jessica Marquez at Miniature Rhino

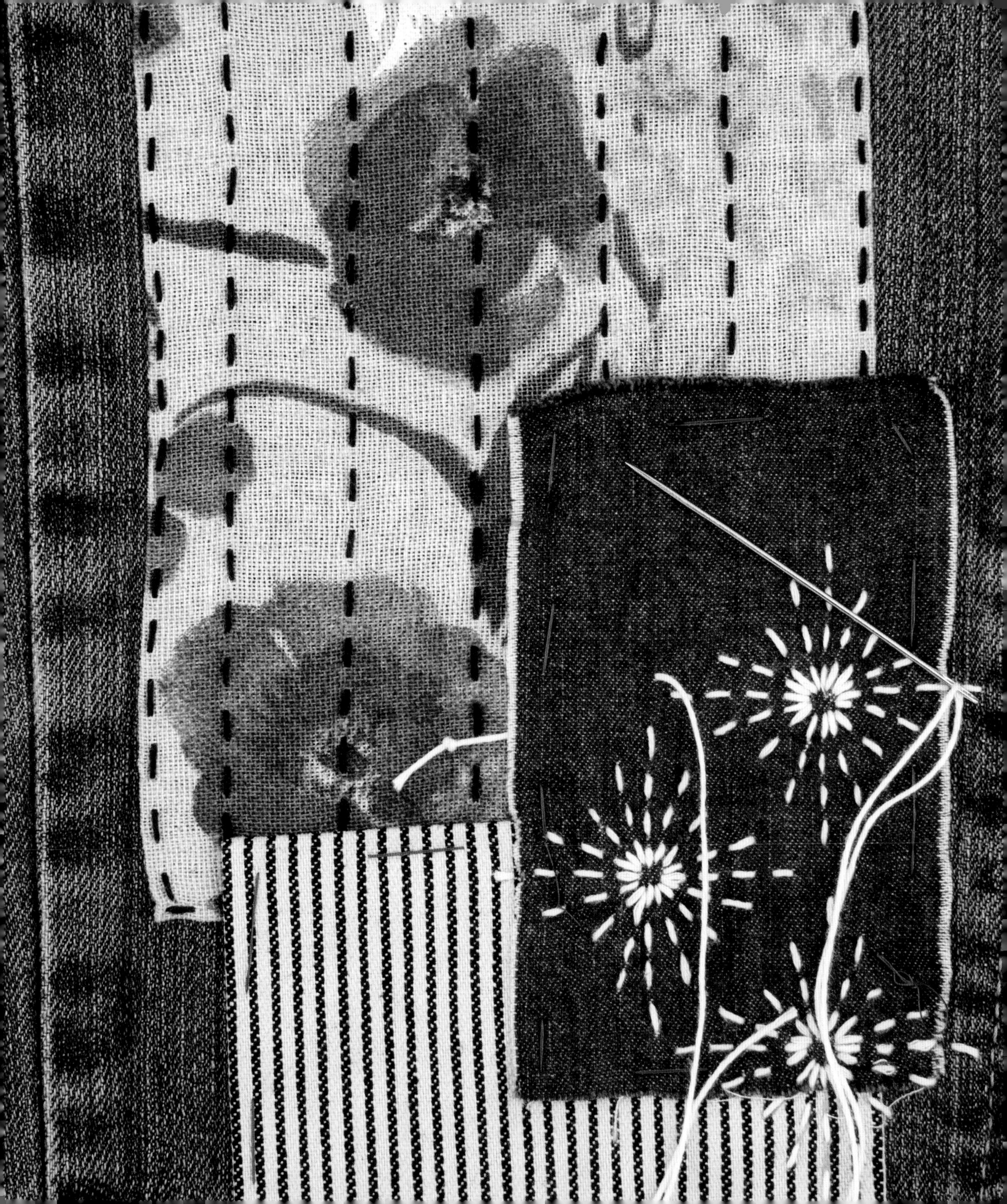

Visible Mending: Jeans

Breathe new life into an old pair of jeans. Mending not only keeps a beloved piece of clothing in your wardrobe, but it can also turn it into a one-of-a-kind work of art.

YOU WILL NEED

A pair of jeans you would like to repair

Extra denim

Embroidery thread

Embroidery needle

Small scissors

1 Trim an extra piece of denim to a size slightly larger than your hole. Additional denim can be purchased or salvaged from another pair of jeans. Place the patch inside your pants underneath the hole and pin in place.

2 Choose a color of embroidery thread that complements your jeans. Separate the embroidery floss into three strands and thread your needle.

3 Tie a knot in your thread and thread the needle through the inside of your jeans, about 1" to 2" above the hole. Using a running stitch, sew a vertical line straight across. Continue sewing until you have sewn across the hole

and past it about 1" to 2". Once you reach the other side, turn the needle and sew back across, about ¼" to ½" from your first line. Continue sewing in this way, catching the patch and the original jeans fabric, until you've covered the hole with stitches. When needed, tie a knot and hide it on the backside to finish a piece of thread.

4 The jeans are now ready for wear, or you can continue strengthening the fabric with additional stitches or decorative embellishments. Continue mending until you are happy with the way your jeans look and feel.

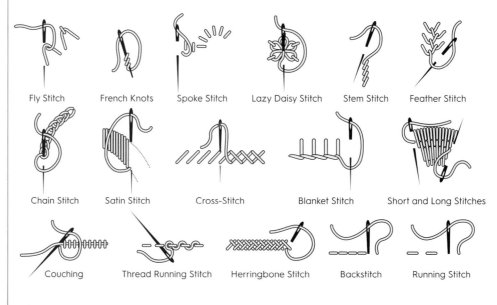

Fly Stitch   French Knots   Spoke Stitch   Lazy Daisy Stitch   Stem Stitch   Feather Stitch

Chain Stitch   Satin Stitch   Cross-Stitch   Blanket Stitch   Short and Long Stitches

Couching   Thread Running Stitch   Herringbone Stitch   Backstitch   Running Stitch

▲ This project uses the Backstitch and Running Stitch, but have fun experimenting with these other decorative stitches.

Kite

Throughout U.S. history, kites have had many uses—for measuring distances, research, military services, and of course in the infamous kite experiment, where Benjamin Franklin allegedly discovered electricity (don't try this at home). Most commonly, however, kites have been used for fun. Here's how to make a traditional, vintage-inspired kite to fly on the next breezy day.

YOU WILL NEED

2 dowels ¼"×36" (cut one to 30")

Box cutter, X-acto knife, or serrated kitchen knife

Masking tape

Cotton or polyester string for construction

1 yard of light cotton or linen fabric, or at least 34"×40"

Pinking shears

Fabric glue (optional)

Long spool of thread for flying

Ribbon

Fabric strips for tail

1 Cut small notches in each end of the dowels to hold the string that will become the outer frame. Notches should be about ¼" deep.

2 Place small notches in the dowels where they will cross to form a "T". For the 30" dowel, cut the notch in the middle (15" from either end). For the 36" dowel, cut the notch 12" down from the top.

3 Cross the dowels and position them so the notches are aligned. Tape them in place with masking tape. (For additional support, you can use string and masking tape together to secure the two pieces tightly.)

4 Form the outer frame of the kite. Using your cotton or polyester string, wrap a piece of string tightly all the way around the frame, placing the string in the notches at each end of the dowel. Start and end at the bottom, tying the string together and trimming to size.

5 Spread out your fabric and lay the kite frame on top. Using pinking shears, cut the fabric about 1" larger than the frame on all sides.

6 Fold the excess fabric over the outer string and secure using fabric glue or a simple running stitch. Continue all the way around the frame until all edges are tight and secure.

7 Cut a length of string about 25" to 30" long. Tie it to the long dowel using a slip knot that you can adjust as needed to allow the kite to fly in your conditions. This will be the string that attaches to your spool thread.

8 Cut a length of ribbon for the tail (about 30"). Tie about 6 to 8 fabric scraps tightly to the ribbon. This will act as a weight and keep your kite from spinning or flipping. Tie the ribbon to the bottom of your kite.

9 Tie one end of your spool thread to the flying thread. Take your kite outside on a breezy day and enjoy.

Scrapbook Shadowbox

Scrapbook pages have taken different shapes over time, but at their heart, they are meant to preserve memories. This modern take on a scrapbook page keeps those memories front and center by allowing them to be displayed on a wall or mantel.

YOU WILL NEED

Shadowbox (any size will work, but it should be big enough to hold photos and memorabilia)

Photos, memorabilia, and/or clippings

Decorative paper or cardstock

Cardboard for the background

Glue dots or double-sided tape

Scissors

Hot-glue gun and glue sticks (optional)

Embellishments such as ribbon, paper, and stickers

1 Select the photos, clippings, and/or memorabilia you would like to display in your scrapbook shadowbox. We recommend choosing a single theme or event for each shadowbox, but the possibilities are endless! (For this shadowbox, we chose a woman and included a birth certificate, photo, and items meaningful to her.)

2 We recommend loading your items through the front, so place your shadowbox face up on your work surface. If you would like a decorative background, adhere your preferred paper or background first onto a piece of cardboard cut to the appropriate size for your shadowbox.

3 Place the background in the shadowbox and begin arranging paper items or photos on top. You can create a layered effect by using glue dots or bits of cardboard between layers. Glue or tape your items securely in place.

4 Set your shadowbox upright and add any objects that you would like to stand upright in the shadowbox. Affix these to the "floor" of your shadowbox with glue or tape. Continue adding and arranging items until you are satisfied with your piece.

5 Finish the project by hanging it on a wall or standing it on a mantel to display. Enjoy!

"Paper dolls weren't just toys for children. Think of them as the Pinterest of the past. They provided style inspiration and a steady stream of celebrity-approved fashions."

— Catherine Keen, Archivist, National Museum of American History

Paper doll and outfits by Xenia Cage, from the Cooper Hewitt, Smithsonian Design Museum.

Contemporaries

Quilters throughout history have used fabric, needle, and thread to create beautiful quilts at the intersection of form and function. Today's quilters are embracing this historic American craft and making quilts that function equally well at home on a wall or a bed.

▲ *Improv Log Cabin* by Tara Faughnan at Quilt-Con 2016 in Pasadena, California

In the 2000s, quilters started creating quilt designs based on modern art and graphic design, featuring areas of negative space, alternative layouts, and improvisation. These quilts had roots in traditional quilt designs, but they had a cool factor that gave quilting a fresh appeal for a new generation. Inspired by early modern quilters and art quilters like Nancy Crow, Gwen Marston, Denyse Schmidt, and the bold work of Amish quilters and the quilters of Gee's Bend, these new quilters promoted a new style of "modern" quilt for the 21st century.

Young makers adopted these contemporary designs and began quilting for themselves, their families, and their friends. They began quilting, often learning from a family member, or by teaching themselves through online blogs, videos, and tutorials, which were cropping up as social media and personal blogs began to grow in popularity. Soon there were

"Modern quilts are creative expressions made with needle and thread, fabric, and time, expressing today's aesthetic through a generations-old traditional craft."

—*Modern Quilts: Designs of the New Century*

a plethora of websites devoted solely to modern quilting and a new online community of makers taking up the craft.

THE MODERN QUILT GUILD

In 2009, a membership group called the Modern Quilt Guild (MQG) began in Los Angeles, providing modern quilters with a place to gather, learn, and make quilts together. In 2013, the MQG hosted the first QuiltCon, a quilt show and convention dedicated entirely to modern quilting. Since then, QuiltCon has grown into an annual international show attracting thousands of people and showcasing more than 500 quilts over four days. Quilters compete for top prizes in 12 categories, and attendees can participate in workshops and lectures by leading modern quilters and designers.

As an organization, the MQG now comprises more than 15,000 members in more than 200 local guilds worldwide.

WHAT IS MODERN QUILTING?

Many of today's quilters and designers follow trends in the art, design, and interior design worlds, developing contemporary designs that speak to a new generation of quilters. Hallmarks of modern quilting include high-contrast designs, solid fabrics, geometric elements, and clean lines. Modern quilts often feature "matchstick," or straight-line quilting, to complement straight-line designs within the piecing.

Some modern quilters use quilting as a medium for political commentary, reflecting an age-old quilting tradition with a new aesthetic. As America continues to change and evolve over time, so do its quilts and quilters, just one segment of a growing population of makers changing the way we think about craft.

Charity quilts by members of the Modern Quilt Guild hang at QuiltCon 2018 in Pasadena, California.

▲ *One Earth* by Kathy York at QuiltCon 2016 in Pasasdena, California

◀ Attendees view modern quilts in the exhibit hall at QuiltCon 2018 in Pasadena, California.

GET INVOLVED

Want to learn more about modern quilting? Check out the Modern Quilt Guild online at themodernquiltguild.com and learn more about the annual quilt show and conference, QuiltCon, at quiltcon.com.

Cooking & Food

Procuring and preparing food is an essential function of human existence. From the country's earliest days of hunting and gathering to innovations that made food production faster and easier to the cultivation of cooking as an art form, what we eat is a reflection of who we are, where we came from, and where we will go.

A hand-colored woodcut depicts Native Americans harvesting corn, or maize, perhaps the most important crop cultivated in North America.

An American Chronology

The story of food in the U.S. is a complicated one. It's one of abundance and scarcity, innovations that had good and bad effects, and a search for both sustenance and meaning in one of life's most fundamental elements.

▲ The first half of the 19th century saw steady and significant improvements in stove design. By the 1850s, open-hearth cooking was a thing of the past in most middle-class homes.

THE PRECOLONIAL ERA

The diets of the indigenous people in precolonial America were, as might be expected, highly regionalized, but not confined to hunting and gathering. The research of Rita Laws, Ph.D., a member of the Choctaw Nation of Southeastern Oklahoma, suggests that the Choctaw grew 60 to 80 different crops, for instance. That all changed starting in the late 15th century, when Western European colonization of the Caribbean and North and South America disrupted food cultures on both sides of the Atlantic. The exchange of plants, animals, technology, diseases, and people—both free and enslaved—known as the Columbian Exchange resulted in the vast diversification of diets around the world. Just one example of this—the introduction of cows and wheat to the Americas from Europe—had a profound effect on what would become the North American diet.

THE COLONIAL PERIOD

During the first winter at Plymouth (1620–1621), 45 of the 102 passengers on the *Mayflower* died. Survivors were aided by

Participants in Harvard College's midsummer Commencement banquet in 1688 enjoyed "cherryes... salad herbs...[and] parsley."

the Wampanoag tribe—who had deep and sophisticated agricultural knowledge—in growing foods that thrived in that environment. The port of Boston became a hub for importing and exporting foodstuffs. Commodities such as sugar, molasses, tea, coffee, chocolate, and citrus were among the most valuable imports.

In 1685, the first rice seed was planted in Charleston, South Carolina. Production spread rapidly. By 1695, rice was so valuable that it was used to pay rent to British proprietors. Advancements in technology and production methods—many of them contributed by enslaved people who had knowledge of rice growing in Africa—dramatically increased yields. By the 1780s, annual production had reached 80 million pounds. Then, as now, about half was exported and half consumed here.

THE EARLY REPUBLIC

The purchase of the Louisiana Territory from France in 1803 nearly doubled the size of the United States. A period of westward expansion (1801–1861) was spurred by economic opportunity and the availability of land, created by forcibly removing indigenous communities from it.

Settlers lived on bison; deer; wild turkey; greens such as purslane, dandelion, and pigweed; as well as wild fruits, berries, and nuts. They exercised creativity in trying to make familiar foods when supplies were not available. Wild honey and maple syrup supplanted sugar, and when there was no tea, they steeped sage, sassafras, and mint.

Agricultural expansion created a veritable cornucopia. Extension of the rail network, along with developments in canning in the early to mid-19th century, meant foods such as canned oysters could be served alongside these frontier foods.

▲ Settlers traveling during the period of westward expansion lived on wild game, including wild turkey.

THE ERA OF MASS MIGRATION

Nothing has had more impact on the landscape of American food than immigration—in particular, the mass immigration of the second half of the 19th century. Between 1870 and 1900, nearly 12 million immigrants arrived on the shores of the United States.

◀ Innovations in the canned-food industry in the early to mid-19th century meant prepared foods could be transported all over the country.

SOUP FOR THE ROAD

Among Lewis and Clark's provisions on their expedition west in 1804 was 193 pounds of "portable soup," a concoction of beef broth, eggs, and vegetables that was boiled down and dehydrated until gelatinous for long-term storage—a precursor of bouillon cubes. It was a meal of last resort.

4 DOZ CANS NET CONTENTS EACH 11 OZ. AVOIR.
SNIDER
(PROCESS)
PORK AND BEANS
WITH TOMATO SAUCE
THE T.A. SNIDER PRESERVE CO
CHICAGO, U.S.A.

In 1849, Chinese workers began migrating in large numbers to the United States to work in gold mines, agriculture, and factories, and, most famously, to build railroads in the West. The entrepreneurial among them started businesses, including restaurants—the first of which was Canton Restaurant, opened

---

Adolphus Busch (1839–1913) left the Rhineland in 1857 and settled in St. Louis, where he married the daughter of a successful brewer.

---

in San Francisco in 1849. By 1882, when the Chinese Exclusion Act put an end to Chinese immigration for 60 years, there were 14 Chinese restaurants in the city. Today, there are more than 45,000 across the country.

The failure in the mid-19th century of revolutions to establish democracy in Germany caused thousands of Germans to flee to America in the following decades. One of these was Adolphus Busch (1839–1913), who left the Rhineland in 1857 and landed in St. Louis,

▲ During the 1930s, nearly one-third of cookbook recipes were gelatin-based. As fresh fruits and vegetables became more prominent in the American diet, congealed salads were considered an elegant way to present them.

where he married the daughter of a successful brewer. By 1890, nearly 3 million German-born immigrants lived in the United States. Street vendors began offering pretzels and sausages, including the frankfurter.

Italian immigrants began to arrive en masse around 1880. By 1920, more than 4 million Italians had come here. And while many of the dishes identified as Italian may not exactly mirror traditional foodways in Italy, the mark made by Italian immigrants—pizza, pasta, meatballs, risotto, espresso, olive oil, cheeses, balsamic vinegar—is immeasurable.

THE 20TH CENTURY

The years between 1900 and 2000 saw almost unprecedented changes in how Americans procure food and their attitudes about it.

Prior to 1900, most Americans produced their own food on small farms or purchased it from a farmer or gardener. Growth of cities due to industrialization and mass immigration forced a different way. In 1916, Clarence Saunders opened the first supermarket—a Piggly Wiggly—in Memphis, Tennessee. Others followed, and soon most Americans got all of their food at supermarkets—much of which was heavily processed due to innovations in food production and storage. The canned and frozen foods that reigned supreme throughout the 1950s and early 1960s gave way to the natural-foods movement of the 1970s. In the 1980s, chefs and home cooks alike began embracing the concept of New American cuisine—a fusion of the influences of traditional American foods and cooking techniques with those from around the world. It is an idea that has been expanded upon and continues to be embraced by the American public to this day.

▼ L.A. Chef Roy Choi's Kogi BBQ Taco Trucks synthesize two developments of the last 30 years: the fusion of flavors and cooking techniques from differing cuisines and the food-truck phenomenon that really took off in about 2010. Choi's food blends Korean barbecue with Mexican foods such as tacos and burritos.

PAST IS PRESENT

It might be said that much of what has happened—and is continuing to happen—in American food so far this century is a return to less-processed, more seasonal, and locally grown foods. Consumers are weighing the environmental impacts of their food choices, and the obesity epidemic is forcing a national conversation about what constitutes healthy eating.

The Food Network came on the air in 1993, turning cooking into entertainment and the hosts of its shows, such as Rachael Ray—pictured here in 2007—into celebrities.

Bison Stew with Butternut Squash and Sage

It's estimated that in the 16th century, between 30 and 60 million bison roamed across North America. For centuries, native people relied heavily on bison as a food source. But by the beginning of the 20th century, the bison population had dwindled to just a few hundred animals. A drought killed off their grassland habitat, farmers and ranchers killed them to accommodate horses and cattle, and passengers shot them from the windows of trains, leaving the bodies to rot. Thanks to organizations such as the American Bison Society—founded in 1905—the population has grown to more than 500,000. About 4 percent roam wild in parks and private reserves, while the remaining animals are raised as livestock. This recipe is inspired by a traditional hunter's stew—with a few vegetables added for texture and flavor.

YOU WILL NEED

- ½ ounce dried mushrooms, such as morels or chanterelles
- ½ cup boiling water
- 2 slices thick-cut bacon, coarsely chopped
- 1 pound bison or beef stew meat, cut into 1½-inch cubes
- ½ teaspoon sea salt
- ½ teaspoon black pepper
- 1 leek, trimmed, washed, and sliced (white and light green parts)
- 4 ounces fresh mushrooms, trimmed and sliced
- 1 tablespoon chopped fresh sage
- 4 cups beef broth
- 2 cups cubed butternut squash

  Polenta (recipe follows)

  Chopped fresh parsley

1 Place the dried mushrooms in a small bowl and cover with the boiling water. Let soak for 20 minutes. Drain, reserving the soaking liquid. Coarsely chop the mushrooms.

2 While the mushrooms soak, cook the bacon in a large pot over medium-high heat. Remove the bacon with a slotted spoon and drain on a paper towel-lined plate. Season the bison with the salt and pepper. Add half of the meat to the pot and cook in the bacon fat until browned all over, about 10 minutes. Remove the browned meat to a plate. Repeat with the remaining half of the meat.

3 Add the leek, mushrooms, and sage to the pot and cook until vegetables are softened, 3 to 5 minutes. Add all of the meat and any accumulated juices to the pot along with the broth and reserved mushroom soaking liquid. Bring to boiling. Reduce heat to a simmer and cook, covered, for about 1¾ hours. (When the stew has been cooking for about 1 hour, prepare the Polenta.)

4 When stew has been cooking for 1¾ hours, stir in the squash and cook for an additional 15 minutes or until meat is fork-tender and squash is cooked through.

5 Serve stew over Polenta. Sprinkle with parsley.

Polenta Bring 3½ cups of water to a boil in a medium-heavy pot over high heat. Stir in ½ teaspoon sea salt, then whisk in ¾ cup polenta or fine cornmeal. Continue stirring as the mixture thickens, 2 to 3 minutes. Turn heat to low and cook the polenta for 45 minutes, stirring every 10 minutes. (If it becomes too thick, thin with a little water.) Stir in ¼ teaspoon black pepper and 2 tablespoons walnut oil or butter.

Enslaved Cooks

THERE WOULD BE NO AMERICAN CUISINE AS WE KNOW IT WITHOUT THE CONTRIBUTIONS OF ENSLAVED AFRICANS AND THEIR DESCENDANTS—IN FACT, SOME SCHOLARS ARGUE THAT THE COOKING OF ENSLAVED PEOPLE IS THE BASIS OF AMERICAN COOKING. THEY BROUGHT INGREDIENTS, AGRICULTURAL AND COOKING TECHNIQUES, AND DISHES FROM THEIR NATIVE COUNTRIES AND HELPED CREATE A DISTINCT CUISINE APART FROM ANY OTHER.

▼ A 19th-century hand-colored woodcut depicts a slave family in their quarters of the Knickerbocker mansion in 1700s New York.

A slave kitchen at Magnolia Mound Plantation in Baton Rouge, Louisiana

A COMPLICATED LEGACY

When Thomas Jefferson went to Paris in 1784 to be Minister to France, he brought James Hemings—an enslaved cook at Monticello—with him. Jefferson struck a bargain with James: If James learned the art of French cooking and taught it to another of Jefferson's slaves, he would earn his freedom. James was freed in 1796, but his younger brother, Peter, took over the kitchen. In 1801, when Jefferson moved to the White House, he brought two enslaved young women—Edith Fossett and Fanny Hern—to cook under the tutelage of a French chef. They cooked for him until his death in 1826. Hercules, George Washington's cook, was also formally trained, but was no more free. Before him, it was Doll, an enslaved woman brought to the Washington marriage by Martha Dandridge Custis. It wasn't just these African American cooks associated with the white leaders of the fledging country who made their mark on American cuisine. Countless black plantation cooks—relegated to 16-foot-wide kitchen cottages that doubled as living quarters and whose hearths burned 24 hours a day with a 1,000°F fire—created sumptuous feasts for the families that enslaved them, while their sustenance consisted of kitchen scraps and what they were able to cultivate in their gardens—foods such as melons, okra, yams, and black-eyed peas, the seeds of which were brought on slave ships from Africa. These fruits and vegetables soon became incorporated into the American diet, as did dishes adapted from their home countries. Gumbo is a derivative of okra stews popular in West Africa; jambalaya a descendant of jollof rice—a spicy rice dish studded with vegetables and meat. Cooking methods such as deep-frying and barbecuing were documented in West Africa before the transatlantic slave trade began. Enslaved cooks took English meat pie and made it with sweet potatoes. They weren't just providing labor, but were creating and crafting what would become the American way of eating.

Gumbo

The art of gumbo making—which requires choosing the protein, a thickener, and season-ings—can seem more of a debate than a recipe. This most-famous Louisiana dish varies greatly from one region to the next and even from cook to cook—and is often subject to the competitive natures of those same cooks. While it is a thickened stew, the rest is up for discussion. The name derives from the West African word for okra, the seeds of which were brought to the South by African slaves, but okra is not always an ingredient. When okra is used, it helps thicken and flavor the dish, but some recipes start with a richly colored roux as a thickener or end with filé powder made from the ground dried leaves of the sassafras tree. While seafood, chicken, and sausage are all common in modern recipes, the combination and varieties vary as much as a cook's unique blend of seasonings.

YOU WILL NEED

- 1 medium onion, finely chopped (1 cup)
- 1 small green bell pepper, chopped (¾ cup)
- 2 stalks celery, chopped (¾ cup)
- 2 cloves garlic, minced
- 1 teaspoon black pepper
- ½ teaspoon salt
- ½ teaspoon dried thyme, crushed
- ½ teaspoon dried oregano, crushed
- ¼ to ½ teaspoon cayenne pepper
- ⅓ cup cooking oil, lard, or strained bacon drippings
- ⅓ cup all-purpose flour
- 6 cups low-sodium chicken broth or seafood stock
- 1 pound skinless, boneless chicken thighs, cut into bite-size pieces
- 1 cup thinly sliced fresh or frozen okra*
- 12 ounces Andouille smoked sausage or other smoked pork sausage, halved and sliced
- 1 dozen shucked oysters with the liquor (liquid that drains off)**
- 1 pound peeled and deveined medium shrimp or crabmeat (or a combination)
- Hot cooked rice
- Italian parsley, chopped (optional)
- Bottled hot sauce (optional)

CAJUN OR CREOLE?

While Cajun and Creole cooking share many similarities and ingredients, there are some distinct differences. Both rely heavily on what's referred to as the "holy trinity" of Louisiana cooking—onion, celery, and bell pepper—as a flavor base. Creole cuisine developed out of the populations of people born to settlers in French colonial Louisi-ana—specifically New Orleans. It's considered "city food." Cajun cuisine came out of the rural, swampy areas of Louisiana, where French Acadians settled after being forcibly removed by the British from areas of Nova Scotia and New Brunswick for their Catholic faith. The word "Cajun" is an Anglicization of the French *Acadien*.

1 In a medium bowl combine onion, bell pepper, celery, and garlic. In a small bowl combine black pepper, salt, thyme, oregano, and cayenne. Set bowls aside.

2 To make a roux, in a large heavy skillet heat fat over medium-high heat until hot. Carefully whisk in flour. Cook, whisking constantly, until the roux is a deep reddish-brown, about 15 minutes. Watch carefully so roux doesn't scorch (no black flecks). Immediately stir in onion mixture in two batches, stirring constantly. Cook and stir about 2 minutes. Stir in black pepper mixture; cook and stir 2 minutes more. Remove from heat.

3 In a Dutch oven bring broth to boiling. Gradually add roux-vegetable mixture by the spoonful, whisking after each addition to dissolve. When roux is all dissolved, add chicken and okra to boiling broth; reduce heat and simmer, covered, 30 minutes. Add sausage to the broth mixture. Cover and simmer 20 minutes more. Add oysters and shrimp to simmering gumbo. Cook about 3 minutes or until seafood is cooked through. Season to taste with salt and black pepper. Serve over rice in bowls. If desired, sprinkle with parsley and serve with bottled hot sauce.

*Note You can omit the okra and either increase the fat and flour in the roux to ½ cup each or use filé powder to thicken the gumbo. If using filé powder, stir 1 tablespoon into a few spoonfuls of the gumbo liquid and add along with the oysters and shrimp. (Do not let the gumbo boil after adding the filé powder or it can take on a strange texture.)

**Note Not an oyster fan? Omit the oysters and increase the Andouille sausage to 1 pound or add 8 ounces crabmeat along with the shrimp.

▲ The roux is ready for the vegetables when it is a deep reddish-brown—about the color of a penny.

▲ Stir the vegetables into the roux in two batches, stirring constantly to evenly coat the vegetables and avoid burning.

▶ Add the roux-vegetable mixture to the boiling broth by the spoonful, whisking after each addition to dissolve the roux and prevent clumping.

Fruit Cordial

In the early days of America, cordials made with herbs and botanicals were considered to be medicinal and were "taken" as a way to settle the stomach, invigorate the body, or cure diseases. Eventually they evolved into recreational drinks sweetened with fruit and sipped for their flavor and intoxicating effects. This simple recipe is made by soaking fruit in spirits and adding sugar syrup.

YOU WILL NEED

Ripe fresh fruit of choice (see opposite)

Fresh herbs and/or spices of choice (see opposite), optional

Spirit, such as, vodka, brandy, or gin

Simple Syrup (recipe follows)

SPECIAL EQUIPMENT

Quart glass jar with a tight-fitting lid

Large glass measuring cup

Fine-mesh strainer

Cheesecloth

Rubber band

1 Sterilize the jar and lid, completely submerged, in a pot of boiling water 10 minutes. Remove from water with tongs and set aside on a clean kitchen towel to dry completely.

2 Pick through the fruit and remove any soft or moldy pieces. Wash the fruit thoroughly under cool running water (no need to dry). Remove any pits or seeds if necessary and lightly mash or chop the fruit if desired. Fill the jar with fruit up to about ½ inch from the top. (Don't pack it in too tightly—you want the spirits to fill in around the fruit.) Add any herbs or spices if desired.

3 Pour the spirit in the jar to completely cover the fruit (if any fruit is exposed to air, it might get moldy). Tightly seal the jar. Allow to steep in a cool, dark place for 3 to 6 weeks, flipping the jar over from top to bottom every few days.

4 Pour the steeped spirit through the fine-mesh strainer into the glass measuring cup. Rinse the steeping jar with water to remove any bits of fruit clinging to the insides. Cover the mouth of the steeping jar with a double thickness of cheesecloth (use the rubber band to hold the cheesecloth in place). Pour the steeped spirit through the cheesecloth into the steeping jar to strain out any remaining pieces of fruit.

5 Stir in about ½ cup of the Simple Syrup or to taste. (More or less to your taste. If you are tasting it as you go, use a clean spoon every time you taste it.)

6 Tightly seal the jar and steep in a cool, dry place at least 2 months before using.

Simple Syrup In a small saucepan combine 1 cup sugar and 1 cup water. Heat over medium heat, stirring, until the sugar has dissolved. Cool completely and store, tightly sealed, in the refrigerator.

Ideas for Using Fruit Cordial

- Sip straight up from a cordial glass
- Stir into sparkling water or seltzer and serve over ice
- Pour over ice cream
- Add to cocktails

▲ Lightly pack the jar with fruit and any additional flavorings, leaving space for the spirit.

▲ Pour the spirit into the jar to completely cover the fruit mixture.

▲ After the first steeping, pour the mixture through a fine-mesh strainer into a large measuring cup.

▲ Before the second steeping, pour the liquid into the steeping jar through cheesecloth.

FRUIT OPTIONS	HERB AND SPICE OPTIONS
Apricot	Anise, cardamom pods, rosemary
Blackberry	Cinnamon, clove, ginger, mint
Blueberry	Lemon, orange, lavender
Lemon	Basil, thyme, rosemary
Orange	Ginger, basil, coffee beans
Peach	Star anise, ginger, basil, tarragon, nutmeg
Pear	Cinnamon, nutmeg, ginger, split vanilla bean
Pineapple	Rosemary, ginger, seeded hot chile pepper
Pomegranate	Cardamom, cinnamon, ginger, mint
Raspberry	Lemon, orange, thyme, split vanilla bean, mint
Strawberry	Basil, mint, rosemary
Sweet cherry	Lemon, black pepper, sage, split vanilla bean

Syllabub

In colonial America, wine was a luxury afforded only by the monied class, as it had to be imported from Europe. While there were early attempts to establish vineyards, the plants succumbed to disease. No one could quite figure out how to produce wine with American-grown grapes, so the masses imbibed beverages made from grains and apples—beer, cider, and whiskey. Thomas Jefferson—credited with introducing fine wines to this country upon his return in 1789 from a four-year stint as the United States' Minister to France—enjoyed his wine straight up and undiluted. But those budding oenophiles who lacked the likes of Jefferson's bank account figured out ways to stretch those precious bottles. One of the most enduring inventions was a frothy, milkshake-like dessert called syllabub, made from cream, brandy, wine, lemon, and sugar. Syllabub first emerged in the 1500s in England and remained a popular dessert there and here into the 19th century.

YOU WILL NEED

- ½ cup dry white wine or sherry
- 2 tablespoons brandy or cognac
- 1 tablespoon lemon zest, plus additional for garnish
- 2 tablespoons fresh lemon juice
- ⅓ to ½ cup superfine sugar
- 1 cup chilled heavy whipping cream
- ⅛ teaspoon freshly grated nutmeg
- Mixed fresh berries (optional)

1 The day before you plan to serve the syllabub, in a small bowl stir together wine, brandy, 1 tablespoon lemon zest, and lemon juice. Cover and let stand at room temperature overnight.

▲ Soft-peak whipped cream will stay on the whisk just briefly before dropping back into the bowl.

2 Transfer the mixture to a large mixing bowl. Add sugar to taste and stir until dissolved. Slowly whisk in cream. Add nutmeg. Beat mixture with a large whisk until it holds a soft peak when whisk is lifted from the bowl. (This may take 5 minutes or more.)

3 To serve, divide among four 3-ounce glass dishes. Garnish with lemon zest. If desired, fill the glasses halfway. Top with a few berries, then top with remaining syllabub and lemon zest.

Pound Cake

Pound cake was brought to America with the British colonists and became a staple for home cooks as an ideal companion to a cup of tea. It was appropriately named after its ingredients list, one that was simple enough to memorize: one pound each sugar, butter, flour, and eggs. The first known printed recipes for this buttery loaf were featured in Amelia Simmons' *American Cookery* in 1796. Over time, cooks lightened the texture by adjusting the ingredient amounts and adding baking powder, as well as embellishments such as citrus peel, vanilla, chocolate, icing, and other flavorings. Pound cake has long been popular in the South, and according to *The Gift of Southern Cooking* by Edna Lewis and Scott Peacock, "a standard by which many a good cook is measured."

Before you start baking, make sure that all the ingredients are at room temperature for easy mixing and that the butter is soft but not melty. Beating is key. Beating the butter and sugar well helps develop volume and a good crumb. Beating in the eggs, one at a time and thoroughly, is important for a proper rise. Finally, gently add the dry ingredients because overmixing at this point can deflate an otherwise beautifully aerated batter.

YOU WILL NEED

- 2 cups all-purpose flour or 2¼ cups cake flour
- 1 teaspoon baking powder
- ¼ teaspoon salt
- 1 cup unsalted butter, at room temperature
- 1¼ cups granulated sugar
- 1½ teaspoons vanilla or vanilla bean paste
- 1 teaspoon grated lemon and/or orange zest
- ¼ teaspoon ground nutmeg (optional)
- 4 eggs, at room temperature
- Citrus Glaze (recipe follows) or Powdered sugar

1 Preheat oven to 325°F. Grease and lightly flour a 9×5×3-inch loaf pan; set aside. In a medium bowl combine flour, baking powder, and salt; set aside.

2 In a large mixing bowl beat butter with an electric mixer on medium-high speed 30 seconds. Gradually add granulated sugar, beating until very light and fluffy, about 7 minutes. Add vanilla, citrus peel, and, if using, nutmeg. Add eggs, one at a time, beating a full minute after each addition, scraping sides frequently. Beat in flour mixture on low speed (or stir in by hand), about ¼ cup at a time, just until combined, being careful not to overmix.

Spoon batter into prepared pan, smoothing top with back of the spoon.

3 Place pan on top of a baking sheet (this helps keep the bottom from overbrowning). Bake 60 to 75 minutes or until a wooden toothpick comes out clean. Cool cake in pan on a wire rack 10 minutes. Remove from pan; cool thoroughly on rack. Drizzle with Citrus Glaze or dust with powdered sugar.

Citrus Glaze In a small saucepan combine ¾ cup granulated sugar and ¼ cup orange or lemon juice. Heat and stir just until sugar dissolves. Remove from heat. Stir in ½ teaspoon vanilla.

Apple Pie

Apple pie—uniquely symbolic to American heritage—is not original to the United States. English colonists brought apple seeds and the concept of apple pie with them, but their version tended toward the savory and featured a tough crust that served more as a vessel than an integral part of the dish. Apples were easy to grow and cross-pollinate to create new varieties and were so versatile they were in demand in New England and on the frontier. With the increased availability of sugar and the development of more-refined and flaky pastries, pie eventually became the dessert today's Americans relate to, usually with a double crust, soft and plentiful apples, and thickened sweet cinnamon juices bubbling through the slits in the top pastry. Many Americans enjoy their apple pie with a wedge of cheddar. This recipe incorporates it into the crust.

YOU WILL NEED

Cheddar Pastry (recipe follows)

2½ pounds cooking apples (5 to 6 medium), peeled, cored, and sliced ¼ inch thick

1 tablespoon freshly squeezed lemon juice

⅓ cup granulated sugar

¼ cup packed brown sugar or granulated sugar

2 tablespoons all-purpose flour

½ teaspoon ground cinnamon or ¾ teaspoon apple pie spice

⅛ teaspoon salt

1 tablespoon butter, cut up (optional)

Milk (optional)

Coarse sugar or granulated sugar (optional)

1 Preheat oven to 425°F and place rack in lower third of the oven. Prepare Cheddar Pastry. On a lightly floured surface, slightly flatten one pastry ball. With a rolling pin, roll pastry from center to edges to a 13-inch circle. Wrap pastry around rolling pin and unroll evenly into a 9-inch pie plate. Trim excess pastry to about ¾ inch larger than pie plate. For top crust, roll remaining pastry to a 12-inch round. Refrigerate both while making the filling.

2 In a large bowl sprinkle apples with lemon juice. In a small bowl combine granulated sugar, brown sugar, flour, cinnamon, and salt. Toss apples with sugar mixture to coat. Let stand about 10 minutes so apples will soften slightly, tossing occasionally.

3 Transfer filling to pastry-lined pie plate and press apple mixture gently to fill the plate evenly. If desired, for a richer pie, dot filling with the butter pieces. Brush edge of pastry with cold water. Cut slits (vents for steam) or cutout designs in remaining pastry and place pastry evenly over filling. Pinch edges where pastry meets to seal. Trim excess pastry to ¾ inch and fold pastry under itself to form a folded edge flush with rim of pie plate. Crimp or flute edge as desired. If desired, brush top with milk and sprinkle with coarse sugar.

4 Bake pie 25 minutes. Place baking sheet under pie plate. Reduce oven temperature to 325°F. Bake pie 25 to 35 minutes more or until top is golden brown and thickened filling looks bubbly through the pastry slits. Cool completely (about 3 to 4 hours) on a wire rack.

Cheddar Pastry In a large bowl stir together 2 cups all-purpose flour, 1 cup shredded sharp white cheddar cheese, and ½ teaspoon salt. Cut ¼ cup cold butter into small pieces. Using a pastry blender, cut in ½ cup shortening or lard and ¼ cup butter into flour mixture until pieces are pea size. Place ⅔ cup ice water in a bowl. Sprinkle 1 tablespoon water over part of flour mixture; toss with a fork. Push moistened pastry to a side of the bowl. Repeat, using just enough water to moisten pastry, to form a ball, kneading gently until it holds together. Divide pastry in half and form two balls.

EVERYTHING OLD IS NEW AGAIN

Health-Food Trends

Health-food movements have always intended to improve physical health, but depending on when they take root, there can be additional goals as well. The current millennial-era Clean Living Movement also seeks to improve the health of the planet by eating less (or no) meat and embracing a plant-based diet.

MORAL PURITY THROUGH WHOLE GRAINS

It was a different story in the last half of the 19th century, when the country was witness to a wave of health crusades that were aimed at improving physical health and also one's personal morality—and in particular, putting a damper on sexual desire. Sanitariums, which were a type of health resort, began popping up everywhere.

Sylvester Graham (1795–1851) was a Presbyterian minister who preached temperance and advocated vegetarianism, frequent baths, and sex only for the purpose of procreation. He was particularly strident about the hazards of eating processed flours and developed one made from the entire wheat seed, not just the endosperm (see page 106). Thousands attended his lectures and his disciples—known as Grahamites—slavishly followed his edicts.

Not everyone was so enamored. Shortly after the 1837 publication of his pamphlet, *Treatise on Bread and Bread-Making*, which laid out in detail the chemistry of baking bread at home, he was reportedly attacked by an angry mob of Boston bakers and butchers.

Dr. James Caleb Jackson (1811–1895), a New York abolitionist and advocate for temperance, founded Our Home on the Hillside sanitarium, where he baked small multigrain biscuits of graham flour, oats, and cornmeal to supplement the institutional breakfast. His success with the biscuits spurred him to reformulate them by making wafers made solely of graham flour, which he crumbled and twice-baked. He dubbed the hard-as-rock nuggets "granula."

John Harvey Kellogg (1852–1943), a doctor and nutritionist, is best known for inventing cornflakes with his brother, Will Keith Kellogg. John Kellogg not only believed many medical conditions could be treated through diet, but that a proper diet would eliminate all sexual urges, whether they involved another person or not. As superintendent of the Battle Creek Sanitarium—founded by the Seventh-day Adventist Church in Battle Creek, Michigan, he fed his patients yogurt and whole-grain breakfast cereals. One of these consisted of oatmeal and cornmeal baked into biscuits, then crushed into tiny pieces. He also called it "granula." Of course, Jackson threatened to sue, and Kellogg changed the name of his creation to "granola."

Perhaps his regimen worked. Kellogg is said to never have consummated his marriage with his wife. Their children—8 of them—were all adopted.

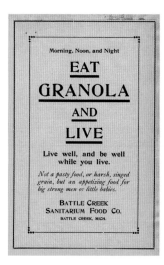

▲ A circa-1902 advertisement from the Battle Creek Sanitarium Food Company touts the benefits of eating granola.

▲ Presbyterian minister Sylvester Graham exhorted his followers to avoid alcohol and meat and to indulge in frequent baths.

Nearly all of the major health-food movements of the 19th century advocated vegetarianism. The modern movement toward plant-based diets is a reflection of interest in personal health, animal welfare, and the health of the planet.

Graham Crackers

The nation's most recognizable cracker—especially with milk chocolate and a toasted marshmallow sandwiched between two squares—evolved from a health food created by a Presbyterian minister in the mid-19th century. Sylvester Graham preached that dietary reform was the answer to excessive behaviors (see page 104). He developed a coarsely ground additive-free whole wheat flour he used in a flatbread. Eventually independent bakeries sold "graham" crackers, and in 1925, the Pacific Coast Biscuit Company introduced Honey Maid Graham Crackers. Today's graham crackers still contain some whole grain but evolved to include spice and sugar, which Graham was abhorrently opposed to.

YOU WILL NEED

- 1½ cups stone-ground whole wheat graham flour*
- ½ cup all-purpose flour
- ¼ cup packed dark brown sugar
- 1 teaspoon ground cinnamon
- ¾ teaspoon baking powder
- ¼ teaspoon baking soda
- ¼ teaspoon salt
- ⅓ cup cold butter
- ¼ cup milk, buttermilk, nut milk, or plain yogurt
- ¼ cup honey (for a more intense flavor, use a dark honey such as buckwheat)

1 In a medium bowl stir together flours, brown sugar, cinnamon, baking powder, baking soda, and salt. With a pastry blender, cut in butter until pieces are pea size. Stir together milk and honey. With a fork, stir half the milk mixture into flour mixture. Stir in just enough of the remaining milk mixture to form a ball, kneading gently until it holds together and dough is smooth. Divide pastry in half and form two flattened balls. Wrap in plastic wrap and refrigerate until firm, about 1 hour or up to 24 hours.

2 Preheat oven to 350°F. Line two baking sheets with parchment paper, cutting to fit bottoms of pans. Remove parchment to a flat surface. Place one piece of dough onto one piece of parchment. Using a rolling pin (lightly flour if sticking) roll to a 12×9-inch rectangle (about 1/16 inch thick). Trim as needed. Dough should be thin. With a pastry cutter or knife cut rectangle into 12 squares (3×3 inches each). Cut each square in half so you end up with 24 small rectangles (still touching). Using a fork, prick each with an × or + design. Slide dough-topped parchment back onto a baking sheet. Repeat with remaining dough and parchment. Bake 12 to 15 minutes until crisp and lightly browned. Transfer crackers to a wire rack and cool completely.

*Note Bob's Red Mill, Hodgson Mill, and Anson Mills sell whole wheat graham flour.

▲ Cut each of 12 rectangles in half to create 24 small rectangles.

▲ Use a fork to prick each small rectangle.

▲ If crackers aren't crisp after cooling, return to the baking sheet and bake an additional 5 to 7 minutes.

Sourdough Bread

Indigenous communities have longstanding traditions of cooking with cornmeal, so it's not surprising that unleavened breads made from it were the first breads embraced by European settlers in the colonies. Eventually, chewy, tuggy leavened breads made from wheat and leavened with sourdough starter became the standard. In 1849, the legendary Boudin Bakery opened in San Francisco selling a tangy bread made from starter borrowed from local gold miners. The bakery uses that same starter to this day! Although the introduction of commercially produced yeast in 1868 by the Fleischmann brothers made breadmaking faster, sourdough bread has retained its appeal over the centuries for its unique taste and texture.

YOU WILL NEED

100 grams Sourdough Starter (recipe page 110)

250 grams water

8 grams kosher salt

400 grams unbleached bread flour, plus additional for shaping

Rice flour

SPECIAL EQUIPMENT

Digital kitchen scale

1 (10-inch) banneton (proofing basket)

1 In a large bowl combine sourdough starter, water, salt, and bread flour. Stir until well blended (dough will be very sticky). Cover the bowl with foil and let rest 4 hours at 70°F to 75°F.

2 Wet your hands and fold the dough over on itself three or four times. Cover with foil and let ferment 2 hours.

3 Dust the banneton with rice flour.

4 Scrape dough onto a lightly floured surface. Shape into a ball with a smooth, unbroken surface, using just enough flour to keep it from sticking. Transfer, smooth side down, to the banneton. Pinch the rough edges of the surface toward the center to smooth them.

5 Cover with foil and refrigerate 12 hours.

6 Remove dough from the refrigerator and let rise in a warm spot until the dough springs back slowly and retains a slight indentation when poked gently with a finger, about 3 to 5 hours.

7 Preheat oven to 450°F. Line a rimmed baking sheet with parchment paper. Dust the surface of the dough with bread flour. Gently invert the banneton over the baking sheet, transferring dough to the lined baking sheet. Gently brush off any excess rice flour. Using a sharp knife, score the top of the dough with a single ⅛-inch-deep slash. Using a clean spray bottle, mist the entire surface of the dough lightly with water.

8 Bake until browned and the loaf sounds hollow when tapped on the bottom, 25 to 30 minutes.

9 Cool completely on a wire rack before slicing.

▲ After the first rise, fold the dough over in the bowl three or four times.

▲ Dust the proofing basket with rice flour to prevent the dough from sticking.

▲ After the dough has raised in the refrigerator 12 hours, raise at room temperature 3 to 5 hours.

▲ Use a pastry brush to gently brush off any excess rice flour before baking.

Sourdough Starter

The yeast that leavens sourdough bread is wild yeast—it comes from the air, the flour, the baker's hands. It takes longer to make bread with starter than with commercial yeast, but the complex flavor and sturdy texture are worth it. If you don't have active starter, you'll need to make this recipe at least 5 days ahead of when you want to bake bread. Be sure to use a digital kitchen scale to measure everything by weight in grams; it is much more precise than measuring by volume.

ACTIVE TIME

45 minutes

TOTAL TIME

5 days 45 minutes

YOU WILL NEED

105   grams whole rye or whole wheat flour

120   grams cool water*

Unbleached all-purpose flour

SPECIAL EQUIPMENT

1-   to 2-quart glass, ceramic, or stainless-steel container (nonreactive materials)

Cheesecloth and large rubber band (or plastic wrap)

Digital kitchen scale

1 Day 1: Thoroughly stir together the whole-grain flour and water in a nonreactive container. Be sure no dry flour remains. Cover the container with the cheesecloth and rubber band or loosely with plastic wrap. Let stand in a warm place (70°F to 75°F) 24 hours. (The top of the refrigerator works well for this.)

2 Day 2: The starter may show some signs of growth or bubbling after 24 hours—or it may not. Either way, use the kitchen scale to weigh out 120 grams of the starter (about ½ cup) and discard. Add 125 grams of the all-purpose flour and 120 grams cool water to the remaining starter. (If your house is cold, add lukewarm water.) Stir well to combine and let the mixture stand in a warm place 24 hours.

3 Day 3: By this day, you'll probably see some bubbling. The mixture should have a fresh, fruity aroma and likely will have expanded some. On this day, you will begin feeding the starter every 12 hours, spaced as evenly as your schedule allows. Weigh out 120 grams of the starter. Discard the remaining starter. To the 120 grams of starter, add 125 grams all-purpose flour and 120 grams water. Stir thoroughly to combine. Cover and let stand at room temperature about 12 hours. Repeat.

4 Day 4: Weigh out 120 grams of the starter; discard any remaining starter. Repeat Step 3.

5 Day 5: Weigh out 120 grams of the starter; discard any remaining starter. Repeat Step 3. By the end of this day, the starter should have doubled in volume. There will be lots of bubbles. It should have a tangy aroma—pleasingly acidic but not ammonia-like. If the starter hasn't risen much and doesn't have a lot of bubbles, repeat the discarding and feeding step every 12 hours for two more days or until you have a very active starter.

6 When the starter is very active, it needs one last feeding before use. Measure out 120 grams by weight and discard the rest. Feed with 125 grams flour and 120 grams water. Let stand, covered, at room temperature, 6 to 8 hours. It should have bubbles breaking the surface. The starter is now ready for use. If you do not use it right away, store it, tightly covered, in the refrigerator. Take it out of the refrigerator 2 days before you plan to use it to activate it. Every time you use the starter, feed it following the method in Step 3. If you don't use it every week, feed it once a week according to Step 3 to keep it active.

*Tip Unless your tap water is highly treated with chemicals, it is fine to use for the starter. If it is highly treated, use purified water for both the starter and for baking bread.

Southern Fried Chicken

Two groups of people who arrived in the South in very different ways had a hand in growing the popularity of fried chicken. Scottish immigrants brought their habit of frying meat in fat to the region (most Europeans baked or boiled it), and so did the enslaved cooks whose ancestors in West Africa used the same cooking method. Enslaved cooks in the South were the experts in its preparation. Fried chicken became an iconic food of African Americans, often in a racially charged depiction, but also as a source of income and a beloved staple. After the Civil War, African American women in Gordonsville, Virginia, a major train stop, turned fried chicken into a business. There were no dining cars onboard, so the women toted baskets of food to the trains, passing fried chicken and other homemade dishes to passengers through open windows. Recognizing the broad appeal of fried chicken, Colonel Harlan Sanders, founder of Kentucky Fried Chicken, created a restaurant concept solely on the dish. Other restaurant concepts followed, including those associated with famous people such as Minnie Pearl (Minnie Pearl's Fried Chicken), Mahalia Jackson (Glori-Fried Chicken), Mickey Mantle (Mickey Mantle's Country Cookin' Family Restaurants), and James Brown (Gold Platter Restaurant).

YOU WILL NEED

- 3 cups buttermilk
- 2 teaspoons salt
- 1 tablespoon bottled hot sauce or ½ to 1 teaspoon cayenne pepper (optional)
- 3 to 3½ pounds bone-in meaty chicken pieces (thighs, drumsticks, breast halves)
- 2 cups all-purpose flour
- ½ teaspoon black pepper
- 2 teaspoons cornstarch
- 1½ pounds lard or vegetable shortening or 3 cups vegetable oil or peanut oil*

1 In a large bowl whisk together buttermilk, 1 teaspoon of the salt, and, if using, hot sauce. Add chicken pieces and toss to cover on all sides. Cover and refrigerate 4 to 12 hours.

2 In a large resealable plastic bag combine remaining salt, flour, black pepper, and cornstarch. Remove chicken from buttermilk mixture, letting excess liquid drain off. Discard buttermilk mixture. Place chicken pieces, a few at a time, in flour mixture, shaking to cover all sides of each piece. Tap pieces to remove excess flour mixture. Place coated chicken on a wire rack set over a baking sheet. Let stand at room temperature until needed.

3 Heat fat in a 12- to 14-inch cast-iron skillet (or heavy, deep skillet) over medium-high heat until a deep-fry thermometer registers 350°F. Gently lay chicken pieces in hot fat skin, sides down, and in a single layer without touching (you may have to cook in batches). Cover and let cook 10 minutes, checking halfway through, adjusting for hot spots, and making sure fat is bubbling and about 300°F. After the 10 minutes, use tongs to turn chicken pieces. Cook, uncovered, about 10 minutes more until chicken is deep golden brown on all sides and is no longer pink inside. Transfer to a clean wire rack set over a baking sheet lined with paper towels. If cooking chicken in batches, keep cooked chicken warm in a 300°F oven.

*Note If using shortening, cooking oil, or peanut oil, adding a couple tablespoons bacon drippings helps to flavor the fat.

Chop Suey

Most historians agree that chop suey was created and popularized on American soil by Chinese cooks. Chinese immigrants who worked on the Transcontinental Railroad that linked the Atlantic and Pacific coasts before its completion in 1869 settled in San Francisco and other western towns. One story claims chop suey—which translates in Cantonese to something like "odds and ends"—originated in the camp kitchens of workers building the Pacific railroad line. Chinese cooks at the camps may have tossed together available ingredients for a quick meal. Chop suey was more of a concept than a specific dish—usually a mix of stir-fried vegetables, available meats, possibly egg, and a sauce served over rice (not noodles). By the 1880s and into the early 20th century, during a time fraught with racism and language barriers, the popularity of this dish spread across the nation, even with non-Chinese Americans.

YOU WILL NEED

½ cup low-sodium chicken broth

¼ cup reduced-sodium soy sauce

2 tablespoons sherry, 1 teaspoon toasted sesame oil, and/ or ¼ teaspoon crushed red pepper (optional)

12 ounces chicken, pork tenderloin, or beef sirloin, cut into ½-inch cubes

2 tablespoons peanut or vegetable oil

½ medium onion, sliced into thick wedges

2 stalks celery, bias-sliced (1 cup)

1 cup sliced mushrooms or enoki mushrooms

1 cup snow peas, trimmed; shredded bok choy; and/ or diced mixed fresh vegetables (optional)

1 8-ounce can bamboo shoots, rinsed and drained

1 8-ounce can sliced water chestnuts, rinsed and drained

1 cup fresh bean sprouts or canned bean sprouts, rinsed and drained

Hot cooked rice

1 In a small bowl stir together broth, soy sauce, and, if desired, sherry.

2 In a large skillet cook chicken in 1 tablespoon hot oil until browned, about 3 to 4 minutes. Remove from skillet; set aside. Add remaining 1 tablespoon oil to skillet. Add onion and cook 1 minute in hot oil. Add celery to onion; cook 1 minute. Add mushrooms; cook 1 minute. If using, add snow peas (or desired vegetables); cook 1 minute. Add browned chicken, bamboo shoots, water chestnuts, and bean sprouts. Stir sauce and add to skillet. Cook and stir until bubbly. Cook about 4 minutes more, stirring frequently, until thickened and chicken and vegetables are cooked through. Serve over rice.

Optional toppings While the chop suey is tasty just as it is, embellish it if you like with a sprinkling of chopped green onion, chopped fresh cilantro, and/or toasted sesame seeds and serve it with chile paste for added heat.

Spaghetti and Meatballs

The red sauce-laden dish of spaghetti topped with meatballs that Americans consider "Italian" came about from ingenuity and availability of ingredients. Between 1880 and 1920, millions of Italians immigrated to America due to lack of opportunity at home. They were delighted with the cheap price of food. They could eat meat regularly, which altered many traditional Italian recipes. The sauce was based on widely available canned tomatoes. The meatballs may have been an adaptation of *polpette*, a bready version served without sauce in Italy. Italian immigrants shared this new beloved food with other Americans. People of all backgrounds fell in love with pasta for its low cost and comforting carbs. While it had been an appetizer in Italy, it became a main dish in America. Three immigrant brothers, Hector, Paul, and Mario Boiardi, brought Italian convenience food to homes across America when they started bottling red sauce in 1928 under the name Chef Boyardee.

YOU WILL NEED

- 1 medium onion, chopped (1 cup)
- 2 tablespoons olive oil
- 1 medium carrot, chopped (½ cup)
- 1 stalk celery, chopped (½ cup)
- 4 cloves garlic, minced
- 1 28-ounce can crushed Italian-style (San Marzano) tomatoes or fire-roasted tomatoes, undrained
- 3 tablespoons tomato paste
- 1 cup dry red wine or water
- ¼ cup chopped fresh Italian parsley
- 1 tablespoon Italian seasoning
- ½ teaspoon salt
- ¼ teaspoon crushed red pepper

  Italian Meatballs (recipe follows)
- ⅓ cup chopped fresh basil
- 1 16-ounce package spaghetti, whole wheat spaghetti, or gluten-free spaghetti

  Freshly grated Parmesan cheese

1 In a large saucepan cook onion in hot oil over medium heat 1 minute. Stir in carrot, celery, and garlic; cook, uncovered, 8 minutes or until very tender but not brown, stirring occasionally.

2 Stir in tomatoes, tomato paste, wine, parsley, Italian seasoning, salt, and crushed red pepper. Bring sauce to boiling; reduce heat. Simmer sauce, uncovered, 30 minutes, stirring occasionally.*

3 While sauce is cooking, prepare Italian Meatballs. Stir meatballs and basil into sauce. Simmer, uncovered, 15 minutes more. If sauce seems too thick, add water (or pasta cooking water) to desired consistency.

4 In a large pot cook pasta according to package directions; drain. Serve sauce over pasta. Top with Parmesan cheese.

Italian Meatballs Preheat oven to 400°F. In a large bowl beat 1 egg with a fork. Add ⅓ cup soft bread crumbs, ¼ cup freshly grated Parmesan cheese, ¼ cup finely chopped onion, and ¼ cup chopped fresh Italian parsley or basil. Add ¾ pound lean ground beef and ½ pound bulk sweet Italian sausage; mix well. Shape into 18 meatballs, about 1 rounded tablespoon each. Bake 12 minutes or until brown and cooked through. Meatballs can be made ahead, cooled, and transferred to a storage container. Cover and refrigerate up to 3 days or freeze up to 6 months.

*To make sauce ahead Sauce can be cooled at this point and transferred to a storage container. Cover and refrigerate up to 4 days or freeze up to 9 months. If frozen, thaw in refrigerator overnight. To use, transfer to a large saucepan and add meatballs and basil. Bring to boiling; reduce heat and simmer, uncovered, 15 minutes.

A MOMENT IN TIME

The Great Depression

The stock market crash in October 1929 triggered not only the worst financial crisis in the country's history but also a fundamental shift in what Americans eat, how they think about nutrition, and the government's role in helping feed the nation.

In June 1930, President Herbert Hoover met with a delegation requesting a federal public works program. "Gentlemen, you have come 60 days too late," he said. "The Depression is over." He then contended that "nobody is actually starving." He was wrong.

In 1931, breadlines in New York were serving 85,000 meals a day. But resistance to having government involved in helping the citizenry in the basic task of feeding itself continued. In a radio address, Hoover said, "The spread of government destroys initiative and thus destroys character."

By 1933, 30 percent of the workforce was unemployed. Average family income had tumbled by 40 percent, from $2,300 in 1929 to $1,500. A relief worker in Arkansas found a widow and her seven children with a pint of flour and a few chicken bones in the pantry. Diseases of malnutrition—such as pellagra, which is caused by a deficiency in niacin and can cause dementia, diarrhea, and inflamed skin—skyrocketed.

It became apparent that the need was too great to refuse to compromise on the point of self-reliance. Private charities could not respond effectively to the crisis.

GOVERNMENT INTERVENTION

Help finally arrived in the form of the Federal Emergency Relief Administration (FERA), established by the Roosevelt Administration in 1933. (It was replaced by the Works Progress Administration [WPA] in 1935.)

An army of (mostly) female agents from the Bureau of Home Economics—a branch of the

▲ A homeless man cooks his dinner over an improvised campfire during the Great Depression, circa 1935.

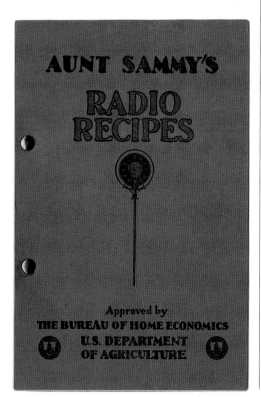

◄ A recipe booklet from *Housekeeper's Chat*—a radio show hosted by the fictional Aunt Sammy. The show broadcast recipes featuring foodstuffs being distributed by relief agencies.

USDA—was dispatched to teach home cooks how to prepare nutritious meals on scant budgets. Aunt Sammy—a radio personality created by the USDA and a companion to Uncle Sam—appeared on a program called *Housekeeper's Chat* to provide recipes for foodstuffs being distributed by FERA.

The emphasis during this era of want was not on flavor but rather what had been determined at the time was the science of good nutrition. In fact, good taste was seen as a dubious quality. Spices and garlic were considered stimulants, which would only increase hunger. Government-supplied food was deliberately bland because it was believed blandness would spur the recipients to find a job and earn money to buy seasonings. Relief boxes didn't include flavorings such as mustard and vinegar because government agents didn't want anyone to be too happy about accepting relief.

Among the most vulnerable were children. An article in a 1936 issue of the *Journal of Home Economics* about the national WPA School Lunch Project cited a survey in Colorado that "revealed that 50 percent of all children attending school in the state were receiving insufficient food and that almost as many were dangerously undernourished."

The supervisor of the same WPA hot lunch project in Utah reported on the results of the program. "The improvement of the children is immeasurable," she wrote. "The teachers cannot find words to express the change in pupils since they are being properly fed. Their application has improved; their deportment, their general health, and their interest in everything has increased."

DIETARY CHANGES

Certain dishes became popular during this era because they adapted easily to affordable and available ingredients. Meat was out of reach for most people, so loaves made of peanuts, liver, or beans could be stretched with additional ingredients. Casseroles became staples. Leftovers or less-than-appetizing foods could be cloaked under a creamy coating of white sauce, a Depression-era staple made with flour, butter or margarine, and milk. The legacy of these dishes lives on in the casseroles and "hot dishes" made with canned soup and noodles that remain staples in many American homes to this day.

◀ Men line up outside a Chicago soup kitchen opened in 1930 by gangster Al Capone. "The Madison Street hobo type was conspicuously absent from these lines of men," reported the *Chicago Tribune*. An associate told another Chicago paper that Capone "couldn't stand to see those poor devils starving, and nobody else seemed to be doing much, so the big boy decided to do it himself." The soup kitchen served three meals a day to 2,200 Chicagoans.

Chicago Dogs

Political upheaval in Germany in the 1840s brought an influx of German immigrants—and their sausage-making prowess—to Chicago. The pork-and-beef Vienna-style frankfurter was especially popular, and Chicago—known as a global meatpacking capital—helped turn this trendy tube steak into a nationwide craze. Hot dog carts became an integral part of immigrant communities both as a social network and as a way to support whole families. Jewish immigrants upped the game with their all-beef hot dog with natural casing, which became the standard for Chicago dogs. Hot dog buns came about as a solution to eating hot sausages on the go. Polish immigrant Sam Rosen created his famous soft white bun with poppy seeds in his Chicago bakery, which became the signature for the Chicago dog.

During the Great Depression, vendors bulked up their hot dogs with condiments and vegetables, which came to be called having your dog "dragged through the garden." Fluky's on Maxwell and Halsted streets offered the first "Depression Sandwich"—a hot dog with assorted toppings and fries for five cents. The Chicago dog is still a Windy City institution, especially at the ballpark, with the sacred combo of toppings: yellow mustard, pickle relish (the greener the better), onion, tomato, dill pickle, sport peppers, and celery salt. Just remember: Always dress the dog, not the bun, and no ketchup ever—or the locals will know you're a tourist.

YOU WILL NEED

- 4 Vienna-style all-beef hot dogs with natural casing*
- 4 poppy seed buns*
- 4 teaspoons yellow mustard*
- ¼ cup sweet pickle relish*
- ¼ cup diced white onion
- 1 medium tomato, cored and cut into 8 thin wedges
- 4 kosher-style dill pickle spears
- 8 sport peppers (medium-hot, bite-size peppers packed in brine)*
- Celery salt*

1 Fill a large pan about one fourth of the way with water and bring to boiling. Add the hot dogs. Cook 5 to 7 minutes or until they float to the top of the water.** Use tongs to remove hot dogs from the water; keep warm.

2 Pour out all but 1 or 2 inches of water from the pan. Add a steamer basket, making sure it sits above the water. Bring water to simmering. Add the buns to the basket. Cover; steam about 2 minutes or just until warmed through (don't let them get soggy). Remove buns from basket.

3 Gently pull buns open and fill with hot dogs. Top each hot dog with mustard and relish; sprinkle with onion. Place two tomato wedges on one side of each hot dog and a pickle on the other side. Top with sport peppers and celery salt.

*Note The original Poppy Seed Mary Ann Buns by Sam Rosen are still available at srosens.com. Vienna-style all-beef frankfurters with natural casings, yellow mustard, Chicago-style relish, sport peppers, and celery salt are all available at viennabeef.com.

**Note Chicago dogs are typically boiled or steamed. To steam, place a steamer basket in a pan of boiling water, making sure basket sits above the water. Add hot dogs to the basket and cook, covered, about 5 minutes or until heated through (160°F).

Tuna Noodle Casserole with Potato Chip Topping

In its classic 1950s canned-soup iteration, tuna noodle casserole is fast to fix, filling, and satisfying—an amalgam of toothsome noodles, tuna, and crunchy sweet peas swathed in a creamy, cheesy sauce and topped with a crispy topping of potato chips, cornflakes, or shoestring potatoes laced together with more melted cheese. The first printed recipe for tuna noodle casserole appeared in a 1930 issue of *Sunset Magazine*. Mrs. W.F.S. from Kennewick, Washington, contributed a recipe for Noodles and Tuna Fish en Casserole, and the rest, as they say, is history. The introduction of Campbell's cream of mushroom soup in 1934 locked this comfort-food casserole into the American culinary canon. By the early 1950s, it was ubiquitous and wildly popular. Quick-to-fix meals using convenience products became staples of the dinner table, the theory being that American housewives—after being out of the house and in the workforce during World War II—were just not all that excited about returning to one of the more laborious daily tasks of domestic life. Even if that was the case, a lot of Americans of all backgrounds continue to get pretty excited when this comfort-food classic is on the menu.

YOU WILL NEED

- 1 (10.5-ounce) can condensed cream of mushroom soup
- ½ cup whole milk
- 1 cup frozen green peas
- 2 tablespoons chopped pimientos
- 1 (4.5-ounce) can sliced mushrooms, drained
- ¼ cup finely chopped onion
- 2 (5-ounce) cans water-packed tuna, drained
- 2 cups medium egg noodles, cooked and drained
- 2 cups shredded cheddar cheese
- 1 cup crushed potato chips

1 Preheat oven to 400°F. In a 1½-quart casserole stir together the soup, milk, peas, pimientos, mushrooms, onion, tuna, noodles, and 1 cup of the cheese. Top with the remaining 1 cup cheese and the potato chips.

2 Bake 25 to 30 minutes or until casserole is bubbling and topping is lightly browned. Let stand 5 minutes before serving.

Clarence Birdseye

AN ADVENTURER AND INVENTOR COMBINED HIS KNOWLEDGE OF BIOLOGY, INTEREST IN FOOD, AND A STRONG ENTREPRENEURIAL SPIRIT TO REVOLUTIONIZE THE FROZEN FOOD INDUSTRY AND THE WAY THE WORLD EATS.

▼ Birdseye experimenting with chopped carrots to determine the effects of various stirring speeds and air velocities on the food

► United States patent #1,773,079 was issued to Clarence Birdseye for the production of quick-frozen fish.

Fig. 1

A FLASH OF GENIUS

Humans have been freezing foods as a means of preservation for thousands of years, but up until fairly recently, it was a decidedly imperfect process.

Freezing food was a slow process that resulted in the loss of proteins and nutrients. Ice crystals formed on the food and ruptured its cell membranes. When thawed, the food was left mushy and flavorless.

Clarence Birdseye changed all of that. In 1912, at the age of 26, he found work as a fur trader in the northeastern Canadian province of Labrador. While living there, he watched the local Inuit people fish trout from holes in the ice. The fish froze instantly in the -30°F air. When it was thawed and cooked, he was pleasantly surprised that it tasted nearly as good as fresh-caught. The key was the speed at which the fish froze—so quickly that only the tiniest ice crystals formed, leaving its taste and texture largely intact.

Birdseye returned to the United States in 1917. While working with the U.S. Fisheries Association, he had an epiphany: The way to increase the demand for fish was to figure out a way to transport it over long distances and have its "intrinsic freshness" intact. He developed a method for flash-freezing—patented in 1927—that involved holding food under pressure between two hollow metal plates chilled to -25°F by evaporating ammonia. His company, General Seafood Corporation, first applied this method to fish but soon expanded it to other foods.

In 1929, he sold the company to the Goldman Sachs Trading Corporation and the Postum Cereal Company for $22 million. It eventually became part of General Foods Corporation. The frozen foods division was trademarked Birds Eye.

By the late 1940s, Americans were buying chest freezers for their homes. Companies began offering prepared foods—frozen hors d'oeuvres, entrées (the first "TV Dinner" appeared in 1954), and pizza (1950s). Birdseye's innovations changed everything about how people around the world eat.

HIDDEN HISTORY

The First "TV Dinner"

As with most cultural phenomena, the story of the first frozen meal that was heated in the oven and served in a compartmentalized disposable tray in front of a television set is more complicated than its original telling.

For almost a half-century, from 1953, when C.A. Swanson & Sons introduced its first "TV Brand Frozen Dinner," to the early 2000s, when inconsistencies in his story began to come to light, former Swanson salesman Gerry Thomas laid claim to having invented the TV dinner. He declared that in 1953, someone at Swanson greatly overestimated the market for Thanksgiving turkeys, leaving 260 tons of frozen birds languishing in 10 refrigerated railroad cars. Panicked Swanson executives solicited ideas from employees for using the frozen birds. According to Thomas, he came up with the idea to create frozen meals of the type served on commercial airlines. The company ordered 5,000 aluminum trays and combined the turkey with cornbread dressing and gravy, peas, and mashed sweet potatoes and debuted the TV dinner at a price of 98 cents. The 5,000 dinners sold out.

> "Mrs. Eisenhower was happy to be with her husband alone at every meal, and many times the President and First Lady took their dinner on trays while watching television. Gossips say the trays contained frozen TV dinners."—*The Presidents' Cookbook*, 1968

The following year, in 1954—after a massive ad campaign, the company sold more than 10 million TV dinners.

Swanson family members, historians, and frozen-food industry officials from the 1950s have all disputed Thomas' story. In 1944, the W.L. Maxson Co. created the first frozen

◀ In 1944, the W.L. Maxson Co. created the first frozen dinner, which was initially sold to the Navy and then to commercial airlines. Here, a TWA "air hostess" prepares to serve a meal.

▲ For almost 50 years, the story went that the first TV dinner was invented to use up an excess of 260 tons of frozen turkeys owned by Swanson.

dinner, which was initially sold to the Navy and then to the airlines. Admittedly, they weren't eaten in front of a television screen, so they couldn't rightly be called a "TV dinner." Former Swanson employees say the company had eight stories of freezers in Omaha and would not have needed the refrigerated trains to store the surplus of birds. Betty Cronin, a bacteriologist who worked for Swanson, asserted that it was the Swanson brothers themselves—Gilbert and Clarke—who conceptualized the TV dinner and set their marketing and advertising team to name and design the product.

In 2003, when the *Los Angeles Times* asked Thomas about the discrepancies, he said the railcar story was "a metaphor."

Perhaps the "TV dinner" is more a product of smart marketing and a confluence of cultural factors than any one person's invention. However those first TV dinners came to be, they took the country by storm. By 1956, Swanson alone was selling 13 million TV dinners annually. Other companies got into the game too, including those that introduced individual frozen meals that reflected the country's growing interest in the foods of non-European cultures such as Chinese and Mexican cuisine. Every year between 1953 and 2008—when they began to decline—the sales of frozen meals increased.

WHY "TV DINNER"?

The growth in sales of frozen meals and the proliferation of televisions in American homes during the 1950s were on an almost-parallel track.

From 1942 to 1949, a total of about 3.7 million television sets were sold. In 1950 alone, the number was almost 8 million. In 1953—the year the Swanson TV dinner debuted—more than 28 million sets were sold. By the end of the decade in 1959, Americans bought more than 67 million televisions. After just 25 minutes in the oven, TV dinners could be enjoyed on "TV trays" in front of *I Love Lucy*, *The Ed Sullivan Show*, or *You Bet Your Life*. There was no cooking beforehand and no cleanup afterward. Just *The $64,000 Question* or the thrill of *Alfred Hitchcock Presents* accompanied by an effortless hot meal of meat loaf, buttered peas, and mashed potatoes.

"...Swanson's brave new product was aided immeasurably by another increasingly powerful package, the television set."

—*Smithsonian Magazine,* December 2004

By the late 1940s, Americans were buying freezers for their homes, making the advent of the frozen meal possible.

Tomato Soup and Grilled Cheese

This classic American combination is the result of innovation, necessity, and thrift, starting in Camden, New Jersey, with Joseph Campbell, a fruit merchant, and Abraham Anderson, an icebox manufacturer, forming what would become the Campbell Soup Company in 1869. In 1895, the company introduced the first can of ready-to-serve tomato soup. Not too many years later and halfway across the country in Chicago, a young man named James L. Kraft lost his job. He figured a good way to make a living would be to buy cheese wholesale, then deliver it to grocers and restaurants via mule. He soon discovered, though, that spoilage was a serious problem for his customers. Most of them did not have refrigerators, so the cheese they bought had to be used within a day of purchase. In 1915, Kraft came up with a way to manufacture a pasteurized product he called processed or American cheese. It could be transported across the country without spoiling. Families began making their toasted cheese sandwiches with Kraft's smooth cheese.

During the Depression, grilled cheese sandwiches became popular because the ingredients were so inexpensive. After World War II, school cafeterias began serving tomato soup with grilled cheese sandwiches to satisfy the vitamin C and protein requirements for school lunches. No one knows who the first genius was to dip the sandwich in the soup, but it was clearly a magical moment.

YOU WILL NEED

- 1   stalk celery, finely diced
- 1   tablespoon butter
- 1   (15-ounce) can tomato sauce
- 1   (6-ounce) can tomato paste
- 1   cup water
- ½   teaspoon garlic salt
- 2   tablespoons light brown sugar
- ¼   teaspoon salt
- 2   cups whole milk

1 In a medium saucepan cook celery in hot butter over medium heat, stirring frequently, until softened. Reduce the heat to medium-low and add tomato sauce, tomato paste, water, garlic salt, sugar, and salt. Bring to a simmer.

2 Remove from heat and puree with an immersion blender until completely smooth. (Alternatively, transfer to a blender and blend until smooth. Be sure to leave a crack in the lid to allow steam to escape. Return to the saucepan.)

3 Slowly whisk in the milk. Heat, stirring frequently, until steaming (do not boil).

4 Serve with Classic Grilled Cheese (recipe below).

Classic Grilled Cheese For each sandwich, layer 2 slices of processed American cheese on a slice of white sandwich bread. Top with another slice of white sandwich bread. Butter each side of the sandwich with 1 teaspoon softened butter. Cook in a skillet until cheese is melted and sandwich is golden brown on both sides, about 3 minutes per side.

HIDDEN HISTORY

Frederick McKinley Jones

A self-taught engineer revolutionized the way the world eats. His mobile refrigeration unit prevented food waste and made fresh fruits, vegetables, and meats available year-round.

On a hot May day in 1938, Minnesota transportation boss Harry Werner got news that one of his trucks had broken down on the way from Minneapolis to Chicago, and its ice-chilled cargo of 35,000 pounds of raw chicken was rotting. Incidents such as these were common at the time.

A CHALLENGE ACCEPTED

Enter Frederick McKinley Jones, an ingenious tinkerer who was working for Minneapolis entrepreneur Joseph Numero of Cinema Supplies. By this time, the 45-year-old Jones already had a couple of inventions under his belt.

Werner and Numero knew each other socially. When Werner recounted the story of the rotting meat, Numero made a half-joking remark that Werner needed refrigerators for his trucks. Numero wasn't joking.

In 1991, Jones was posthumously awarded the National Medal of Technology and Innovation by President George H.W. Bush. He was the first African American to receive it.

Werner showed up at Numero's business with a truck and a challenge to Jones to create a cooling unit that could withstand the bumps and jolts of over-the-road travel. Jones did it. He received a patent for the invention—the first of more than 60 patents over his career—in 1940.

THE POWER OF POSITIVITY

Jones and Numero went into business together, calling their new company U.S. Thermo Control Company—later known as Thermo King—with Jones as chief engineer and vice president of engineering. By 1949, the company had earned $3 million. Jones' invention

◀ Jones' invention made it possible to transport produce over long distances without spoiling, giving the public access to fresh fruits and vegetables year-round.

▶ Frederick McKinley Jones stands in front of a truck outfitted with his cooling unit. Jones and business partner, Joseph Numero, manufactured the units at their Minneapolis company, Thermo King, and sold them to numerous transportation companies. His invention was later applied to boats, planes, and boxcars.

was later applied to boats, planes, and boxcars. Millions of people worldwide now had access to fresh food.

"Doughboys and leathernecks down in the steaming jungles of the South Pacific have fresh vegetables and meat on their bill of fare because of the inventive genius of a Minneapolis man," touted a January 1, 1945 article in the *Minneapolis Star Journal*. "He is Frederick Jones— veritably a black Thomas Edison."

Jones was born in Covington, Kentucky, in 1893 in a country still simmering from the Civil War and that had entrenched ideas about the proper place of a black man. Although racism impacted his life, he did not let it define him—and neither did his challenging childhood.

His mother left the family shortly after he was born, and his father struggled to raise him alone. When Frederick was age 7, his father sent him to live with the priests at a Catholic school and rectory. He attended school there for four years but ran away at age 11. He had an agile and highly curious mind but not much patience for the constraints of formal education and its rules.

He found work cleaning an auto garage. There, he further experimented with mechanics and by age 14 was employed full-time as a mechanic. By 15, he was a foreman. At 19, he left the garage and spent the next 20 years repairing the mechanisms of steamships, furnaces, and farm machinery. It was during this period that he met Numero.

In a 1953 speech he gave as he accepted the Merit Award from the Phillis Wheatley Auxiliary in Minneapolis for his "outstanding achievements which serve as an inspiration for youth," Jones outlined the three elements of success. "First, don't be afraid to get your hands dirty. Don't be afraid to work. Try lots of jobs. Work for nothing if you have to, but get the experience. You never know when what you have learned will come in handy. Second, you have to read. Find out what others know. You don't have to buy books. Use libraries! You can educate yourself by reading. All my life has been study and work. That's what I get fun out of. And third, you have to believe in yourself. Don't listen to others tell you you're wrong. Remember, nothing is impossible. Go ahead and prove you're right."

Barbecue Ribs

American barbecue is most closely associated with the South. The featured meat is usually pork, cooked low and slow over a wood fire, often built in a pit. Enslaved men were the early pitmasters, often cooking large amounts of barbecue for gatherings hosted by the plantation owner. During the first half of the 20th century—when large numbers of African Americans migrated from the South to northern industrial cities, they took barbecue knowledge with them. Kansas City became especially well-known for barbecue and attributes its style to Henry Perry. Originally from an area near Memphis, Perry, who worked on steamboats, relocated to an African American neighborhood in Kansas City and in 1908 started serving slow-cooked ribs on pages of newsprint for 25 cents. Today, the Kansas City Barbeque Society boasts more than 10,000 members and says it is dedicated to "promoting barbecue as America's cuisine and having fun while doing so."

YOU WILL NEED

- 3 tablespoons smoked paprika
- 2 tablespoons packed dark brown sugar
- 1 tablespoon kosher salt
- 1 tablespoon chili powder
- 1 tablespoon onion powder
- 1 tablespoon granulated garlic
- 1 teaspoon black pepper
- ½ teaspoon dried thyme
- ½ teaspoon cayenne pepper
- 2 to 3 racks baby back ribs (3 pounds each)
- 1 cup hickory chips

MOP SAUCE

- Barbecue Sauce (recipe follows)
- ¾ cup apple cider or water
- ¼ cup cider vinegar

1 In a medium bowl stir together the smoked paprika, brown sugar, salt, chili powder, onion powder, garlic, black pepper, thyme, and cayenne pepper. Use a table knife to loosen the membrane covering the backside of each rack of ribs. Use a towel to grasp a corner of the membrane and pull it off; discard. Sprinkle racks all over with rub and massage into meat, using enough rub so it sticks. Let stand at room temperature 1 hour. Soak wood chips in water to cover 1 hour.

2 Prepare grill for indirect cooking over low heat (250°F to 300°F). If using a charcoal grill, make sure charcoal covers no more than one-third of the grate. Place a disposable drip pan on the empty side of the grate. Fill the pan about halfway with warm water.

3 Drain the wood chips and add half to the charcoal or to the smoker box of a gas grill, following manufacturer's instructions; close grill lid. If using a charcoal grill, place racks of ribs in a rib rack facing the same direction. When smoke appears, for a gas grill place ribs over indirect low heat. For charcoal, place the rib rack over foil pan with bone sides facing charcoal. Close the lid and cook 1 hour, maintaining low heat.

4 For the Mop Sauce, in a medium bowl stir together ¼ cup of the Barbecue Sauce, cider, and vinegar.

5 After the first hour of cooking ribs, brush ribs on all sides with mop sauce. Add remaining wood chips to charcoal or smoker box. If using a charcoal grill, replenish charcoal as needed to maintain steady temperature (about 8 briquettes every hour or so) and add more water to drip pan as needed. Cook 1½ hours more, brushing with mop sauce two more times during cooking and turning and rotating ribs. Brush ribs with barbecue sauce and cook 30 to 60 minutes more or until tender and meat tears easily. Brush again with barbecue sauce at end of cook time. If desired, serve ribs with additional sauce.

Barbecue Sauce In a medium saucepan cook ½ cup finely chopped onion in 1 tablespoon hot oil over medium-low heat until tender. Add ½ cup ketchup, 1 (6-ounce) can tomato paste, ½ cup apple cider or water, ½ cup cider vinegar, ¼ cup dark brown sugar, 2 tablespoons molasses, 2 tablespoons Worcestershire sauce, 1 teaspoon chili powder, 1 teaspoon smoked paprika, and ¼ teaspoon cayenne pepper. Bring to a simmer over medium heat. Simmer 30 minutes.

Tostadas and Salsa

There was a time when tortilla chips (tostadas) were simply tortillas made by home cooks from leftover masa (corn dough) that were fried. Then, in 1912, José Bartolomé Martínez—known as the Corn King of San Antonio, Texas—started selling commercially produced corn tortilla chips. Competitors followed, including C. Elmer Doolin, who in 1932 bought a recipe and developed a device for extruding masa into strips and the process for frying them. He used a factory line to make his Fritos, named after a Mexican street food called *fritas*. Eventually the company became Frito-Lay and started producing "authentic" corn tortilla chips under the name Tostitos. As for salsa, it was the Aztecs who first made a condiment out of tomatoes and chile peppers to season their dishes. Americans embraced salsa as a taco topper and dip for chips. By 1991, it was outselling ketchup as a condiment.

CORN TORTILLAS

2 cups masa harina or blue corn masa harina

1¼ cups warm water

TOSTADAS

   Peanut oil or vegetable oil for frying

12 Corn Tortillas

   Salt

   Salsa Fresca

CORN TORTILLAS

1 To a medium bowl add masa harina and make a well in the center. Add water all at once and stir. Knead mixture to form a dough that is firm enough to form a smooth ball without cracks. If too dry, add more warm water 1 tablespoon at a time.

2 To shape tortillas, divide dough into 12 portions and roll each into a ball. Cover to keep from drying out. Place one ball of dough between two pieces of plastic wrap or parchment paper. Using a tortilla press, the bottom of a dinner plate, or a rolling pin, flatten each ball into a circle, about 6 inches in diameter.

3 Remove plastic wrap from one side, flip over onto your hand, and remove other piece of plastic. On a hot ungreased comal or heavy skillet (such as cast-iron), cook tortilla about 2 minutes or until light brown and set (dry looking), turning one or two times so both sides cook evenly. Repeat with remaining dough balls. Makes 12 tortillas.

TOSTADAS (FRIED CORN CHIPS)

1 In a deep heavy skillet heat 1 to 2 inches oil to 350°F. Meanwhile, cut each tortilla into six wedges. Line a plate with paper towels.

2 Fry a few wedges at a time until lightly browned, about 1 to 2 minutes, turning occasionally. With a slotted spoon transfer cooked tostada wedges to paper towel-lined plate. Sprinkle with salt. Cool completely. Serve with Salsa Fresca. Store in an airtight container. Makes 72 tostadas.

Salsa Fresca In a medium bowl combine 1 pound chopped or diced ripe tomatoes, ½ cup finely chopped onion, 1 large seeded and chopped poblano or Anaheim pepper, 1 or 2 seeded and chopped jalapeños, 2 tablespoons lime juice, 2 tablespoons chopped fresh cilantro, 1 tablespoon olive oil, 2 cloves minced garlic, ½ teaspoon salt; and 1 teaspoon cumin seeds, toasted and crushed. Let stand 30 minutes to meld flavors. Serve with tostadas. Makes about 4 cups.

▲ Plastic wrap keeps the dough from sticking to the tortilla press.

▲ Cook tortillas on an ungreased heavy skillet.

▲ Fry a few wedges at a time until lightly browned. Don't overcrowd the pan.

Ray Kroc

IT COULD BE ARGUED WHETHER OR NOT THE VISION OF THIS CONSUMMATE BUSINESSMAN WAS GOOD FOR THE HEALTH OF THE NATION, BUT WHAT CAN'T BE DISPUTED IS THAT HE HAD A PROFOUND EFFECT ON THE CULTURE OF EATING WORLDWIDE. MCDONALD'S WAS THE FIRST GLOBAL FAST-FOOD FRANCHISE.

▶ "I can't pretend to know what it is—certainly, it's not some divine vision," Kroc recalled in a memoir published by *The New York Times* about his epiphany at the McDonald brothers' California restaurant. "Whatever it was, I saw it in the McDonald's operation, and in that moment, I suppose, I became an entrepreneur. I decided to go for broke."

▶ Ronald McDonald made his national debut in 1966 during a nationwide television commercial that was part of an advertising campaign created to appeal to children.

The actual structure of the first Ray Kroc-affiliated McDonald's franchise in Des Plaines, Illinois, was torn down in 1984. A replica was built and served as the McDonald's Store No. 1 Museum until it, too, was demolished in 2018 due to repeated flooding at the site.

▼ The first McDonald's drive-thru was installed in 1975 at the franchise in Sierra Vista, Arizona. Now, more than 60 percent of McDonald's' business comes from customers who take their food and drive away.

SHAKING UP THE RESTAURANT WORLD

It all started with a milkshake—or, more specifically, a few milkshake mixers. In 1954, Ray Kroc—a Multimixer salesman from Illinois—visited a small but successful restaurant in San Bernadino, California, owned by Dick and Mac McDonald, two brothers who had created a concept for a limited-menu establishment that allowed them to focus on consistency and quick service. Although it started out as a barbecue restaurant in 1940, the brothers discovered by 1948 that their highest-profit items were hamburgers. They streamlined their menu to hamburgers, potato chips, and orange drink. The next year, they added French fries and Coca-Cola.™

Kroc was impressed by the operation. The brothers were looking for a new franchising agent and Kroc seized the opportunity. The first McDonald's restaurant founded by McDonald's System, Inc.—predecessor to McDonald's Corporation—was opened in Des Plaines, Illinois, in April 1955. A menu from that era touted a "Pure Beef Hamburger" for 15 cents, a "Tempting Cheeseburger" for 19 cents, and "Golden French Fries" for 10 cents.

By 1958, McDonald's franchises had sold 100 million hamburgers. As the number of restaurants grew, Kroc maintained the assembly-line production system pioneered by the McDonald brothers. Franchisees attended a training course called Hamburger University in Elk Grove, Illinois, which led to a "Bachelor of Hamburgerology with a minor in french fries."

Kroc bought the brothers out in 1961. More than 36,000 McDonald's restaurants in 101 countries around the world serve 69 million people daily, according to 2019 figures.

"There is nothing at McDonald's that makes it necessary to have teeth," the nutritionist Jean Mayer is quoted as saying in a 1973 *Time* magazine article, referencing the fact that the food is specifically engineered to be eaten quickly and on the go. "I am nonfanatical about McDonald's. As a weekend treat, it is clean and fast."

EVERYTHING OLD IS NEW AGAIN

Food Preservation

Shortly after the financial crisis of 2008—and for several years following it—the country was in the throes of a renaissance in home food preservation. Home cooks embraced all methods, but especially canning. By the middle of 2009, sales of Ball and Kerr canning supplies were up by almost 50 percent over the previous year.

Economic necessity likely drove much of the resurgence in home food preservation during this time, but that wasn't the sole factor. In the late 1990s, there was a reawakening of interest in buying seasonal, locally grown, and minimally processed food. Farmers markets both increased in number exponentially and expanded into communities around the country (see page 150). Home cooks were canning tomatoes, green beans, and beets they bought at their local market or grew themselves.

This early-21st-century boom may have been the most recent comeback of canning and other traditional methods of home food preservation, but it is not the only one in the country's history. During both world wars, the government encouraged Americans to grow Victory Gardens (see page 248) and to preserve the harvest to make wartime rations go farther, among other rationale.

In the 1970s—with its antiestablishment ethos and sense of homespun chic—home food preservation experienced another rebirth, this time as a means of both accessing wholesome foods and rejecting mainstream culture. Back-to-the-landers grew their own food and canned their homegrown crops as a way of removing themselves from the commercial food economy—or at least lessening their participation in it.

Whether the motivation to preserve fresh foods at home is practical, political, personal, or simply a matter of taste, the process always offers a powerful connection to the past.

▲ During World War II, the U.S. government encouraged Americans to grow Victory Gardens and preserve the harvest to make wartime rations go further.

▶ Canning, dehydrating, freezing, and pickling are all methods of food preservation. Herbs are best preserved by dehydrating.

Classic Dill Pickles

In the mid-19th century, Jewish immigrants from Eastern Europe introduced New York City to long-fermented kosher dill pickles. They filled wooden barrels with cucumbers, garlic, dill, water, kosher salt, and seasonings, leaving them to ferment over a month to produce a strongly sour pickle that they peddled on carts as a street snack. During this era, inventors were making innovations in canning, which eventually allowed home gardeners and cooks to put up pickles—and more—for long-term storage.

YOU WILL NEED

- 4 pounds (4-inch) pickling cucumbers (about 48)
- 4 cups water
- 4 cups white vinegar
- ⅓ cup pickling salt
- 3 tablespoons sugar
- 8 to 16 heads fresh dill or 8 tablespoons dill seeds
- 8 teaspoons assorted color or black peppercorns
- 8 cloves garlic, peeled and halved
- 8 teaspoons mustard seeds

SPECIAL EQUIPMENT

- 8 pint canning jars with new lids* and screw bands

  Boiling water canner

  Jar lifter

1 Rinse cucumbers thoroughly with cold water; drain. Remove stems and cut off a slice from the blossom ends (see Note). In a large stainless-steel or enamel pan stir together water, vinegar, salt, and sugar. Bring to boiling, stirring to dissolve sugar.

2 Pack cucumbers loosely into hot, sterilized pint jars, leaving a ½-inch headspace. To each jar, add 1 or 2 heads dill (or 1 tablespoon dill seeds), 1 teaspoon peppercorns, 2 garlic clove halves, and 1 teaspoon mustard seeds. Pour hot vinegar mixture over cucumbers, leaving a ½-inch headspace. Wipe jars and tighten lids just to fingertip tight (not too tight or they won't create a vacuum seal).

3 Process jars in a boiling water canner 10 minutes, beginning timing when water returns to boiling. Remove jars with a jar lifter and transfer to a wire rack to cool. Check to see that the jar has sealed properly after it has cooled. If the center of the lid is depressed and does not make a popping sound when pressed, it has sealed properly. Let stand at room temperature at least 2 weeks before using to develop flavor.

Note If desired, cut cucumbers into spears lengthwise. An optional extra brining step helps to ensure crisp pickle spears. To brine, place cucumbers in an extra-large non-metal food-safe container. In a large pitcher combine 1 gallon water and ⅓ cup pickling salt, stirring to dissolve. Pour over cucumbers and let stand at room temperature 24 hours. Drain and rinse well with cold water; drain.

*Note Always use new lids every time you can. The jars and screw tops can be reused, but the lids have a special sticky compound that seals the jar.

▲ Pack the cucumbers loosely into the jars, leaving a ½-inch headspace.

▲ Pour the hot vinegar mixture over the cucumbers, leaving a ½-inch headspace.

▲ Press on the centers of the lids to test the seals. They should be depressed and not make a popping sound.

Peppered Maple Jerky

Before refrigeration, air-drying meat was the best way to preserve it. American Indians made what is now called jerky from venison, bison, deer, elk, or antelope by cutting it into very thin strips and hanging it in the sun over a small smoky fire until it was dried out. The name "jerky" comes from the American Spanish *charqui* (jerked meat) adapted from the Incan Quechua *ch'arki* (dried flesh). Europeans who moved West and settled on native lands learned the technique from local tribes. Sarah Cummins, who traveled with her family in 1845 across Kansas in a wagon, ate dried buffalo meat and wrote about it. "To prepare this dried or jerked meat, the newly dressed meat is first dipped into a solution of strong brine, then hung over a frame of small poles and allowed to drain. A fire of hardwood now supplies the drying curing smoke." Today, you can safely make jerky in a dehydrator.

YOU WILL NEED

- 2 pounds venison (eye round or rump roast) or boneless beef chuck roast or sirloin roast
- 1 cup reduced-sodium soy sauce
- 2 tablespoons pure maple syrup
- 2 tablespoons sunflower oil
- 4 cloves garlic, minced
- 2 teaspoons cracked black peppercorns
- 2 teaspoons sea salt
- 1 teaspoon crushed dried thyme

1 Place a steamer insert in an extra-large skillet. Add water so the level comes just below the insert. Bring the water to a boil. Place the roast in the steamer. Cover and steam 20 to 30 minutes or until a meat thermometer inserted into the center of the roast registers 160°F. Let the roast stand on a cutting board 10 minutes. Place the roast on a plate and freeze 30 to 45 minutes or until it is partially frozen. (This makes it easier to slice very thinly.)

2 Trim excess fat from meat. Cut across the grain into 6-inch-long, ⅛-inch-thick strips.

3 In a large bowl whisk together the soy sauce, maple syrup, oil, garlic, peppercorns, sea salt, and thyme. Add the meat and stir well to coat. Cover and marinate in the refrigerator 2 hours. Drain, discarding the marinade.

4 Place the meat slices in a single layer on mesh-lined dehydrator trays.

5 Dehydrate at 160°F 5 to 6 hours or until dry. To check doneness, remove one slice from the dehydrator. When the jerky is done, it should easily break in half. Let meat slices cool. Store the cooled jerky in an airtight container at room temperature up to 3 weeks.

▲ Be sure all of the slices of meat are thoroughly coated in the marinade.

▲ Arrange meat strips in a single layer in the dehydrator to ensure even drying.

▲ Allow meat strips to cool completely before storing in an airtight container.

Julia Child

IN THE EARLY 1960S, A PASSIONATE BUT UNLIKELY
ADVOCATE FOR FINE FRENCH COOKING BURST ONTO
THE SCENE WITH A GROUNDBREAKING COOKBOOK
AND TELEVISION SHOW. WITH WIT, CANDOR, AND
CONTAGIOUS ENTHUSIASM, SHE CHANGED AMERICA'S
RELATIONSHIP TO FOOD AT A TIME WHEN NEW
TECHNOLOGIES, THE WIDESPREAD ACCEPTANCE
OF CONVENIENCE FOODS, AND CHANGING IDEAS
ABOUT THE VALUE OF TIME SPENT IN THE KITCHEN
THREATENED TO WIPE OUT REAL COOKING.

◀ In 2014, the U.S.
Postal service issued a
series of limited-edition
stamps featuring five
chefs—including Child—
who revolutionized the
nation's understanding
of food.

Julia Child
FOREVER

Courtesy of HILLS BROS COFFEE
Gourmet cooking is Child's play. Just watch Ju...

THE FRENCH CHE

THURSDAYS 8:30 P. M. KQED
[Repeats Mondays at 4:30 p.m.]

Compliments of HILLS BROS COFFEE

JULIA CHILD · THE FRENCH CHEF
Presented by KQED · San Francisco

BON APPÉTIT!

In 1962, when Julia Child made an appearance on WGBH in Boston to promote her new cookbook *Mastering the Art of French Cooking*, she demonstrated how to make a proper omelette. Viewers demanded more. In 1963, the station launched *The French Chef*—initially contracting with Child to create 26 episodes at $50 each. In the first episode, she demonstrated how to make a rich French beef stew, *boeuf bourguignon*. The series ran for 10 years.

Child came to cooking by curiosity and appetite. After graduating from Smith College in 1934, she worked a series of jobs in her native California, in Massachusetts, and in New York City. In 1941, she moved to Washington, D.C., to work as a research assistant for the Office of Strategic Services, the forerunner of the CIA. She and her colleagues were sent on assignments around the world. They—including her future husband, Paul—reveled in the experience of eating new foods while helping the war effort.

The Childs married in 1946. His work for the United States Information Service took them to Paris in 1948. "As soon as we got over there and I tasted that food," Child said, "I just couldn't get over it."

She enrolled at the prestigious Cordon Bleu cooking school and also met Simone Beck and Louisette Bertholle—her future collaborators on *Mastering the Art of French Cooking*.

It was after the Childs had settled in Cambridge, Massachusetts, in the early 1960s that she made that first appearance on WGBH. In 2001, she turned her Cambridge kitchen over to the Smithsonian, where it is on display at the National Museum of American History. Everything is arranged exactly as it was for the many episodes of the multiple television shows in which she chopped, stirred, whipped, and served up encouragement.

HIDDEN HISTORY

Jan Longone

When culinary experts need primary-source information about the history of American gastronomy, they turn to the collection of more than 30,000 cookbooks and other materials amassed over the lifetime of a passionate but accidental archivist.

Jan Longone didn't set out to create the most exhaustive and important collection of printed culinary artifacts in the country, but that's what happened—and it all started with a birthday gift of volume 1 of *The Gourmet Cookbook* from her husband, Daniel, shortly after they got married in 1954.

A SPARK IS LIT

The book came with a coupon for $2 off of a lifetime subscription to *Gourmet* magazine. They were poor graduate students at Cornell University at the time, but they scraped together the $48 to purchase the subscription.

"The minute I got the magazine, I read every single word of every single issue. I wasn't so much interested in cookbooks at first, but I was interested in the history," says Longone, who holds a bachelor's degree in history and did work toward a Ph.D. in Chinese history.

> James Beard called the collection "an unequaled feat of culinary scholarship."

She and Dan began searching for out-of-print cookbooks and other food-related ephemera—menus, posters, and pamphlets. Jan's reputation began to precede her.

"In New England there were lots of wonderful book shops. We would go booking—we called it going 'booking'—and I would have a very good eye," Longone says. "I don't understand why, but I did. We went to bookstores and [the owners] would say, 'Oh, you're the woman who wants food and wine books. We have some books for you.' And I would always buy the interesting books."

▲ Longone's donated collection includes not just cookbooks but posters, pamphlets, and menus as well. This menu is from chef Alice Waters' highly influential restaurant in Berkeley, California.

CHEZ : PANISSE
MENU NEW YEAR'S EVE 1974

▶ Vintage recipe booklets from food companies are a whimsical and often entertaining peek into the history of advertising, such as this circa 1934 collection of tuna recipes.

86 new *proven tuna* recipes
and THE ROMANCE OF TUNA

▼ Although Longone and her husband donated their collection of vintage cookbooks and ephemera to the University of Michigan, she still has several thousand items in her house. "This is a problem," she says, laughing. "My house is a mess."

COOKING & FOOD | 147

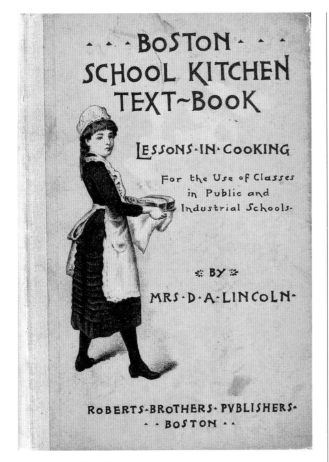

BOSTON SCHOOL KITCHEN TEXT~BOOK

LESSONS·IN·COOKING

For the Use of Classes in Public and Industrial Schools·

❧ BY ❧

MRS·D·A·LINCOLN·

ROBERTS·BROTHERS·PUBLISHERS· ··BOSTON··

A GIFT OF HISTORY

In 1959, the couple moved to Ann Arbor, Michigan, where Dan got a position in the University of Michigan's department of chemistry. The collection kept growing. Julia Child, James Beard, and *New York Times* food writer Craig Claiborne were all early fans. In 1972, Longone created The Wine and Food Library, which sold books through mail order or appointment.

While Longone appreciated the recipes, what she found truly compelling was the story cookbooks told about American history and culture. The rise of charity cookbooks by churches, synagogues, and other community organizations, for instance, came at a time during which women had no rights—no vote, no control over money, no place to meet outside the home. Putting together a cookbook for a cause was a way to exert some power.

In 2000, the Longones donated the collection to the University of Michigan. It was named the Janice Bluestein Longone Culinary Archive, and Longone was appointed curator.

There are many pieces in the collection that she holds dear, but her most prized acquisition is *A Domestic Cook Book: Containing a Careful Selection of Useful Receipts for the Kitchen* by Mrs. Malinda Russell, an Experienced Cook, published in 1866.

Mrs. Russell was a free black woman, and her cookbook is the oldest known cookbook by an African American woman. Its 39 pages contain 265 recipes—mostly for cakes and pastries, as she owned a pastry shop for six years. She also tells her personal story and why she was forced to leave her home in Tennessee.

By "hard labor and economy," she writes, she saved a "considerable sum of money for the support of myself and son, which was taken from me on the 16th of January, 1864, by a guerrilla party, who threatened my life if I revealed who they were. Under those circumstances we were obliged to leave home, following a flag of truce out of the Southern borders, being attacked several times by the enemy."

Mrs. Russell and her son eventually settled in Michigan, where she wrote and published her book.

To this day, Longone continues to look for more details about Malinda Russell's life. "She's one of my two favorite people [the other being her husband]," she says. "This is a woman I so admire. I call her my inspiration."

The same might be said of Longone, whose contribution to the caretaking of America's culinary history is immeasurable.

"My collection is truly beautiful. I tell people it's probably the best collection [of cookbooks] in the world," she says. "I am so proud of it."

> "I'm going to do all I can to talk about culinary history because we all have to eat."
>
> —*Jan Longone*

Bagels

Jewish immigrants from Eastern Europe brought the chewy roll with a hole—that is first boiled and then baked—to the United States. Between 1880 and 1914, about 2 million Ashkenazi Jews arrived in the U.S., many escaping persecution. Russian and Polish bakers were already pros at making bagels, and since many Jewish families settled in Manhattan's Lower East Side, bagel bakeries and street vendors soon followed. The hole in the middle helped bagels bake evenly but also allowed vendors to stack them up on dowels or hang them on strings. In the early 1900s, the Local 338 Union in Manhattan was formed, a federation of 300 bagel makers. Early bagels were half the size of today's bagels and were all made by hand. It took decades for bagels to make their way into shops and home freezers across America, but by the 1990s the country was in the middle of a veritable bagel craze.

YOU WILL NEED

- 1½ cups warm water (120°F–130°F)
- 2 tablespoons malt syrup, sugar, or honey
- 1 package active dry yeast (2¼ teaspoons)
- 1 teaspoon salt
- 3½ to 4 cups bread flour or all-purpose flour
- 8 cups water
- 1½ tablespoons malt syrup or sugar

1 In a small bowl stir together the 1½ cups warm water, malt syrup, yeast, and salt. In a large mixing bowl add 2 cups of the flour and water-yeast mixture; beat with an electric mixer on low speed 30 seconds, scraping sides of the bowl as needed. Beat on high speed 3 minutes. Using a wooden spoon or mixer fitted with a dough hook, on low speed, stir in as much of the remaining flour as possible.

2 Turn dough onto a floured surface. Knead in enough of the remaining flour to make moderately stiff dough that is smooth and elastic, about 7 to 9 minutes. (Or knead using an electric mixer fitted with a dough hook on medium-low speed.) Place dough in a lightly oiled large bowl. Cover and let rise 1 hour.

3 Stir down the dough with a wooden spoon. Divide dough into 12 portions. Shape each portion into a smooth ball. Let stand 5 minutes to relax. Punch a hole into the center of each ball and insert both thumbs. Use thumbs to stretch and pat dough until the hole is about 2 inches in diameter. On the work surface, cover bagels and let rise about 10 minutes.

4 Meanwhile, preheat oven to 400°F. Line a baking sheet with lightly oiled parchment paper or plastic wrap. In a Dutch oven or large saucepan bring the 8 cups water to boiling. Stir in the 1½ tablespoons malt syrup. Reduce heat to a simmer. With a skimmer or slotted spoon, add bagels, two to four at a time (don't crowd them). The bagels should sink, then rise back to the surface. Cook 1 minute; turn over and cook 1 minute more. Turn bagels so rounded sides are up and remove from water. Drain excess water and place on prepared baking sheet. Repeat with remaining bagels.

5 Bake 25 to 30 minutes or until tops are golden. Transfer to a wire rack and cool.

Optional Toppings Whisk together 1 egg white and 1 teaspoon water. Before baking, brush bagels on the baking sheet with the egg wash. Sprinkle with seeds such as poppy seeds, sesame seeds, and/or caraway seeds. Or sprinkle with cinnamon sugar or kosher salt.

Whole Wheat Bagels Substitute 1½ cups whole wheat flour for 1½ cups of the bread flour added at the end of Step 1.

EVERYTHING OLD IS NEW AGAIN

Farm-to-Table Food

Eating locally grown food produced on a small scale used to be a necessity until industrialization and technological innovation replaced the practice. Now it's back in full force.

FEEDING A GROWING POPULATION

Before the industrial boom of the late 19th century, most Americans grew their own food or purchased it from farmers who produced it within just a few miles of their homes. Then, between 1870 and 1920, 11 million people moved from rural to urban areas. By 1920, more Americans lived in cities than rural areas for the first time in U.S. history. In 1900, the population of the United States was 76 million. By 2000, it was 280 million. In 1940, one farmer fed 19 people. In 2013, one farmer fed 170 people.

TO MARKET, TO MARKET

Over the last century, the ways in which many Americans access food have changed dramatically. Prior to 1900, there were specialty stores—the butcher, the baker, the vegetable market. In 1916, Clarence Saunders opened the first supermarket—a Piggly Wiggly—in Memphis, Tennessee. Others—King Kullen, Safeway, and Kroger—followed. After World War II, a growing number of refrigerators and automobiles for more American homes meant more Americans got all of their food at a supermarket—much of which was heavily processed due to innovations in food production and storage. Canned and frozen foods gained popularity throughout the 1950s and early 1960s.

In 1962, Rachel Carson published her book, *Silent Spring*, which highlighted the dangers of pesticides. That, combined with the rise of a counterculture in America in the late 1960s and early 1970s, created a groundswell of interest among some members of the population—mostly white and middle class—in "getting back to the land." Alice Waters opened what could be called the first farm-to-table restaurant in the country, Chez Panisse, in 1971 in Berkeley, California. In 1973, the California Certified Organic Farmers was formed. Americans from all walks of life started demanding to know more about where their food came from.

The more recent farm-to-table movement has largely referred to restaurants that source their ingredients locally, but it's more than that. The way Americans source the foods they prepare at home has changed as well.

The explosion in the number of farmers markets and CSAs (community-supported agriculture) reflects the growing interest among many people in eating healthy, fresh, and locally grown foods. If they can't grow the food themselves—and if they have access, many people will visit a farmers market or sign up for a CSA—which involves receiving a box of seasonal, local produce from a small-scale grower every week.

Farmers markets give Americans an opportunity to buy fresh, locally grown foods that are in season and to interact with the farmers. They're also community gathering places—which boosts health in a different way.

▲ Clarence Saunders opened the first supermarket—a Piggly Wiggly—in 1916 in Memphis, Tennessee. This image of the Piggly Wiggly located at 106 South Austin in Chicago, Illinois, was taken in 1926.

According to the *USDA Farmers Market Directory*, between 1994 and 2014, the number of farmers markets in the United States grew from about 1,700 to 8,250 and increased in number by 180 percent from 2006 to 2014.

Kombucha

This effervescent, sweet-sour beverage made from a fermented fusion of tea and sugar was first made in China around 220 BCE and was prized for its healing properties. A culture called a SCOBY (symbiotic culture of bacteria and yeast) drives the fermentation process. Its name likely derives from Dr. Kombu, a Korean physician who brought it to Japan in 414 CE as a curative for Emperor Ingyō. A Swiss study in the 1960s demonstrated that it had health benefits comparable to yogurt, but it wasn't until the mid-1990s that it was embraced in the United States. The last decade has seen an explosion in both commercial and home-produced varieties. Like other fermented foods, it contains probiotics that promote a healthy digestive system.

YOU WILL NEED

- 16 cups purified water
- 6 tea bags* or 6 teaspoons loose-leaf* tea
- 1 cup sugar
- 1 to 2 cups starter liquid**
- 1 SCOBY

1 In a medium saucepan bring 4 cups water just to boiling over medium-high heat. Remove from heat; add the tea bags and let steep 15 minutes. Remove and discard tea bags or strain tea leaves. Add the sugar and stir to dissolve completely.

2 Meanwhile, add the remaining 12 cups water to a 1-gallon glass container. Add the sweet tea to the water. Check the temperature of the water mixture; it should be no warmer than body temperature (about 100°F). Add the starter liquid; stir to combine. Add the SCOBY.

3 Cover container opening with a paper towel, paper napkin, or tightly woven cloth; secure with a rubber band. Place the container in a warm (75°F to 80°F) ventilated area out of direct sunlight for 7 days. (The "mother" SCOBY may rise to the top, sink to the bottom, or float sideways, and a new "baby" SCOBY will form on the top.) Gently slide a straw under the SCOBYs to taste the brew. When it has the right-for-you balance of sweet-sour it is ready to decant; if it's not ready after 7 days, simply re-cover and continue fermentation, tasting every 2 days.

4 To decant the brew, use clean hands to transfer the SCOBYs to a glass container along with 1 to 2 cups of the kombucha (this will serve as the starter liquid for the next batch). If making another batch of kombucha right away, cover the container with a paper towel, paper napkin, or tightly woven cloth and set aside. If not, add a lid to the container and refrigerate up to 1 month.

5 If you're flavoring the kombucha in the bottle, add the desired flavoring to each bottle. Place bottles in a sink and insert a funnel. Ladle kombucha into bottles, filling nearly to the top. Secure the lids and store out of direct sunlight for 1 to 3 days, burping the bottles daily to release carbonation and prevent explosions. Transfer the bottles to the refrigerator and chill at least 4 hours. If desired, strain the flavoring from the kombucha before drinking. Kombucha will keep, refrigerated, up to 3 weeks.

* Use all green tea, all black tea, or a combination of green, black, and white teas. Do not use herbal teas.

** The starter liquid can be the liquid that came with a purchased SCOBY, reserved kombucha from a previous batch, or purchased plain kombucha.

Raspberry-Hibiscus In each 16-ounce glass bottle place 1 tablespoon gently mashed raspberry and ½ teaspoon dried hibiscus petals.

Lavender In each 16-ounce glass bottle place 1 teaspoon dried lavender flowers.

Turmeric-Ginger In each 16-ounce glass bottle place 1½ teaspoons grated fresh turmeric root and 2 teaspoons grated fresh gingerroot.

Contemporaries

Two Native American chefs come from different backgrounds but with a shared vision of educating the public about indigenous foods and bringing good health to their communities by returning to ancestral foodways.

The mission of Red Mesa Cuisine, the catering company where Lois Ellen Frank and Walter Whitewater work together in Santa Fe, New Mexico, is "to bring Native American Cuisine into the contemporary Southwest kitchen and to help sustain traditional Native American food, traditional Native agricultural practices, as well as keep alive ancestral culinary techniques from Native communities all over the Americas."

They prepare and serve foods for private events, parties, corporate meetings, and gallery openings, but educating the public about indigenous foods and ingredients and helping Native communities return to the traditional ways of eating is their true passion.

"I think everyone should have access to healthy, culturally appropriate foods," Frank says. "We teach Native people about foods that are culturally appropriate to them." The two worked together on a book authored by Frank—*Foods of the Southwest Indian*

▲ Chiles both fresh and dried—here they are strung on a ristra—are a central ingredient in Red Mesa Cuisine's cooking.

> "As I age, the next thing will be to make sure this all gets passed on and that young chefs step forward."
>
> —*Lois Ellen Frank*

This recipe for Hazruquive (Hominy, Bean Sprout, and Corncob Stew) is a Hopi stew made in late winter for the Powamu Ceremony, or Bean Dance. It's traditionally made with dried corncobs, but Frank adapted it for fresh corncobs, which are more available.

Nations—that won a James Beard Award in the Americana category in 2003.

"I [want to] introduce the old Native cooking," says Whitewater, who is Diné (Navajo). "The old people used to live off the land and had very little meat and mostly the greens and vegetables," he says. "For the Navajo people, whatever they had was taken away, and now it's fast food."

CULINARY AMBASSADORS

They came to this place from different backgrounds but with a shared vision. Frank, whose father is Sephardic and mother Kiowa, grew up on the East Coast. She holds a Ph.D. in culinary anthropology from the University of New Mexico. Whitewater was born in Pinon, Arizona, and raised on the Navajo reservation. He came up through the ranks cooking in high-end kitchens in the Southwest.

Currently, they are focused on helping to resolve pervasive health problems in Native communities—most notably diabetes. They have worked with the Physicians Committee for Responsible Medicine (PCRM) developing educational DVDs and plant-based recipes for their website, nativepowerplate.org. Frank teaches a 4-credit college class on indigenous foods to Native students from all over the country at the Institute of American Indian Arts (IAIA) in Santa Fe. They have been sent on trips by the U.S. State Department as culinary ambassadors to Ukraine, Russia, and the U.K. Whitewater has taught cooking classes at Diné College in Tsaile, Arizona.

"I want to reintroduce how we eat to the younger generation. We go back to how the foods were without the sugar, without the cream. At Diné, I showed [the students] what our food would be like in high-end restaurants—how it would look. I wanted to let them know that we have beautiful food too," he says. "I had a full crowd in my session and everybody went wild. We went back to plant-based foods. I think the Creator put me here to [reintroduce] that to my people."

◀ Chef Whitewater speaks at a Journey to Wellness Diabetes Awareness event with the Salt River Pima-Maricopa Indian Community.

▲ Chefs Lois Ellen Frank and Walter Whitewater met in the early 1990s at an Apache coming-of-age celebration and have been working together since.

THE MAGIC EIGHT

Frank and Whitewater mostly eat plants—a little wild game, but no commercial meat. They focus on the indigenous plants that did not exist outside of the pre-Columbian Americas. They refer to them as the "magic eight": corn, beans, squash, chiles, tomatoes, potatoes, vanilla, and cacao. "Those are the primary ingredients we use," Frank says.

Design & Decorating

The history of how we adorn spaces is a glimpse into how the country evolved. From molding natural materials to creating furniture out of modern materials, design offers a look into how architects and artists outfitted and adapted America's homes.

Hopewell Furnace National Historic Site in Pennsylvania, established in 1771 to produce iron for the growing nation, provides a look into early industrialization in colonial times.

An American Chronology

The history of design in America parallels the cultural and social developments that shaped the nation. Each era builds on the past, resulting in the current melting pot of architecture and design.

AN EARLY LOOK

Not surprisingly, the first colonists to this continent needed to set up their homes quickly. Early settlements featured the most-elemental designs, with simple one-room structures that were quick to build and basic furnishings made by hand. As the colonies grew in population, skilled artisans provided more skills and services, giving settlers access to builders, furniture makers, blacksmiths, and potters. Homes became more elaborate, with the addition of second stories, symmetrical multi-pane windows, and hipped or gambrel roofs. Ornamentation such as stenciled patterns, homespun fabrics, furniture with scrollwork, embroidery, and wall color brought personality into homes. Today, visitors to Williamsburg, Virginia, can see prime examples of the style.

As more religious sects emigrated to the country in the 1600s and 1700s, alternative design aesthetics developed. The Quakers

▲ Introduced to North America by the English in the early 1700s, the Windsor chair became a design staple throughout the colonies. American Windsor chairs were typically painted solid colors or stenciled with simple designs.

> "Design creates culture. Culture shapes values. Values determine the future."
>
> *—Robert L. Peters*

brought an emphasis on simplicity, which allowed them to focus on what was most important—their interior, not exterior, lives. And the Shakers of the late 1700s, formerly part of the British Quakers, designed and built clean-line, pure furnishings that continue to endure. They relied on beautiful materials and crisp colors to create their cabinets, chests of drawers, and ladderback chairs with woven seats. Shaker style has influenced American furniture designers ever since.

A MOVE TO ORNAMENTATION

As cities and towns in America became more established, homes in turn became more decorative. Furniture makers throughout the East Coast developed fine casegoods with more embellishments, such as carved animal feet, decorative inlays, Greek key patterns, and star or circle motifs. The Victorian age of the mid-1800s brought mass production, giving access and affordability to furnishings and home decor to the rising middle class.

RISE OF THE ARTS

As scholars began to question the impact of industrialization, new movements focused on handmade goods. The Arts and Crafts Movement, originating in England, brought an emphasis on individual artists and a focus on nature motifs. New York glassmaker Louis Comfort Tiffany was an American icon of the movement who gained international acclaim.

GETTING INTO MODERNISM

The roaring twenties saw a wealth of design. The geometric shapes, reflective surfaces, and bright colors of Art Deco moved nearly every area of life in a contemporary direction. Skyscrapers such as New York's Chrysler and Empire State buildings, movie theaters in small towns and cities, and everyday household items such as table clocks, cocktail shakers, and appliances featured the Modernist forms. New materials such as plastic, chrome, and Bakelite put an emphasis on innovation. Toward the end of the 1940s, the world war in Europe changed sensibilities. Architects, furniture makers, and industrial

◀ The Victorian Era introduced mass production of goods, allowing the growing middle class to decorate their homes with popular ornamental designs of the day, which often featured elaborate carving and intricate patterns.

AMERICAN ICONS

Built in 1800, the White House embodies neoclassical style and the best of American art and design throughout the past two centuries. First decorated with French wall coverings and furniture during Thomas Jefferson's presidency, the White House has been renovated by several administrations to suit contemporary tastes. The most recent renovation by Jacqueline Kennedy in 1961 turned the home into a museum that showcases fine arts and antiques. Some of the country's pioneering painters and furniture makers on display include Georgia O'Keeffe, John and Thomas Seymour, and Duncan Phyfe.

and interior designers moved to cleaner, linear, streamlined shapes. After the war, modern suburbs boomed, bringing a major emphasis on new furniture styles that complemented the contemporary homes.

BEYOND MIDCENTURY

As the century moved on and America's star rose as a superpower, styles and colors moved to bold, happy, and pattern-rich. Hollywood and art culture introduced pop art to the

> Today's style reflects an individualist spirit, combining styles from different eras and cultures.

masses. Shag carpets, small appliances, and rooms drenched with colors as well as televisions all saw a surge, as did architecture that better combined interior and exterior spaces. A greater environmental awareness focused designers on materials from nature, greater energy efficiency, and smarter planning

to conserve resources. Organic shapes and hues based on nature permeated interiors. In the 1980s, fashion and romanticism ruled the day. Designers such as Laura Ashley returned to florals—placed everywhere—and preppy looks and colors such as pinks, mint greens, and mauves influenced heavily from fashion. British designer Rachel Ashwell, founder of Shabby Chic, evolved the look with the use of antiques, flea market finds, and heavy doses of whites and neutrals for a cleaner design.

DESIGN IN THE 21ST CENTURY

Anything goes is really the look of today. Contemporary designers and homeowners mix styles with ease in an anything-goes attitude. Boho fabrics from the Middle East and 1970s-look macramé combine for a fresh look; transitional style pairs traditional and midcentury pieces with ease; modern industrial embraces the past with fresh interpretations with no rules or limits.

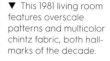

▼ This 1981 living room features overscale patterns and multicolor chintz fabric, both hallmarks of the decade.

DESIGNS THAT ENDURE

Midcentury classics continue to inspire contemporary design trends today. Businesses such as Herman Miller, Knoll, and Design Within Reach offer shapes made popular in the 1940s, including the Eames chair, Nelson Bubble Lamp, and Florence Knoll Relaxed sofa.

◀ Natural materials, clean lines, minimal pattern, and open floor plans embody midcentury design.

A mix of textures and a few pops of black add warmth to this modern white-on-white living room.

EVERYTHING OLD IS NEW AGAIN

Shaker to Maker

"'Tis a gift to be simple" isn't just a song lyric to the Shakers of late 1700s to early 1800s New England. Their beloved hymn "Simple Gifts" embodies their culture, their aesthetic, and their commitment to quality craftsmanship and inspires current furniture-makers to this day.

The most successful communal living arrangement in U.S. history, self-sufficient Shakers (former English Quakers) are famous for the furniture, furnishings, and fabrics created for their austere environments, with the tenets of honesty, utility, and simplicity guiding the designs. Devoid of pattern or ornamentation, Shaker furnishings showcase natural materials such as pine, cherry, and maple and feature clean lines, simple forms, and perfect proportion. Vibrant paint hues such as bright yellow and red add pops of color. Drawers on chests are intentionally asymmetrical, with turned wood knobs versus imported brass. Ladderback chairs, a hallmark of the style, become decoration when hung from peg rails on the walls.

MOVING ON TO THE MAKERS

While the Shaker culture diminished due to the Civil War and the impact of the industrial revolution, the furniture styles have inspired furniture makers throughout the 21st century. Herman Miller produced a Shaker-influenced collection in the 1930s, and famous American furniture designer George Nakashima, known as the father of the American craft movement, found influence in the simple, utilitarian designs. Today Shaker pieces are highly collectible, and current reproductions fit in modern, traditional, and transitional homes.

Today's maker trend—with artisans finding beauty in simple materials and clean lines—connects to the Shaker aesthetic. Young woodworkers throughout the country are building simple, beautiful forms, and DIYers eager to learn a new craft can find countless building plans for the famous cabinets, tables, and chairs. And the iconic clean lines continue as a top cabinetry style in home builds and kitchen remodels.

▲ The religious sect influenced 20th-century furniture designer Nakashima, the father of the American craft movement.

The Shakers focused their furniture building on functional form and proportion.

Stenciling

Stenciling is an ancient art. Two thousand years ago, the Chinese used paper to transfer designs to cloth. Eventually, stencils entered the mass-produced machine age. But they remain a beautiful way to add pattern and artistry that's all your own to a piece of furniture.

YOU WILL NEED

Furniture piece to stencil

Screwdriver

Fine-grit sandpaper

Paintbrush

Primer

Paint for furniture piece

Stencil

Removable tape or stencil adhesive

Paint for stencil

Foam roller

1 Decide where you want to place the stencil on the furniture piece. Remove any hardware such as screws or knobs from the furniture piece. Take apart the furniture piece if necessary (take the drawers out of a dresser or, if stenciling on a door, remove the door from the hinges).

2 Thoroughly clean the furniture piece. Lightly sand with fine-grit sandpaper. Using the paintbrush and/or the foam roller, prime furniture piece, allowing to dry according to the manufacturer's directions. Paint the furniture piece the base color; repeat with a second coat if needed.

3 Decide how you want to position the stencil on the furniture. Attach the stencil with removable tape or spray with repositionable stencil adhesive.

4 Using the stencil paint and foam roller, paint over the stencil. If you have different stencils and different colors of paint, apply each separately. Let dry according to the manufacturer's directions.

5 Reattach any hardware and reassemble the furniture piece.

OTHER STENCIL PROJECTS

Ceiling cove
Wall border
Fabric roller shades
Headboard
Top of a table (may need to cover the stencil with thin piece of glass to prevent wear and tear)
Door
Cabinet fronts in a bathroom or kitchen
Chairback

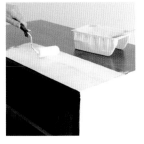

▲ Prime your furniture piece with a latex-based formula.

▲ Using a foam roller or small paintbrush, paint your furniture piece with one or two thin coats of paint.

▲ Start at a corner of your piece, lightly rolling paint over your stencil. Repeat, carefully lining up the pattern.

▲ Carefully peel back the stencil.

HIDDEN HISTORY

The Everyday Artist

Folk art—made and produced for the people—reflects the local culture and community of the time, serving as a means of self-expression for artists with little to no formal training.

Everyday people can create extraordinary art. That's the lesson behind America's (and the larger world's) rich folk art tradition. The art can take nearly any form: ceramics, textiles, furniture, portraits, artwork, wood carvings, metalwork, clothing, and more. But at the core there are a few central tenets. It's made by hand, often by an untrained artist. It can be decorative or utilitarian. It should be produced for local needs and tastes.

ABOUT THE ART
Much of the art originated during the 1700s and 1800s in rural areas, often by common workers or artisans. In many cases, the artists had practical skills, such as house painting or throwing pots. Materials were often at hand and tended to be natural—wood, clay, or straw. It's often called childlike, featuring bright colors, basic techniques,

Folk art expresses the ideas, feelings, and customs of the artist.

and whimsical shapes and forms. Folk art was the common man's (and woman's) art. It's also the work of groups living outside of the mainstream trying to retain their cultures, including American Indians, Mennonites, and the Amish.

CLASSIC FORMS
Paintings are some of the most popular forms of the art. Objects were embellished with designs such as stencils; portraits and cityscapes

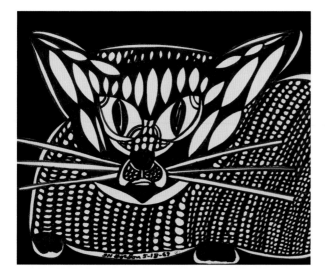

▲ The artist inked this whimsical feline with a simple pen.

▶ This curio cabinet is constructed from wood and painted paper.

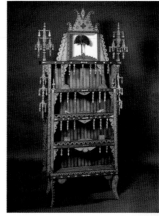

▶ Howard Finster of Georgia assembled and painted electronic television parts, metal, sticks, glitter, mirror glass, wood, cardboard, and ceramic to build this sculpture.

presented simple shapes and motifs; murals represented real-life views. Diego Rivera and other Mexican muralists of the 1930s are all considered folk artists. Rivera's classic (and massive) Detroit Industry Murals depict workers and industry. The murals form the foundation of the Detroit Institute for the Arts Museum. Sculpture and wood carving are other popular types of the craft. Often, they were made in miniature, so the objects are easy to transport and affordable to create. Textiles—quilts, embroidery, felt making, and tapestries—were made from scraps. Printmaking through wood blocks also provided utility, creating games and signs for homeowners. Objects such as whirligigs, weathervanes, and statues provided whimsy and decoration to outdoor spaces. Other forms such as basketmaking, leatherwork, and stained glass gave artists additional ways to work with their hands. Today's tattoo artists, muralists, and other makers can track their crafts to these early folk artists.

MUSEUM EXHIBITS

Several museums provide glimpses into the culture and aesthetics of the folk artists. The Smithsonian American Art Museum displays a variety of folk and self-taught art, including crazy quilts, paintings, and carvings.

New York City's American Folk Art Museum displays crazy quilts, cityscape paintings with stylized bodies, and early furniture pieces. Kansas City's Nelson-Atkins displays a small collection of portrait, still-life, and landscape paintings, as well as carved boxes, trade figures, and whirligigs. And at the Museum of International Folk Art in Santa Fe, visitors can see crafts from 100 countries, with more than 130,000 objects on display. Visitors can see a three-dimensional, miniature model of a Mexican village, highly prized Rio Grande blankets, and rustic glazed urns.

▲ This Tramp Art box from Texas was built from small carved pieces of wood layered into designs.

"Many of the artworks come from before the rise of the middle class, before the rise of mechanization."

—Stephanie Knappe, curator at the Nelson-Atkins Museum of Art, Kansas City

▲ James Castle of Idaho created this painting with found paper, soot, and paint.

◀ Nature motifs often appear in folk-art paintings, as in this acrylic.

EVERYTHING OLD IS NEW AGAIN

Southern Vernacular

Constructed out of utility for the extremes of the climate, historic Southern homes are some of the earliest eco-friendly buildings in the country.

The first Southern colonists faced unexpected and often new challenges they didn't have in their countries of origin—heat, humidity, hurricanes, mosquitoes. As they navigated their new environments, Southerners devised clever buildings that took advantage of local materials and Mother Nature's climate control. Today those same designs lead contemporary architectural trends.

DOGTROT STYLE

Made popular in the 19th and 20th centuries, the simple Gulf Coast home design takes advantage of ocean breezes while keeping insects at bay. The homes are based on a zone system, with two main areas connected by a breezeway or porch that spans from the front to the back of the house. One zone or pod focuses on cooking and dining (thus keeping the heat in one area); the other structure contains living and sleeping areas.

Smart design keeps the home cool and energy-efficient. Siting under trees, an aboveground grade, and deep overhangs on porches ensure shade, breezes, and cross-flow. And builders use local materials, including shells for foundations.

COMFORT AND CHARACTER

The diverse home styles found in the South—plantation, Low Country, neoclassical, Greek Revival, antebellum, French Colonial—feature similar characteristics to dogtrot homes. Porches are deep and welcoming, raised foundations alleviate flooding concerns, high ceilings and windows allow for maximum ventilation, and deep roof overhangs provide necessary shade. While the architecture in the South remains beautiful, its focus on smart design remains at the heart of the structures.

▲ Open porches connect the two structures of dogtrot-style homes, allowing for maximum breezes and ample outdoor living space.

▶ Inspired by the aesthetic of the French and Spanish, most of New Orleans' early ironwork can be traced to enslaved people from West Africa.

Expansive porches,
tall shuttered windows,
columns, and symmet-
rical features all define
Southern Vernacular
architecture.

A MOMENT IN TIME

The World's Fair

World's Fairs were a 19th-century phenomenon that crossed country borders and drew together hundreds of thousands of people to showcase how technology and design could change our homes.

Some World's Fairs—such as the 1851 London World's Fair—were monumental in their design and cultural impact. It's said that Queen Victoria visited more than 30 times. Nearly one-third of Great Britain's population dressed in their Victorian finest to see new inventions such as steam engines, a prototype submarine, and cameras.

Housed in a massive glass and cast-iron structure known as the Crystal Palace, the 1851 Great Exhibition covered 19 acres of Hyde Park. Trees that couldn't be removed during construction were simply glassed over, creating the sense of a dynamic indoor garden housing the top inventions.

AMERICA MAKES ITS MARK

In 1893, the phenomenon made its way to America, this time for the World's Columbian Exposition to mark the 400th anniversary of Columbus' arrival on these shores. Notable

▲ Introduced to the world at the 1851 Great Exhibition in London, the telegraph was just one of the innovations that helped push technology.

The 1851 fair promoted Victorians' hope for a better future and their dominating presence on the world stage.

In addition to the day's newest technologies, decorative arts were also on display, such as this Julien-Nicolas Rivart Louis XV table.

INNOVATIONS AT THE GREAT FAIR

Exhibits featuring working machines wowed visitors to the first World's Fair. The fax machine, microscopes, an early voting machine, a barometer that used leeches to gauge the weather, electric telegraphs, air pumps, and even the world's first pay toilets all highlighted the promise and ingenuity of the Industrial Revolution. As Queen Victoria declared, the Crystal Palace housed "every conceivable invention."

▶ London's Great Industrial Exhibition of 1851 introduced Britons and tourists alike to the greatest innovations of the day.

to many visitors was the color: Everything was white, a clear contrast to the homes most Americans lived in. Over 600 acres in Chicago, American homeowners imagined what a new invention—electricity—might mean to their homes. Visitors could also stroll through gardens designed by Frederick Law Olmsted and imagine what it would be like if their own homes were surrounded by landscapes more welcoming than a simple patch of lawn.

THE NEXT CENTURY OF FAIRS

Fairs continued into the 1900s, influencing what homeowners imagined for the spaces they lived in and showcasing technology that we would all one day consider must-have.

Chicago was again home to the 1933 World's Fair, this one centered around the theme "A Century of Progress." One of its most vaunted additions was the House of Tomorrow, built by George Fred Keck. The glass home was meant to illustrate for visitors what technological and design advances would mean for their own homes: dishwashers, central air, automatic garage door openers to name just a few. Forty million fairgoers attended exhibits meant to bring home the idea that cooperation between science, business, and government could pave the way to a better future.

▲ Housed in a massive glass and cast-iron building known as the Crystal Palace, the 1851 Great Exhibition covered 19 acres of Hyde Park in London.

Lockwood de Forest

A LEADER OF THE AESTHETIC MOVEMENT, A PRECURSOR TO LATE-1800S ARTS AND CRAFTS, THE NEW YORK PAINTER AND IMPORTER INTRODUCED GLOBAL DIVERSITY TO THE COUNTRY.

▲ Twelve pierced brass panels with geometric patterns embellish this window frame.

▲ de Forest found inspiration in British India. This cabinet exhibits the intricate carving and wood prolific in that country.

◀ The artist's New York home was known as the "most Indian house in America."

de Forest frequently painted nature scenes, such as this 1912 work titled *Childs Glacier*.

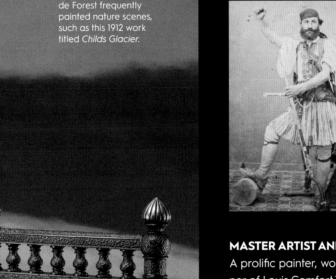

MASTER ARTIST AND IMPORTER

A prolific painter, world traveler, and business partner of Louis Comfort Tiffany, de Forest imparted luxe exotic sensibilities that complemented the popular nature motifs of the day.

Trained as a painter, the New Yorker traveled extensively—Greece, Italy, the Persian Empire, Japan, Korea. It was a two-year honeymoon to British India that inspired his love for the country's signature carvings and teakwood. Upon his return to the United States, de Forest opened a studio featuring Indian goods, working with clients such as Andrew Carnegie and Samuel Clemens. His designs appeared in the Colonial and Indian Exhibition in London's World's Columbian Exposition, and his New York home, featuring a carved wood facade, was known as the "most Indian house in America."

While his imports appear in museums such as the Cooper Hewitt Smithsonian Design Museum, and the Metropolitan Museum of Art in New York City, his paintings are also revered, especially in his later home of Santa Barbara. During his career, his plein-air landscape paintings appeared in 150 group exhibitions, 20 solo shows, World's Fairs, and today in some 20 museums.

▲ This intricate 1880s chair by de Forest displays beautiful carved teakwood with brass detailing.

EVERYTHING OLD IS NEW AGAIN

Arts and Crafts

Developed in Great Britain during the mid-1800s as a social critique of the Industrial Revolution, Arts and Crafts style promoted craftsmanship over mass production and individual artists over factory lines. The movement focused on beauty and simplicity, with influences coming from medieval Gothic style. The nature-based designs infuse architecture and decorative arts, including stained glass, textiles, ceramics, furniture, and mosaic art.

A leader of the movement, which spanned from 1880 to 1920, social and art critic John Ruskin believed mass-produced objects to be "dishonest" and that traditional skills needed to be embraced to promote the livelihood of the worker. As he stated, "Quality is never an accident. It is always the result of intelligent effort."

British designer William Morris was an icon of the movement. His nature-based wall coverings are some of the most noteworthy designs of Arts and Crafts style, featuring swirling greenery, blooming branches, and symmetrical florals.

Today, homeowners wanting to add classic richness and beauty to their walls can find the patterns through Morris & Co.

ACROSS THE POND

In the United States, the Arts and Crafts movement influenced architecture and was also known as Craftsman or Mission style. Known as one of the top American homes, Pasadena's Gamble House by California architects Charles and Henry Greene embodies the movement, featuring stylized leaded art glass, built-in furniture, and rich wood finishes.

In 1897, the American Arts and Crafts Exhibition in Boston showcased works by 160 artisans, with more than 1,000 objects on display. Of note, half were women. The Society of Arts and Crafts developed after the exhibit and continues to promote the movement's philosophies.

Today, collectors prize Steuben glass, Rookwood pottery, and Stickley furniture.

▼ Motifs from nature recur in Arts and Crafts works, such as this Rookwood pottery vase with a berry motif at the neck.

▲ Architects Charles and Henry Greene's Gamble House in California presents an outstanding example of American Arts and Crafts style.

▶ Designed by John Henry Dearle in 1895 for Morris & Co., the design combines leaves and stylized flowers, tulips, and honeysuckle in an all-over pattern.

Pasadena's Gamble House is a masterpiece in wood—the tree design on the leaded art glass entry pays homage to the principal material used in the home's construction.

Louis Henry Sullivan

IN HIS SEARCH FOR GREATNESS, ONE OF THE
19TH CENTURY'S MOST NOTABLE ARCHITECTS WOULD
ABANDON HIS FORMAL EDUCATION AND BUSINESS
PARTNERS BUT LEAVE BEHIND A SERIES OF GAME-CHANGING
BUILDINGS THAT WE STILL TREASURE IN THE 21ST CENTURY.

▼ One of Sullivan's best-known works, Chicago's Auditorium Building is a National Historic Landmark.

▼ Sullivan introduced elaborate designs to staircases and other interior surfaces, such as the Chicago Stock Exchange Building, built in 1893.

▼ Located in downtown St Louis, Missouri, the 10-story Wainwright Building features a terra-cotta facade and intricate frieze design trimming the windows and building top. Frank Lloyd Wright called it "the very first human expression of a tall steel office-building as Architecture."

AN ETHOS: FORM FOLLOWS FUNCTION

Known as father of the modern skyscraper and one of the early Modernists, the Chicago architect revolutionized the way we think about building and how American cities present themselves. He served as a mentor to Frank Lloyd Wright and inspired both the Chicago and Prairie architectural styles.

Sullivan came to the city after the Great Chicago Fire of 1871, working with William LeBaron Jenney, believed to be the first to build with steel, an emerging material in the late 1800s. By the age of 24, he was already a partner in his own firm, Adler and Sullivan, Architects. Adler worked the business side while Sullivan focused on innovation.

The partnership elevated Sullivan's profile and his ability to execute his revolutionary approach, which used steel frameworks to construct the first tall, sleek buildings. In their 14-year partnership, the two built more than 100 structures, including the 10-story Auditorium Building in Chicago, the Chicago Stock Exchange, and the Wainwright Building in St. Louis. Many feature Sullivan's keen eye for ornamentation in the Art Nouveau and Celtic Revival styles. Vines, ivies, and other geometric details in terra-cotta or ironwork provide contrast to the austere structures, as do semicircular arches and ornamental caps. Both are hallmarks of Sullivan's designs. Today the Art Institute of Chicago archives many of Sullivan's drawings and other works, as does the Cooper Hewitt Smithsonian Design Museum.

Reupholstering

Seat cushions are a relatively modern invention; what once were pillows eventually became integrated elements of chairs, sofas, and more. Salvaging the bones of a piece of furniture and updating the upholstery can be a great way to integrate a pattern or color that you like and give a fresh face to a tired-looking room accessory.

YOU WILL NEED

Chair

Screwdriver

Primer

Small paintbrush

Paint

Upholstery fabric

Fabric marker or chalk

Batting

Heavy-duty staples and stapler

Tack strips (optional)

1 Remove the old upholstery and disassemble the pieces. The old fabric piece will serve as your pattern for the new fabric piece, as will the batting. If you are reusing any pieces from the chair, carefully document them and their location. Use the screwdriver to remove any staples or fasteners.

2 Clean and repair the chair. Prime, using a small paintbrush to create light, even coats. Let dry according to the manufacturer's directions. Paint with two coats of the desired color.

3 Using the old batting and the old fabric, cut out pieces of new batting and new fabric. You should lay the old fabric wrong side up on the wrong side of the new fabric. Make sure to cut a generous 3-inch edge on the fabric for fastening.

4 Replace the batting first, stapling into place to mimic the placement of the old batting.

5 Drape the new fabric where it will go on the chair, adjusting spacing. Pull tightly and begin to staple in place, starting in the middle of straight edges and working your way out. Staple closely and securely together.

6 If desired, attach tack strips with staples over edges of fabric on bottom of chair in order to create a clean edge.

OTHER REUPHOLSTERY PROJECTS

Headboard

Sofa

Rocking chair

Stools

Pillows

▲ Using a screwdriver, remove the chair seat from the base of the chair.

▲ Paint the primed chair with two coats of the desired color.

▲ After removing the seat fabric, position the seat base atop batting; cut, leaving a 3-inch surround. Use a staple gun to secure batting to seat.

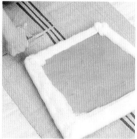

▲ Cut fabric, again leaving a 3-inch surround. Staple to the chair using the same method.

Louis Comfort Tiffany

BORN INTO THE FAMED NEW YORK JEWELER'S FAMILY, THE
ARTIST MADE HIS OWN STAMP ON THE DESIGN WORLD WITH INTRICATE
STAINED GLASS REFLECTING THE BEAUTY FOUND IN NATURE.

▲ Though famously
known as a glass artist,
the New Yorker also
painted and designed
furniture and jewelry.

◄ Tiffany's opalescent
vases and other works
often feature motifs from
nature.

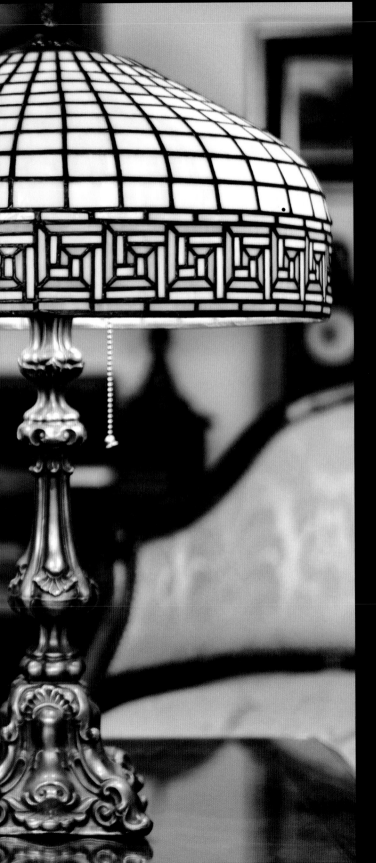

NATURE IN GLASS

His works adorned prominent rooms in the White House, Samuel Clemens' Connecticut home, and churches in New York, Boston, and Cleveland, to name a few. But his opulent craft also adorned everyday people's homes at the turn of the 21st century, as evident in the popularity of his lamps frequently discovered on PBS' *Antiques Roadshow.* Tiffany wanted everyone to have access to his art.

Son of Charles Lewis Tiffany, founder of Tiffany and Company, he originally trained as a painter. The versatile artist (he also decorated interiors and designed furniture) eventually found his passion in glassmaking, founding his Queens studio in 1875. One of the greatest artists in Art Nouveau style, Tiffany invented a new style of art glass named Favrile, creating opalescent glass versus the clear material used by his contemporaries. He used brilliant colors found in nature: intense greens and blues, brilliant fuschias and purples, clean yellows and oranges.

Tiffany molded and fused the glass into rich nature-based scenes with impressionistic effects such as dragonflies, vining flowers, and lush trees. The designs adorn windows and screens as well as lampshades and overhead lighting (in fact, his studio produced thousands of lamps, giving Americans of all economic means an opportunity to decorate with his craft).

His works were so popular he became a true international design star, one of the first American artists to gain acclaim in Europe.

Wall Hanging

Decorative wall coverings have added color, texture, and interest to walls since the 13th century, but they have seen a significant surge in popularity in the last few centuries. Using a pattern you love, create a statement with art panels made from wallpaper.

YOU WILL NEED

2×4-foot plywood boards

Paintbrush

Wallpaper adhesive

Wallpaper

Smoothing tool

Picture molding

Miter box and saw

Paint

Adhesive

Picture hangers

1 Paint plywood boards with wallpaper adhesive; use a heavy coat.
2 Carefully align the wallpaper with the top and side edges of the board. Smooth by hand.
3 Using the smoothing tool, carefully press the wallpaper to the board to remove air bubbles; add more adhesive to the edges if needed.
4 Cover the remaining area of the board with wallpaper adhesive. Line up the wallpapers so the patterns match (you will likely have some waste). Press down by hand and smooth with the tool.

5 Measure the picture molding to make a frame. Use the miter box to cut 45-degree angles.
6 Paint the molding with two coats of paint.
7 Run a thin line of adhesive on the back of the picture molding. Firmly press in place (use clamps if necessary and clean any glue that spreads on the board). Repeat with other molding.
8 Attach picture hangers to back of the board. Hang.

▲ Prime board with wallpaper adhesive.

▲ Attach the first sheet of wallpaper and smooth out with the wallpaper tool.

▲ Align wallpaper pattern and adhere to the board, smoothing out with the tool.

▲ Paint picture molding in the color of choice.

▲ Adhere molding with a strong adhesive.

Frank Lloyd Wright

A BELIEF THAT STRUCTURE AND SPACE COULD CREATE
AND CONVEY CULTURAL VALUES LED WRIGHT TO CREATE
ENTIRELY NEW TYPES OF ARCHITECTURE.

▼ Wright's first home and adjacent studio in Chicago suburb Oak Park allowed him to experiment with new design concepts.

▲ Wright designed New York's Solomon R. Guggenheim Museum in the late 1950s to be a "temple of the spirit."

A UNESCO World Heritage Site, Fallingwater in Mill Run, Pennsylvania, showcases Wright's philosophy of melding architecture with nature. Today it's open for tours.

AN AMERICAN LEGEND

He's known as America's greatest architect. His prolific structures—532 constructed over a seven-decade career—established a new way of thinking about homes and public buildings, inspiring today's innovators, artists, and designers with his new design theories. Midcentury and contemporary design today see influence from the prolific architect, known for creating his own rules of design.

The Wisconsin native found his calling in Chicago, apprenticing with Louis Henry Sullivan before opening his own studio in 1893. He stamped the Chicago suburb Oak Park with his new approach to design based on the prairie landscape, known as Prairie Style. His long, horizontal homes featured lighting, furniture, and rugs all designed for the spaces. Later, his Usonian homes further developed his look, featuring open plans, flat roofs over a simple one-level structure, and built-in furniture.

Wright designed homes and structures in a holistic way, with an emphasis on the environment and natural materials. He stripped out the ornamentation of the Victorian Era, instead focusing on elemental forms such as circles and triangles. His work focuses on natural materials. Two of his most famous buildings, Fallingwater in Pennsylvania and the Guggenheim Museum in New York City, embody his approach to integrating homes into their environments.

A MOMENT IN TIME

The Mason Behind Masonite

A manufacturing mistake led to a material that found countless applications for the home.

Even just 100 years ago, materials for the construction and decoration of homes was limited. Plastic was not widely used. Wood was milled in thoughtful and beautiful ways, and metal and glass offered some variation too. But many of the mass-market materials we take for granted as we stroll through the cavernous warehouses of today's home improvement stores and furnishings shops didn't exist. And then came Masonite.

A NEW WAY OF MANUFACTURING

The credit for the invention of Masonite may be unclear or subject to nationalistic claims: It was either manufactured in England in 1898 through an accidental application of steam to waste paper, or Mississippian William H. Mason created it and the namesake company Masonite in 1924.

Mason held the patent, so it would be his name that came to be associated with the

▲ William H. Mason patented Masonite, an engineered wood made of steam-cooked and pressure-molded wood fibers.

Waste paper and steam would revolutionize the home materials market.

generic product, hardboard. Hardboard, as it is commonly known, was cheap to manufacture and inexpensive for the common homeowner and home builder. The Mason method is sort of a leftover process: Wood chips are stretched into fibers and pressed together with steam to form a board. It's both smooth and strong, so it's very difficult to break. It's also incredibly flexible. And unlike other manufactured woods,

◄ The material allowed for flexible forms to be created, such as this lounge chair made of laminated shaped strips of corrugated cardboard and Masonite on the sides.

the process did not include formaldehyde-based resins to bind the fibers.

HOME INNOVATION

In the mid-20th century, access to new and different products that were cheap to manufacture gave homeowners and builders more options for interior finishes such as doors, walls, cabinets, and other surfaces, as well as outdoor applications such as siding and roofing. Its flexibility allowed builders to create forms for building curving concrete sidewalks.

EVERYDAY APPLICATIONS

The density and stability of hardboard meant it could be used in all sorts of applications. It became temporary flooring for theaters and homes. It became ramps for skateboarders, tops of Ping-Pong tables, and shells of canoes. It became flooring and cabinets for console stereos and bookshelves. And it became bases for wedding cake decorators as well as bodies of guitars and music wobble boards.

Home designers found its texture and color useful too. Look closely at some of the iconic furniture pieces from the midcentury modern era, and you'll see swooping curves of hardboard make an appearance. Artists continue to use it for lino-cut printing.

▲ The material's ability to bend allowed concrete to curve instead of follow a straight path.

MANUFACTURED MOVEMENT

Invented after World War II, engineered wood types allowed floors to be completed quickly to bolster the real estate boom. Since then, additional products for floors and walls include laminate, vinyl, even ceramic tile. All available in planks similar to wood, these manufactured options feature the elegant, natural look of wood but with greater flexibility and strength.

◄ Masonite became the building block of implements for popular recreational activities such as table tennis.

EVERYTHING OLD IS NEW AGAIN

Art Deco

Born out of the booming Great Gatsby era, Art Deco style imparted an ornamental, sophisticated, high-end spirit to nearly every part of 1920s and 1930s culture—its architecture, arts, furniture, fashion, jewelry, even automobile and train design. The glamorous style debuted at Paris' 1925 World's Fair, the International Exhibition of Modern Decorative and Industrial Arts (Exposition Internationale des Arts Décoratifs et Industriels Modernes). Modernist Art Deco designs soon swept the country and larger world, decking skyscraper facades, interiors, as well as marquees of countless movie theaters. Public Art Deco statues loom large. Rio de Janeiro's *Christ the Redeemer* towers over the city; 1933's *Prometheus* statue guards Rockefeller Center in New York.

Inspired by Expressionist, Art Nouveau, the Bauhaus, and Cubism, Art Deco focused on modern, game-changing design themes applied in new, fresh ways. Geometric and stylized motifs came from Native American, Egyptian, classical, and nature themes. Examples include the stepped forms and sunburst motifs on Manhattan's Chrysler Building and zigzags on Miami Beach's Delano hotel. Bright colors penetrate the stylized floral designs, rectangles, chevrons, spheres, and sunburst motifs, and new materials in the 1920s, including stainless steel, chrome, and plastic, added innovation to the designs.

ART DECO TODAY

For collectors, the prolific design trend means a plethora of objects, including Bakelite jewelry and tabletop clocks, sparkly sunburst mirrors, graphic art posters, and figural lamps. New York City provides a hub for the designs, including the Empire State Building, American Radiator Building (now the Bryant Park Hotel), and the Waldorf-Astoria Hotel. Miami's South Beach Art Deco District provides another prime example, with buildings featuring bright pastel colors, curved designs, and graphic motifs made popular in the era.

▲ Now in the Brooklyn Museum, this study is known as a conservative Art Deco look.

▶ Midtown New York's sparkling Chrysler Building was constructed during the city's real estate boom.

▼ The style impacted every aspect of design, including the graphic arts.

Miami Beach's Delano is known for its whimsical Art-Deco styling.

Norman Bel Geddes

A PIONEER OF THE ART DECO MOVEMENT, THE INDUSTRIAL DESIGNER TOUCHED NEARLY EVERY ASPECT OF LIFE IN THE 1920S AND 1930S, ADDING FLAIR TO CONSUMER PRODUCTS, BUILDINGS, AND TRANSPORTATION. HE EVEN REVOLUTIONIZED THE WAY WE TRAVEL.

▲ Bel Geddes worked on streamlining cars, including this teardrop shape.

◀ The Patriot radio, from 1939, is intentionally decked out in a patriotic red, white, and blue palette.

Bel Geddes created his oceanliner in the shape of a porpoise.

▼ This Greyhound station in Arkansas exudes the bright colors, curves, and graphic signage of Art Deco times.

▶ The designer created numerous furniture pieces, including this enameled steel chest of drawers topped by a round mirror.

THE LASTING LEGACY OF THE ULTIMATE CREATOR

Though he worked a century ago, the New York creative left a lasting legacy that touches nearly every American today—thank him for the Interstate Highway System, retractable stadium roofs, multimedia stage productions, even autonomous cars. The best-known designer in his time, Bel Geddes (called the Modernist da Vinci) imparted his streamlined look to myriad products: ocean liners and cars, cocktail shakers and inkwells, radio cabinets and refrigerators. The successful entrepreneur employed nearly 2,000 in his heyday.

Though he got his start in set design, he moved to larger design initiatives. Bel Geddes presented a distinctive interest in transportation. To replace weeklong transatlantic ocean liners, he invented a 9-deck amphibious aircraft complete with a gym, solarium, deck games, and an orchestra that could complete the trip in two days. Though the aircraft was never built, his streamlined yachts and ocean liners were.

For the 1939 New York World's Fair, Bel Geddes created the showstopper Futurama in the General Motors pavilion. Creating a post-war city 20 years out, his model included sleek skyscrapers, green spaces, and one-way roads with clover-leaf intersections. His 1940s book *Magic Motorways* touted improved highways and transportation, a precursor to the Interstate Highway System, and even introduces driver-assist cars.

Dorothy Draper designed the 5-star Greenbrier Hotel resort interior in White Sulphur Springs, West Virginia, in the mid-1940s.

"I always put in one controversial item. It makes people talk."

—Dorothy Draper

EVERYTHING OLD IS NEW AGAIN

Midcentury Modern

It endures: That much can be said for midcentury modern.

In fact, of all the design trends that have influenced home decor, none has perhaps had the same number and frequency of resurgence as midcentury modern design. It can be found in the TV shows we watch, the furniture we covet, the home getaways that we want to stay in.

In architecture, furniture, and design, the influence of midcentury modern began for real in the 1930s. While it has, at times, been in danger of disappearing, it has never been fully absorbed by any other design influence. Today, in the third decade of the 21st century, the influence of midcentury modern remains far-ranging and stronger than ever.

The first iterations of midcentury modern in home decor became apparent immediately after World War I, much sooner than many people often assume.

A couple factors led to the first iteration of midcentury modern. Designers, of course, were shaking off the excess of the Art Deco and Victorian standard-bearers of earlier in the century. They also took cues from European influences such as Bauhaus and International styles. And post-World War II, the housing boom meant that many builders abandoned the complexity and fussiness of the previous century in favor of quicker and cheaper. Thus, the ranch-style house was born and with it the need for furniture that fit.

However, manufacturing and technology played a key role in the development of midcentury modern too. For starters, there were new materials available to the home decorating market. And both old materials such as wood and metal and those new materials, including fiberglass to foam, aluminum, and plastic laminate, could be bent and formed in unusual ways.

Those new contours gave designers a chance to implement silhouettes that were clean-lined and full of unusual contours, which gave home decor elements a new,

▲ Midcentury furniture, accessories, and lighting took on more sculptural forms during the era.

▶ Furniture evolved from being stiff and traditional to curvy and modern.

Smart Furniture Studio in Chattanooga, Tennessee, offers classics such as the Eames Lounge Chair and the Eames Storage Unit, both by Herman Miller.

futuristic profile. The latter also tied into the new focus on what science was doing, and would do, to change everyday life. Astronauts were on the Moon, and we wanted to be reminded of the places we could go—even when we were at home.

Unburdened by the technological constraints that drove the designs of some of their predecessors, midcentury modern designers also celebrated material and form in a way not done before. For once, it was permissible to let assembly shine, not to hide it behind fabric. There was less ornamentation and more of a focus on the interplay of materials.

The heyday of the first period of midcentury modern design ended in the mid-1960s, but the ethos and aesthetic became part of the baby

---

Midcentury architects and designers became household names for their famous works.

---

boomers' upbringing. There remained a strong market for vintage designs too. And then the art world took notice, with high-profile designs that focused on a few of the standout names of the period, including Charles and Ray Eames. That show traveled, too, bringing the message of midcentury modern to a much wider audience. Pop culture rode that same wave, driving familiarity through TV shows such as *Mad Men*.

Today, enthusiasts can still find those vintage pieces, but they're far too pricey for most homeowners of modest means. Instead, today's fans can turn to companies that reproduce those original designs as well as new manufacturers that capitalize on the clean lines, materials, organic forms, and futuristic look of the midcentury modern aesthetic. And while it would have taken a designer or an

architect to actually buy an original midcentury modern piece in the 1950s and 1960s, today's outlets sell directly to consumers.

There's one last piece of the midcentury modern puzzle that we're still feeling today. The design movement and its stars, including George Nelson, the Eames couple, the Saarinen father-and-son duo, Edward Wormley, Harry Bertoia, Eileen Gray, and Arne Jacobsen, became stars and household names. While architects such as Frank Lloyd Wright were celebrities in their own day, the number of star architects and designers was new, and we see it in the 21st century with designers as TV hosts, magazine editors, authors, and social media stars.

▲ Rather than rely on excessive ornamentation or pattern, midcentury furniture designers relied on clean, simple lines and functionality of the piece.

MIDCENTURY DESIGN TODAY

Numerous classics from top midcentury designers such as Charles and Ray Eames, Florence Knoll, George Nelson, and Eero Saarinen are available to homeowners today through retail sites such as Design Within Reach and Herman Miller.

◄ Danish designer Verner Panton created this chandelier with five enameled metal "flowerpot" shades for Louis Poulsen.

Postwar homes featured
open spaces and ample
windows and often were
integrated with nature.

A. Quincy Jones

WITH MORE THAN 5,000 PROJECTS IN HIS REPERTOIRE, THE LOS
ANGELES ARCHITECT INFUSED HIS MIDCENTURY AESTHETIC ON BOTH PUBLIC
AND PRIVATE SPACES THROUGHOUT SOUTHERN CALIFORNIA.

▲ Designed in 1949, the Brody House in Los Angeles presents Hollywood glamour at its finest.

◀ Featured in *Sunset* magazine and Jones' book *Building for Better Living,* the Gross House in Los Angeles integrates interiors and exteriors thanks to ample glass.

Jones' architectural objective was to create aesthetic experiences, as in the open, light-filled plan of the Tyre House in Los Angeles.

CALIFORNIA COOL

He designed for celebrities and the masses alike. The prolific architect, trained in Seattle, shaped the landscape of post-World War II California, building out contemporary plans for neighborhoods, restaurants, churches, schools, as well as for his famous contemporary homes.

Jones embraced a new style of architecture that integrated interior and exterior spaces. His open plans relied on open layouts, warm woods, and plenty of glass. Alternative building materials for the era—including masonry block, plywood, and steel—imparted linear structure and warm texture, while his smart site planning allowed buildings to access optimal light, ventilation, and views. His homes today continue to light up the Hollywood Hills, Bel Air, and Palm Springs.

Jones made his mark on the community and common culture as well, serving as the dean of architecture at the University of Southern California, the city planner for Irvine, and the architect of the Warner Brothers Records Building. He originated the idea of green common spaces so popular in today's community planning.

HIDDEN HISTORY

Gerald Thurston

Gerald Thurston revolutionized one of the home's essential accessories, but remains virtually unknown in decorating history.

If Gerald Thurston had a signature design statement, perhaps it would be the intersection of three legs to form the foundation of a lamp. Or it could have been an elongated triangle used to move the eye visually from floor to light shade. Or perhaps Thurston's true signature was the dash of glam—fluted body elements, a metallic shade. But the fact of the matter is no one seems to have asked one of the most notable lighting designers of the 20th century, Gerald Thurston, very much about what he thought, what he liked, or even where he came from.

A POSTWAR SHIFT

Thurston had the good fortune to display his talents during the heady days of postwar America, when staples were no

The midcentury designer elevated the look of lighting, making it like jewelry for the home.

longer luxuries and home decor designers were able to move away from the dictates of function, function, function to something a little more individualized and beautiful. He was a member of the design team at Lightolier, so perhaps the fact that he didn't have his own firm buried his genius from the wider public view.

The era that Thurston designed in was a heady time for creatives Jackson Pollock, Willem de Kooning, and Mark Rothko, and the followers of Abstract Expressionism

▼ Forms such as the drum shade on this tripod hairpin floor lamp continue to influence lamp designers today.

◀ The designer created lamps that are both functional and elegant, such as this ivory ceramic and brass stacking gourd lamp.

▶ Sculptural forms such as this brass and lacquered steel table lamp are a hallmark of Thurston's designs.

created art unlike anything ever seen before. By the time Thurston joined Lightolier, the company was a half-century into its prowess as one of the foremost lighting houses in the country. Where he came from and what he did before Lightolier isn't really known. Associates note that Thurston drew by hand, but that was where his old-fashioned approach to lighting ended. In place of the ornamentation that so dictated Victorian-era designs, Thurston executed fixtures that were innovative and streamlined.

RADICAL CREATIVITY

Thurston's designs aren't showy, but they do show off particularly the distinctive mix of materials. His work was notable for its contrast in composition—rich metals alongside hefty wood grains, for example. The forms he relied on, such as drum shades and curvaceous bulb hoods as well as infrequent but bold pops of color, continue to influence today's modern accessory marketplace. And Thurston of course benefited from the advance in technological abilities and the introduction of new materials, as well as the capacity of design houses to execute on visions because manufacturing facilities were no longer dedicated solely to the support of the war effort.

As Thurston executed lamp and lighting fixture designs at Lightolier, his aesthetic became more and more sculptural and sleek. The combination of the materials with his deftness at shape assembly allowed the finished pieces to shine. One of his signature collections, the Scandia series of fixtures, is much prized today. And his tenure at Lightolier marked such notable collaborations as the Lightolier work with Arteluce. That was one of the first of many partnerships that American design companies would form with European houses—a trend still apparent with the proliferation of mass market stores such as Ikea.

Today, however, Gerald Thurston languishes in obscurity even as his designs fetch thousands of dollars on resale at auction houses.

The era Thurston designed in was a heady time for creatives.

◄ Original Lightolier pendant, circa 1958. Thurston was influenced by the work of Italian designers Gino Sarfatti and Gaetano Sciolari.

◄ Thurston's tripod design was a popular format and has many variations.

► The Triennale floor lamp features perforated shades that can be articulated so that the light can be directed towards many different focal points.

George Nelson

WITH A 50-YEAR BODY OF WORK, THE DESIGNER SHAPED
MIDCENTURY AMERICA THROUGH MODERN CITY PLANNING,
FURNITURE, AND EVEN READING MATERIALS.

From his start in the 1940s to the 1980s, Nelson partnered with most of the Modernist designers of the time.

MIDCENTURY'S ICONIC DESIGNER

Editor, industrial designer, and furniture designer Nelson wore many hats during his career. He's most famous for sparking the design revolution that is midcentury modern. But it all came about thanks to happenstance. While attending Yale, Nelson ducked into a nearby building during a rainstorm, only to discover an architecture school and a contest for a trip to study in Rome. Good news: He won. During his stay in Rome, Nelson met and interviewed pioneers in Europe's and America's modern architectural movement, meeting with the likes of Ludwig Mies van der Rohe, Le Corbusier, and Frank Lloyd Wright.

In the 1940s, Nelson worked as an editor at *Architectural Forum*, developed the concept of a pedestrian mall to reface urban downtowns, and designed a game-changing modular storage unit featured in *Life* magazine, sparking the furniture industry to move in a modern direction. Nelson designed some of the most iconic midcentury furniture and lighting for Herman Miller: Bubble Lamps, the Marshmallow sofa, and the first L-shape desk. He also worked in accessories for Vitra (including clocks and lamps), with the goal of bringing modern style to homes throughout America with his focus on simple solutions for everyday living.

A MOMENT IN TIME

Florence Knoll

Florence Knoll set the stage for Modernist office design after World War II. Awarded the top prize for artistic excellence in 2003, the designer set the standard for future female artists and entrepreneurs.

Knoll made the most of the opportunities she faced in her 101-year life. Orphaned at age 12, the Saginaw, Michigan, native discovered architecture and design while at school. Her talents sparked the interest of famed architect Eliel Saarinen, whose family embraced the student. Throughout her life Knoll worked with influential midcentury architects and designers and in turn became a pioneer in the world of interior design herself.

MAKING OFFICES WORK

During the height of the war, Knoll (née Schust) moved to New York, where she met Hans Knoll. The two started Knoll Associates and eventually married in 1946. The Knolls created a new way of thinking about work environments, focusing on the needs of each client. Creating her own design studio in the business, she was a first to use "paste-ups" or mood boards to present concepts to her clients.

▲ Knoll's custom-designed chair, from the Rockefeller family offices at Rockefeller Center, exemplifies the comfort and beauty of her work.

"I designed the architectural [elements] that were needed to make rooms work."

The studio worked for significant businesses of the day, including CBS, General Motors, and IBM. Her designs focused on open plans and streamlined furniture, with texture and organic shapes adding interest. Sleek boat-shape tables on slim pedestals replaced the heavy board room standard. Desks featured glass tops and straight legs, and floating staircases allowed spaces to remain open and light-filled. Knoll was much more than a "decorator," the term used for females in her profession. In fact, Knoll was the influence behind the use of the term "interior design."

◄ Knoll worked with many prominent midcentury designers, including Eero Saarinen. This Knoll advertisement appears in the Archives of American Art at the Smithsonian Institution.

► Knoll's office spaces felt like contemporary homes, with comfortable furniture and flooring. This office belongs to Jack Heinz's 1958 work suite.

LEGACY OF GREAT DESIGN

Knoll designed furniture she called "the meat and potatoes" that filled in for some of signature pieces designed by Eero Saarinen, Mies van der Rohe, and Harry Bertoia. She crafted straight-line sofas and chairs with button tufting, hairpin-leg stacking tables, and office tables balanced on pedestal legs. With the death of Hans in 1955, Knoll became president. The business endured as an international powerhouse, with offices in Paris, New York, Chicago, and Los Angeles. It lives on today, selling her popular pieces for homes and offices alike.

FAMOUS EDUCATION

Knoll had the opportunity to train with some of the best in the industry. In Michigan, she studied under Eliel Saarinen, becoming quite close with his son Eero. In Chicago, Mies van der Rohe mentored her at the Illinois Institute of Technology, and she learned Le Corbusier's International Style while living in London.

HONORING THE LEGEND

Knoll's peers in architecture, design, and the arts recognized her unique skill set. The American Institute of Architects awarded her the Gold Medal for Industrial Design, the first woman to receive the honor. Famed Rhode Island School of Design gave her an Athena Award in 1983, and *Interior Design* magazine inducted her into its Hall of Fame in 1985. In 2003, President George W. Bush awarded her the National Medal of Arts.

▲ Knoll revolutionized office design, bringing a Modernist approach to workspaces.

EVOLUTION OF THE WORKING WORLD

Today's trend toward communal spaces, comfortable furniture, and bright colors stems from Knoll's work. But it was a later Herman Miller designer, Robert Propst, who brought the concept of the cubicle to America. Designed in 1964, the cubicle remains the hallmark of corporate offices today, with more than 40 million workers performing tasks in these uni-form spaces. But the trend toward flexible spaces also stems from Propst's design. His design, called the Action Office, in-tended to be flexible and adaptable, with adjustable desks to allow for worker mobility.

Isamu Noguchi

OVERCOMING EARLY CAREER REJECTION AND INSTITUTIONAL
RACISM DURING WORLD WAR II, THE AWARD-WINNING JAPANESE AMERICAN
DESIGNER, SCULPTOR, AND LANDSCAPE ARCHITECT HAS WORKS THAT
ENDURE TODAY IN PARKS AND CONTEMPORARY HOMES.

▲ Chrome-plated steel rods create the central tower for this side table.

▶ Abstract legs and a thick glass top compose Noguchi's famous coffee table.

Installed in Manhattan's Financial District in 1968, *Red Cube* balances on a corner; leading the observer to peer up at the sky.

SHAPING LANDSCAPES AND FAMOUS FURNITURE

His gardens and outdoor sculptures grace spaces throughout the United States and the larger world. His works were memorialized on a 37-cent stamp in 2004. And his signature Japanese paper lamps and coffee table—a sculptural wood base and thick glass top—continue to thrive in modern design.

The midcentury influencer, born in Los Angeles in 1904, developed his interest in sculpture while apprenticing under Gutzon Borglum, creator of Mount Rushmore (he said Noguchi lacked talent), and learning stone carving at New York's Leonardo da Vinci Art School. Receiving a Guggenheim Fellowship in the late 1920s, Noguchi evolved his work in abstract sculpture while in Paris.

During the Great Depression, Noguchi tried to gain a foothold through the Public Works of Art program (without success). And after a voluntary internment during World War II, the artist was accused of espionage by the FBI and eventually cleared with help from the ACLU.

Noguchi found his breakthrough in the 1940s, when he teamed up with Herman Miller, Charles Eames, and George Nelson to produce their groundbreaking modern furniture catalog. Noguchi's designs meld the Japanese aesthetic with Modernist shapes. For example, his light sculptures transform handcrafted washi paper into Modernist ovals. "Everything is sculpture; any material, any idea without hindrance born into space, I consider sculpture," he said.

HIDDEN HISTORY

Eva Zeisel

The 21st-century ceramic artist and industrial designer contributed the modern, clean white aesthetic to tabletops across America.

In her 70-year career, Zeisel broke numerous gender barriers. She became the first Hungarian woman to be admitted to a local trade guild, the first female solo exhibit at New York's Museum of Modern Art, and the first to teach mass production of ceramics at Pratt Institute in New York. Her whimsical and organic shapes such as birds and mother-and-child salt-and-pepper shakers appear in museums and private collections, and she's been honored with awards and degrees all over the world. Despite her tumultuous early life due to the political climate, the Hungarian-born ceramicist created the contemporary white tablescapes so popular today, inspiring a new generation of potters in the process, including Jonathan Adler.

Born into a family with strong female presence (her mother was one of the first Ph.D.s at the University of Budapest), Zeisel gravitated to art early on. Thanks to her

> Eva Zeisel's designs are made for use. The inspiration for her sensuous forms often comes from the curves of the human body.

mother's influence, she chose a practical craft—pottery—over fine art. She apprenticed under a classically trained potter, learning under the Arts and Crafts movement themes of handmade, local materials and focus on form.

LEAVING HER MARK IN EUROPE

In her 20s, Zeisel became a working ceramist in Bavaria, finding inspiration from popular Art Deco motifs such as ovals, concentric circles, and rings. These early works feature fluid lines and sleek white shapes. Wanting to

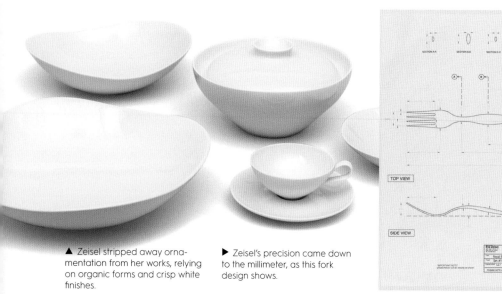

▲ Zeisel stripped away ornamentation from her works, relying on organic forms and crisp white finishes.

▶ Zeisel's precision came down to the millimeter, as this fork design shows.

▼ The designer played with curves and whimsical shapes, such as this salt shaker.

continue with her travels, Zeisel moved to the Soviet Union, where she worked for the government as a lead designer of glass and ceramics. While in the Communist country, she was imprisoned for more than a year after being accused of an assassination attempt against Joseph Stalin. She spent much of her time in solitary confinement before being deported to Vienna shortly before the Nazi invasion. The Jewish potter and her husband fled before the Nazi takeover, eventually settling in New York.

A NEW WORLD OF POTTERY

In the United States, Zeisel began designing clean-lined porcelain china for mass production. Though working in the Modernist era, she aimed for beauty and whimsy. "I didn't accept the purism of modern design," she said. Her shapely, graceful pieces took inspiration from the curves of the human body as well as Hungarian folk art. She created works for Nambé, Red Wing Pottery, KleinReid, and Hall China. Today, her works continue to star on websites such as Design Within Reach, Etsy, Replacements.com, and Evazeiseloriginals.com.

AN ENDURING LEGACY

Zeisel continued designing into her 90s. She created one of Crate and Barrel's most successful lines of dinnerware. Today her works appear in museums throughout the country.

▲ Known for her work with ceramics, Zeisel lived to age 105.

> "I don't create angular things. I'm a more circular person—it's more my character. Even the air between my hands is round."
>
> —Eva Zeisel

▶ Designed for Red Wing Pottery, Zeisel's Town & Country pitchers embody her graceful and fun approach.

HIDDEN HISTORY

Dieter Rams

The German industrial designer set the mark for sleek 1960s appliances, inspiring products today with his legendary 10 principles of good design.

His T3 pocket transistor from Braun looks strikingly similar to the first iPod. His other streamlined consumer products, including small kitchen appliances, electronics, and contemporary furniture, could star in the most high-end modern museum or 1960s throwback movie set.

POSTWAR INNOVATION

Trained as an architect at the Ulm School of Design, Rams joined electronics company Braun in the mid-1950s. Known for its high-tech innovations for everyday consumer products such as coffeepots, juicers, and record players, the company set the standard for 1960s smooth. As director of design for 35 years, Rams created many of the products meant to integrate into the environment versus standing out. He used boxy shapes, simple knobs, and clean white and metal finishes. Given the choice

> The 2018 documentary *Rams* by Gary Hustwit highlights the designer and his sleek 1960s German home filled with products he designed. As *The Guardian* notes, he's "the man who all but invented consumer product design as we know it today."

between multiple knobs or switches for his electronics or a simpler option, he opted for the latter choice. During his tenure at Braun, Rams is credited for such products as a complete stereo system 20 years ahead of its time, a portable radio with a handle for easy transport, and a minimalist black calculator that looks strikingly modern

▲ Designed in 1961, Braun's Tischsuper RT 20 radio exhibits a clean look with minimalist knobs, a vertical dial, and horizontal speaker slits.

▶ Rams' wristwatch—with three hands—combines utility with beautiful, sleek design.

▼ The German industrial designer bases his work on *"Weniger, aber besser"* or "Less, but better."

and is still for sale. His designs for furniture company Vitsoe also endure. His 1960 606 Universal Shelving System; chairs and sofas featuring molded frames, leather upholstery, and swiveling bases; and simple stacking tables continue to thrill customers. As one writes, "How delighted we are with the glorious Dieter Rams chair. Now that I have 'parked' myself in it for the last couple of days, I can write you with genuine experience that the chair is as comfortable as it is beautiful."

HIS 10 PRINCIPLES OF DESIGN

About half a century ago, Rams developed the creed of contemporary product design, which continues to inspire today's generation of industrial designers.

1 Good design is innovative. It should be intentional and rooted in functionality.

2 Good design makes a product useful. It needs to enhance everyday life while possessing beauty.

3 Good design is aesthetic. Products should make us happy and increase everyday joy.

4 Good design makes a product understandable. Ideally, it's intuitive, not needing a consumer manual to understand how to operate.

5 Good design is unobtrusive. Objects need to blend in with the environment and complement the home interior.

6 Good design is honest. It should be true to itself.

7 Good design is long-lasting. Rather than embracing trends of the day, it should be modeled to be classic.

8 Good design is thorough to the last detail. Attention is paid to every single element.

9 Good design is environmentally friendly. In its creation, resources need to be considered and conserved.

10 Good design is as little as possible. Simple, pure forms are a thing of beauty.

▲ Rams' Combi DL5 Razor for Braun proved the designer's affinity for innovation—he continued to improve the product over time.

> "Indifference towards people and the reality in which they live is actually the one and only cardinal sin in design."
>
> —*Dieter Rams*

◀ Flanked by ash wood sides and a hinged cover of clear plastic, the Phonosuper SK55 by Rams and Hans Gugelot also features simple controls. "Good design is thorough down to the last detail," Rams said.

Designed by John Lautner in 1960, the eight-sided Malin residence (known as Chemosphere) sits on a 29-foot-high concrete base.

"To me, architecture is an art, naturally, and it isn't architecture unless it's alive. Alive is what art is. If it's not alive, it's dead, and it's not art."

—John Lautner

A MOMENT IN TIME

Environmental Awakening

The late 1960s and early 1970s yielded a cultural shift in art, music, and politics—and how we integrate the environment into our homes.

Not only did civil rights and political activation gain traction during the era of the Vietnam War, but so did a deeper connection to the world and its environment, as reflected in our homes.

AN ENVIRONMENTAL MOVEMENT

Scientists began finding a shift in the health of the planet and its inhabitants in the 20th century. Between 1500 and 1900, just two species became extinct per century. By 1900 that rate had reached an alarming number in the United States alone: 468. Animals central to the American identity— bison, bald eagles, gray wolves, grizzly bears, peregrine falcons—faced alarmingly low populations, forcing the country to embark on one of its most important environmental success stories, the Endangered Species Act.

A LEGACY OF CONSCIOUSNESS

Public consciousness had changed by the late 1960s. Disasters such as an oil spill off the

▲ Tropical plants came into vogue in the 1960s and 1970s, when Americans gained greater awareness of air quality.

"Nothing is more priceless and more worthy of preservation than the rich array of animal life with which our country has been blessed."

—*Richard Nixon*

◀ High ceilings and ample ventilation, thanks to sliding doors and ceiling fans, reduce the energy footprint of this beach house.

California coast, polluted Great Lakes (Lake Erie actually caught fire), and the greater concern about pesticides and their impact on species coalesced to drive the country to take action. The environment became a nonpartisan issue. "It has become a common cause of all the people of this country," said President Richard Nixon. As part of the push to protect the country's resources, Nixon created the Environmental Protection Agency, the Clean

Air Act, and the Clean Water Act. As he noted, "'Environment' is not an abstract concern, or simply a matter of aesthetics, or of personal taste—although it can and should involve these as well."

It may well be something else about that time that continued to provide lessons for how we live today. There was a shared consciousness about what we did in all aspects of our lives, including home decor and furniture, which shaped the health of the planet.

HOW THE ACT MATTERED TO HOMES

The enactment of the Endangered Species Act of 1973, enforced by the U.S. Fish and Wildlife Service and the National Oceanic and Atmospheric Administration (NOAA), turned a focus onto our natural world and also prompted Americans to think about how they could integrate more of the outdoors into the interior spaces they lived in. It also prompted a rethinking of resource consumption in how we outfit our homes.

STILL IN ACTION TODAY

Some refer to that time as the great environmental awakening. It led to the development of products that have a direct impact on our homes, such as nonpetroleum-based products like paint. It also opened a refocused discussion about how our homes could not only connect us with outdoor spaces, but also influence our health and well-being. And the refocusing on vernacular architecture, on connection with outdoor spaces, and a better focus on manufacture and consumption continues to influence home spaces today.

▲ Repurposing old materials such as shipping pallets reduces the need for new production.

GREEN READS

Nonfiction and children's literature alike embraced the movement to save species and protect the environment, helping change public sentiment.

In 1962, Rachel Carson published *Silent Spring,* which examined the impacts of DDT and other pesticides on species' health (see page 258). And Dr. Seuss' *The Lorax* taught children the importance of speaking for the trees, the fish, the mammals, and more.

◀ Solar panels allow homeowners to create their own renewable energy.

HIDDEN HISTORY

Jasper Morrison

Similar to the Modernists a generation earlier, contemporary British industrial designer Jasper Morrison imparts superb function and simple beauty to everyday objects.

Modern brands Alessi, Vitra, Cappellini, and B&B Italia all feature his designs, as do trams, rest stops, restaurants, and museums, including the Cooper Hewitt Smithsonian Design Museum. Like the Modernists of the 1960s and 1970s, the legendary British creator bases his design approach on simplicity, function, and practicality.

FINDING INSPIRATION

Braun's "Snow White's coffin" record player left an impression. Designed by Dieter Rams and Hans Gugelot in the 1960s, the sleek musical player with wooden side panels possesses many of the tenets of Morrison's designs: clean, simple to use, innovative, and aesthetically pleasing.

While Morrison designs myriad products for both the home and public spaces, all incorporate a similar thread:

> Morrison believes a well-designed object should improve the feel of the room.

They create great atmosphere. Morrison's goal is to create objects that improve the feel of a space. He designs "to produce everyday objects for everyone's use, make things lighter not heavier, softer not harder, inclusive rather than exclusive, generate energy, light and space," he says.

CONTEMPORARY LOOKS

Morrison began showing his works in the late 1980s, working with Vitra for Milan's Furniture Fair. Today he still works with the company, producing icons such as the

▶ Playful curves define the industrial designer's chairs.

◀ Morrison's stream-lined kitchen cabinets and countertops combine wood with black paint.

All Plastic Chair and modular low-slung sofas. His other products include kitchenware, bath fixtures, lighting, storage, appliances, and kitchen cabinets. But his designs reach beyond the home, recently including fashion. "I spent my life thinking of things to sit on, so it's good to turn my attention onto things to wear," he says.

His mobile phones look like calculators and cameras. His portable speaker is a sleek, stylish triangle. "There are better ways to design than putting a big effort into making something look special. Special is generally less useful than normal, and less rewarding in the long term."

Morrison gained inspiration from his grandfather's home. In the 1960s, interiors tended to be gloomy and heavy, with abundant upholstery and curtains. His grandfather's space featured clean-line Scandinavian qualities, including abundant daylight, wood floors with simple white rugs, lightweight seating, and that classic Braun record player.

INTERNATIONAL FLAIR

Named a Royal Designer for Industry (an award through the British Royal Society of Arts), the designer today spends most of his time in Tokyo, taking influence from the country's aesthetic. He also has offices in London and Paris. When possible, he believes in embracing quirks, a term he calls Utilism, which incorporates humor and irony and charm. One of his recent collections involves cork. Using faulty wine bottle corks as his muse, he shapes sculptural chairs and stools, a chaise lounge, and even a fireplace from the rich, textural material.

▲ The British designer works in nearly every medium today, including fashion, electronics, and furniture.

> "Design makes things seem special, and who wants normal if they can have special?"
>
> —Jasper Morrison

Vitra's modular three-piece sofa and book-cases make a statement in simplicity.

Contemporaries

The culmination of design movements and innovations over the past several centuries has yielded the current melting pot, where a combination of technology, punchy color, handmade goods, and personal style shine.

▲ Jonathan Adler's Gala Round Vase relies on a geometric relief pattern of lips to create a surreal style.

Design permeates everything today. On the small scale: The morning alarm clock, the speaker delivering the latest podcast, the touchscreen phone or laptop running everyday functions are all result of a good design, as are the buildings in which we work and live, the urban murals and billboard signage lining our streets, and the latest means of transportation.

But today's look—unlike in past generations when being homogeneous was a good thing—allows for the individual spirit to shine, as evidenced by some of today's top designers.

A POP OF FUN

New York potter, designer, and author Jonathan Adler rules when it comes to whimsy. Rainbows, astrological signs, body parts, and more all weave into his decorative pottery and other home goods. Known for his crisp white pottery shaped into modern forms (he finds inspiration in Eva Zeisel's ceramics and architect Frank Lloyd Wright's freedom to create his own rulebook), the designer has been keen on introducing the fun factor since the inception of his company in 1993.

> "For the longest time design only existed for the elite and for a small insular culture. I have worked hard for the last 20 years trying to make design a public subject."
>
> —Karim Rashid

Opening his New York SOHO shop in 1998, the designer branched out to home furnishings, artwork, and more. Though based on a white foundation, his creations feature punches of color and personality. "So many people shy away from using color in their homes for fear of getting it wrong...But ignorance and fear are no reason to live in a bland box," he says.

◀ Karim Rashid's New York loft exhibits his flair for color, pattern, and sense of humor.

A similar high-key energy shines in Kelly Wearstler's designs. Known for using pops of color, mixing antiques with the modern, and weaving in strong and complex texture, the Southern California designer has elevated the style of homes, hotels, and all types of interior

products. An early project, the Avalon hotel in Beverly Hills, "changed the look of boutique hotels around the world," according to the *New York Times*. Today Wearstler offers a full range of evocative furniture, innovative wall coverings, and decorative lighting.

French designer Philippe Starck makes master works of art from acrylic and plastic, often with whimsical flair. A leader in modern design, the postmodern artist creates decorative yet practical objects, including furniture, lighting, and kitchen accessories for brands such as Kartell, Emeco,

◀ Designed by Kelly Wearstler, Charmaine's—the rooftop at the San Francisco Proper Hotel—offers an eclectic mix of patterns and furniture styles.

DESIGN FOR THE MASSES

Good design is everywhere. From the home aisles of the local discount retailer to direct-mail catalogs focused on overall home design, as well as niche topics such as lighting, rugs, and eco-friendly goods, consumers today have greater access to affordable design than at any other time. Many top artists work with affordability and accessibility in mind. As Philippe Starck notes, "It's not hard to make one object which costs one million dollars, but it's hard to make one million objects which cost just one dollar each."

◀ Wearstler incorporates a curated collection of vintage furniture, textiles, and finishes.

Alessi, and Target. His goal is bringing good design to the masses. Starck's translucent Louis Ghost chair has become an icon, as have his plastic sofas, chairs, and stools.

And for Egyptian-born Karim Rashid, a playful energy exudes from his work—everything from Citibank graphics to Artemide lighting to the packaging on Method cleaners. With more than 3,000 products and 300 awards, the designer infuses color, personality, and joy into his products. His looks nod to the mod days of the 1960s and 1970s but feature contemporary flair.

RETURN TO THE WOODS

Wood, the timeless material, continues to add texture, warmth, and depth to today's interiors. Designers such as Atlas Industries are harnessing the beauty of the material to create their platform beds, modular storage systems, and credenzas. Featuring clean lines that hearken to midcentury modern, the materials are the

> "The woodworker has a special intensity, a striving for perfection, a conviction that any task must be executed with all his skill...to create the best object he is capable of creating."
> —George Nakashima

stars of the New York company's works. Founded in 1993 by Thomas Wright and Joseph Fratesi, the New York Hudson Valley company resides in a century-old factory, which also serves as a hub for other area makers.

INDUSTRIAL GIANTS

A sense of playfulness, a quest for simplicity, and a push to improve everyday objects influence today's new generation of award-winning industrial designers.

Working for the likes of Design Within Reach, Ligne Roset, L'Oréal, and Bernhardt Design, New York designer Brad Ascalon works in simple forms and shapes, relying on a less-is-more philosophy to create his pieces, which include sleek furniture and accessories, such as a modern menorah. "My design work is still highly influenced by the minimalist music movement that I've always been passionate about," he says.

Fellow New Yorker Joe Doucet's diverse works simplify some of the most common objects, turning them into obsessions. His innovations include minimalist playing cards, water bottles, motorcycle helmets, neckties, running gloves, and more. Doucet embraces modern tech, using 3D printers to model prototypes. "I do believe that technology is just going to empower people to do more while using less," he says.

▼ *Interior Design* magazine's Best of the Year Award 2018, Ascalon's Preludia collection features seating and tables for home and commercial applications.

A MODERN MIX

Throwback looks from the 1960s and 1970s continue to drive today's design scene.

Bohemian style allows homeowners an anything-goes approach. Focused on personal styles and passions, boho looks blend family heirlooms, personal collections (especially from travel), and handmade goods with warm earth tones, rich metallics, patterned fabrics, and complex textures.

◀ This white oak and rolled-steel desk configuration from Atlas Industries features the clean lines that hearken to midcentury modern design.

Today's modern look is more relaxed and comfortable, with furniture and accessories that reflect personal passions.

Gardening

Growing food, cultivating flowers, organizing the landscape: The actions of gardening help feed our bodies, nurture our creativity, and allow us to carve out a place of our own in the wilderness.

An American Chronology

Gardening in America is a tapestry of cultivation practices and plants that grew on land populated by Native Americans, along with rootstock and seeds brought by immigrants from the Old World.

Plants grew on Earth long before humans existed. Some plants found in today's gardens have bloomed for millions of years. Mosses are 470 million years old. Sago palms predate dinosaurs. Humans showed up around 200,000 years ago. Gardening in America is a blend of cultivation practices and plants that came from indigenous peoples and immigrants who brought rootstock and seeds from the Old World.

GARDENS IN THE COLONIES

Fast-forward to the newly minted America. Colonists brought European gardening and farming traditions. Native Americans introduced new crops, such as corn, to colonists and taught about the bounty of wild foods in the landscape, including chestnuts, watercress, grapes, strawberries, huckleberries, blackberries, and raspberries. Colonists planted gardens that were a combination of Old World species combined with New World discoveries. Gardens were orderly, influenced by Anglo-Dutch tradition; they were decorative, featuring geometric-shape beds as was the fashion in 17th- and 18th-century Europe.

WESTWARD, HO

As Americans moved westward, so did their gardens. Families traveling in Conestoga wagons brought herb, vegetable, and perennial seeds and plants from gardens out East to plant in their new homes. 'Harison's Yellow' rose, also called the Oregon Trail rose, which was marketed in Long Island, New York, in 1830, was found blooming at abandoned home sites all along the Oregon Trail. Seed catalogs made it possible to get vegetables and flowers, so settlers filled their gardens with newly developed varieties and species.

GARDENS FOR SOCIAL GOOD

Since the 1890s, gardens in America have worked to solve social problems such as economic recession. Community gardens filled vacant lots; in 1896 Detroit was the first city

▲ Native Americans taught European colonists to grow the indigenous grains, including corn, wild rice, and amaranth.

◄ A blanket based on a 19th-century Navajo sand painting design shows sacred maize, one of the Three Sisters crops (corn, beans, and squash) grown by farming Native Americans.

to use vacant lots in a municipally sponsored urban gardening program. Other cities followed suit. During the Great Depression, community gardens offered ground for unemployed folks to grow their own food. In 1934, more than 23 million households used community gardens.

The two World Wars also turned Americans into fruit and vegetable gardeners. Prompted by requests from the government, patriotic Americans tilled and planted front yards and schoolyards into Victory Gardens, which pumped out vegetables for the war effort. Twenty million Victory Gardens grew more than 40 percent of all American produce in 1943. The fruits and vegetables planted there were what we now call "heirlooms."

A LOVE AFFAIR WITH LAWN

The prosperity following World War II meant Americans didn't have to garden for food as much. The suburban development was born, with the first one in Levitttown, New York, which offered homeowners a new house sitting in an oasis of turfgrass. Lawns became a status symbol of wealth in the 1940s and 1950s. Modern landscaping surrounded homes with foundation plantings, such as flowering and evergreen shrubs, and shade trees were planted in rows,

▲ In the 1950s, luxurious green lawns were (and continue to be) a status symbol for suburban Americans.

America's first flower show, held in Philadelphia in 1829, featured exotic and native plants.

COLONIST CROPS

The Jamestown Colony produced vegetable crops that included beans, squash, peas, okra, pumpkins, peppers, tomatoes, and peanuts. Fruit trees in Williamsburg's early gardens were generally European varieties of apple, pear, cherry, apricot, and peach.

◄ A colonist farmer could plant 5 to 10 acres of corn by hand. A horse and plow increased production to 20 acres.

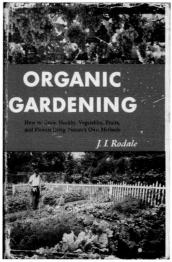

▶ *Organic Farming and Gardening* magazine began publication in 1942 by Rodale Press and promoted an organic, healthy approach to growing food. The magazine was renamed *Organic Gardening*.

creating a canopy of cover. The American elm tree was the most popularly planted tree.

SCIENTIFIC INFLUENCES

In the 1960s, science solved many gardening problems—herbicides and pesticides offered time-saving solutions to hand-weeding and pesky insects. But the dark side of chemical solutions was revealed in Rachel Carson's book *Silent Spring*, published in 1962. Research showed that the use of the pesticide DDT stayed in the food chain, thereby almost making extinct America's icon, the bald eagle. The Environmental Protection Agency (EPA) was formed in the aftermath. The organic movement was born, popularized by J.I. Rodale's publications *Organic Gardening* and *Prevention* magazines. Earth Day in 1970 drew attention to world ecology.

American gardens provided food, reflected fashion, and offered a little piece of paradise.

Americans created organizations around their love of gardens. The National Garden Clubs, Inc. traces its history to 1891. The Garden Club of America was founded in 1913.

GARDENING TODAY

Living the outdoor lifestyle continues to be a trend with today's gardeners, who build and enjoy decks, patios, swimming pools, fire pits, outdoor kitchens, and grilling areas. Outdoors has all the comforts of indoors thanks to weatherproof fabrics, rugs, and outdoor appliances. Gardening trends have scaled to fit urban spaces; small-space, container, and vertical gardens snug into postage-stamp-size yards and turn terraces into jungles. Xeriscaping solves gardening problems in water-restricted areas. For the modern homesteader, heirloom vegetables and fruits return flavors of the past to kitchen gardens. A whole new generation is embracing homegrown herbs to use in cooking and aromatherapy. And just as apothecary gardens of the past provided medicinal cures, herbs and perennials are once again being investigated for medicinal uses. Indoor gardening with houseplants is more popular than ever.

Americans are gardeners. Our love of wild and tamed spaces, delicious foods, fragrant flowers, and exotic plants links us to our gardening ancestors who loved all the same things for the same reasons. And as Americans always do, we put our own spin on gardens, indoors and out.

▲ Growing windowsill herb gardens of basil and thyme combines the love of raising fresh food with the trend of indoor gardening.

◄ Backyard raised-bed gardening makes planting easier and adds to landscape appeal. Homeowners can raise a bounty of fruit of vegetables in a small space.

Thomas Jefferson

JEFFERSON WAS A LIFELONG GARDENER. HIS GARDEN JOURNAL, WHICH HE
OBSESSIVELY AND METICULOUSLY WROTE IN FOR 58 YEARS, REVEALS CAREFUL ENTRIES
ABOUT PLANTING AND FLOWERING TIMES, HARVEST DATES, AND YIELDS.

▲ A spring garden
blooms in front of the
Monticello home near
Charlottesville, Virginia.

Monticello's 1,000-foot-long garden terrace grew 330 vegetable varieties. The orchards produced fruit from 170 different varieties.

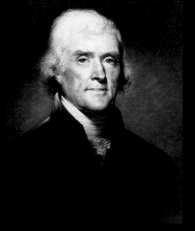

▼ Jefferson recorded seed sowing, amendments, harvest dates, successes, and failures in his "Garden Kalendar."

FROM FORMER PRESIDENT TO FARMER

When Jefferson built his home, Monticello, the garden wasn't just a landscaping project. Jefferson was a farmer, interested in every aspect of planting, from seed sowing, flowering times, date to table, yield, and flavor. But he was also a scientist, statesman, and world traveler, and his collection of plants reflected that.

His 1,000-foot-long, south-facing vegetable garden was built in 1770 and terraced in 1806. The gardens at Monticello were both ornamental in their layout and utilitarian in their purpose. The gardens were testing plots for new species and varieties of vegetables, fruits, flowers, and trees both indigenous and imported.

Plants from Africa, Europe, and the Americas grew shoulder to shoulder. According to Peter J. Hatch, former Director of Gardens and Grounds at Monticello, the garden was "an Ellis Island of introductions." Jefferson's garden journal featured detailed entries from 1766 to 1824. He died in 1826 at the age of 83. Yet he remained enchanted by gardening his whole life: He wrote, "Tho' an old man, I am but a young gardener." His garden in Monticello exists as a living museum of plant varieties and species for all to visit.

HIDDEN HISTORY

Bernard McMahon

A gardening mentor of Thomas Jefferson, Bernard McMahon was a Philadelphia nurseryman who wrote perhaps the first how-to gardening book in this country. Jefferson referred to this book as his gardening "bible."

Bernard McMahon (also M'Mahon) was born in Ireland in 1775 and emigrated to America when he was 21, in 1796. He settled in Philadelphia and in 1802 he started a nursery and seed business. He and his wife, Ann, ran the business together while McMahon also worked on various publishing projects that helped build his horticultural reputation in America and abroad. His shop was frequented by botanists, horticulturalists, and others interested in his hundreds of unique seed varieties.

THE ROOTS OF THE SEED BUSINESS

McMahon promoted his seed business by creating America's first seed list/booklet in 1802, called the *Catalogue of Garden Grass, Herb, Flower, Tree & Shrub-Seeds, Flower Roots, &c.*

To honor McMahon, botanist Thomas Nuttall bestowed the genus name *Mahonia* on a now-popular West Coast evergreen shrub.

This alphabetically ordered list featured 720 species and varieties for sale. There were no plant descriptions or illustrations, but McMahon is generally credited for creating America's first seed catalog. Two years later, he published a 30-page booklet of seeds that were native to America. Seed collection, sales, and marketing helped focus the interest in specific species, including native plants, which helped popularize them in Europe.

▼ Irish-born Philadelphia nurseryman Bernard McMahon (1775–1816) was Thomas Jefferson's gardening mentor. His book *The American Gardener's Calendar* was described as Jefferson's horticultural "bible."

THE AMERICAN GARDENER'S CALENDAR; ADAPTED TO THE CLIMATES AND SEASONS OF THE UNITED STATES.

◄ McMahon published *The American Gardener's Calendar* in 1806 for "all the work necessary to be done" for vegetable, fruit, and flower gardening. Detailed instructions were written for every month of the year. The book has 648 pages.

▲ Lewis and Clark's Corps of Discovery expedition sent back specimens and seeds to Jefferson who passed them on to McMahon and other horticulturalists to grow.

▶ Captain Meriwether Lewis kept a botanical journal of plant notes and sketches, such as the sword leaf fern.

AMERICA'S FIRST GARDENING BOOK

McMahon was an avid grower and note taker and In 1806, he published *The American Gardener's Calendar*, a 648-page book written in a month-by-month format, detailing every action required for raising vegetables, fruits, flowers, and trees. The book told eager gardeners when to plant, how to plant, when to prune, how to make good soil, when to divide plants, and more.

This detailed narrative of monthly gardening activities interested one particular reader: Thomas Jefferson, who referred to McMahon's book in his growing decisions at Monticello. Jefferson and McMahon become correspondents, seed sharers, and plant friends. In fact, McMahon's book is often referred to as Jefferson's gardening "bible." *The American Gardener's Calendar* was considered a best-seller and was consequently updated with 11 editions, the last in 1857. It is considered the most comprehensive gardening guide of its time.

LEWIS AND CLARK'S PLANTS AND SEEDS

When Thomas Jefferson hired Meriwether Lewis and William Clark to embark upon the Corps of Discovery expedition (the first expedition to cross the country going westward, lasting from May 1804 to September 1806), they were charged with collecting and documenting flora and fauna for scientific research as well as identifying potential commerce value. The plants discovered and collected by Lewis were sent to Washington to Thomas Jefferson, who, in turn, sent them to Bernard McMahon, appointing him as the curator of plants from the expedition. Lewis and Clark found 174 plants, 94 of which were new to science. McMahon grew many of these, as directed by Jefferson. Botanist Thomas Nuttall memorialized McMahon's contributions to botany and horticulture by naming a genus of shrubs after him: *Mahonia*.

▲ Meriwether Lewis (1774–1809), (top) and William Clark (1770–1838). Portraits by Charles Willson Peale

Lewis and Clark found 174 plants. McMahon was their curator.

commencing at the bottom and from thence to the extremity sessile. The rib is terminated by a single undivided lanceolate gagged leafet. The leafets are lanceolate, from 2 to 4 Inches in length gagged and have a small accute angular projection on the upper edge near the base where it is spurred on the side which has the projection and obliquely cut at the base on the other side of the rib of the leafet: or which will give a better idea in this form. the upper surface is smooth and of a deep green the under disk of a pale green and covered with a brown pubescence of a woolly appearance particularly near the cental fiber or rib. These

A MOMENT IN TIME

Catalogs

Plants and seeds were sold locally until the U.S. Postal Service opened up a world of planting possibilities by delivering seed catalogs to every corner of the country.

The history of American gardening was written in yearly installments through the publication of seed catalogs each year. Sent through the mail directly to customers, these catalogs arrived in mailboxes in midwinter (just as they do today) to winter-weary gardeners who could spend weeks poring over the pages of planting possibilities, then order seeds and receive packets in the mail in time for planting that spring. The colorful covers told the story of America's changing fashions, fads, and flora discoveries and development. Seed catalogs from the past are also a window into the history of advertising graphic arts and the development of horticultural marketing through the text and illustrations.

THE FIRST SEED COMPANY AND MAIL-ORDER CATALOG

In 1784, English immigrant David Landreth started the first American seed company in Philadelphia. It was called D. Landreth Seed Co., and the products in the mail-order catalogs included vegetables, flowers, and ornamental shrub seeds. In addition to supplying seeds throughout the country, the company also introduced exciting new species and varieties to the American gardening public. David Landreth was the first to sell zinnias (which came from Mexico) in 1798. Other "firsts" were the white potato in 1811, the tomato in 1820, and 'Bloomsdale' spinach in 1826. The catalog sold Osage orange seeds from stock discovered and collected by Lewis and Clark in 1808 from the banks of the Osage River.

SEEDING THEIR WAY WESTWARD

American pioneers moved westward by handcart, wagons, and eventually trains. Seed catalogs offered a way to plant the flavors and flowers of the home they were leaving, as well as an opportunity to try new varieties in the

▲ David Landreth was born in England in 1752. He is credited with creating the first mail-order seed company in America.

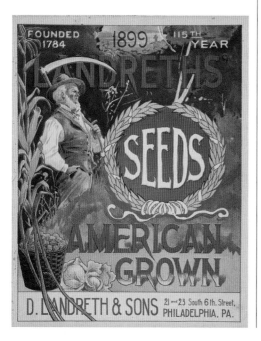

◀ D. Landreth Seed Co. introduced the zinnia, white potato, and tomato (called the love apple) to American gardeners.

soil of their new land. Catalogs helped settlers literally set down new roots.

BIGGER, BETTER, BEST

As companies and catalogs sprouted up following the Civil War, the mail-order market became more competitive. "Bigger is better" was a marketing hook, and vegetable and flower varieties began to take on names such as 'Mammoth,' 'Giant,' and 'Perfection' to help distinguish themselves as superior in a growing competitive market. Catalogs employed other "new" marketing techniques such as customer testimonials, special offers, plant collections, and home-hybridizer growing contests.

SEED SOLUTIONS

Catalogs sold seeds that offered solutions to troubled times. According to Alice Krinsky Formiga of the Oregon State University Department of Horticulture, "Although many catalogues made no mention of the stock market crash of 1929 and the subsequent Depression, some referred to hard times and offered customers seeds, plants, and bulbs at low or reduced prices." Catalogs were marketed to home gardeners who wanted to grow their own food, as well as to a growing market of garden businesses. The 'Mortgage Lifter' tomato, developed in the 1930s by a West Virginia home hybridizer named M.C. Byles (aka Radiator Charlie), who paid off his $6,000 mortgage in six years, appealed to both markets.

▲ W. Atlee Burpee & Co. announced a competition in its 1954 catalog for home gardeners to develop a truly white marigold. The prize was $10,000.

$10K WHITE MARIGOLD

In 1954, W. Atlee Burpee & Co.'s catalog encouraged home-garden hybridizers to create a new plant variety. The catalog offered a $10,000 prize for the first white marigold flower. It took 21 years to produce a winner. Sixty-seven-year-old Alice Vonk of Sully, Iowa, spent two decades on the process. "I used to look in the seed catalogs for the largest yellow marigolds I could find. I would let the palest flowers go to seed, then collect the seeds," she said. In 1975, she was able to achieve a pure-white flower, beating out 8,200 other entries.

The first seed catalogs offered plant material to gardeners who couldn't get it any other way.

◀ Families traveling westward depended on seed catalogs to get the flowers and flavors from back home. Photo by George Barnard, 1862.

Gertrude Jekyll

AN ENGLISH GARDEN DESIGNER, HORTICULTURIST, AND WRITER,
GERTRUDE JEKYLL INFLUENCED FLOWER GARDENING—SPECIFICALLY
PERENNIAL GARDENING—IN ENGLAND, EUROPE, AND AMERICA.

Hestercombe Gardens near Taunton, Somerset, England is a collaboration between Gertrude Jekyll and architect Edwin Lutyens. Jekyll designed more than 400 gardens across the U.K., Europe, and America, widely influencing American gardens.

GARDENING TAKES A TURN FOR THE ORNAMENTAL

Born in 1843, Gertrude Jekyll influenced how American gardens would look for decades. She wrote extensively about gardening and garden design, contributing articles to English and American gardening journals. Her many books were published in Great Britain and America.

Jekyll designed more than 400 gardens in the United Kingdom and Europe. Although she never came to America to work, she designed three gardens in the United States from abroad. In 1914, she created a garden design for a house in Elmhurst, Ohio. In 1925, she designed the garden at Cotswold Cottage in Greenwich, Connecticut. And in 1926, she designed the garden at Glebe House (now Glebe House Museum) in Woodbury, Connecticut. This garden was restored in the 1990s and is the only American garden planned by Gertrude Jekyll that is still in existence.

Jekyll's influence on American gardens included design elements still used today: combining hot and cool colors, massing plants, and repeating elements. Jekyll was honored by a number of American gardening organizations, including the Garden Club of America and the Massachusetts Horticultural Society.

EVERYTHING OLD IS NEW AGAIN

Perennial Gardens

Big, lush border gardens became all the rage in the early 1900s, following an English tradition. And while still trendy, perennial gardens have grown and changed with the times.

WHEN PERENNIALS BECAME THE "IT" PLANTS

Gardeners have always had a mix of flower types to choose from: annuals that bloom all season, then die; perennials that bloom year after year; and biennials, which take two years to complete their life cycle. From 1865 to 1900, Victorian gardeners popularized annual bedding plants as a landscape style. But the cost, time, and repetitiveness of replanting regimented beds every year made way for a new gardening fashion: using primarily perennials in the garden. In 1890, garden designer George Nicholson reintroduced gardeners to perennial gardening at the Royal Botanic Gardens, Kew, in England. This started the still-popular trend of creating perennial borders and island gardens that capitalized on perennial plant talents: a specific season of bloom, varying heights, and the ability to overwinter and return each year. Old-school English-inspired perennial border gardens generally consisted of a wide, long bed planted against a wall or hedge. Tall plants were positioned in back, with shorter plants in front. This garden design was popular in Great Britain, Europe, and America.

MODERN PERENNIAL GARDENS

As perennial gardens became more popular, they also morphed in shape and size. Island gardens began showing up in American backyards in the 1950s. These smaller perennial beds could be installed anywhere in the yard and looked good from all angles. As urban living grew, perennial gardens have become smaller, but also more diverse. Modern small-space gardens are more inclusive, adding annuals for color, succulents for texture, and edibles, such as herbs and small-size fruits and vegetables, for great taste. Contemporary garden designers, armed with a palette of new and old perennials, have created perennial gardens with modern appeal. Gardens have grown wilder. For example, Dutch garden designer Piet Oudolf used regionally native plants that attract wildlife and change looks through the seasons in New York City's High Line and Chicago's Lurie Garden in Millennium Park.

▲ Colorful, large English-style perennial borders became standard elements of American public and estate gardens, such as Old Westbury Gardens.

▶ Xeriscaping is a garden technique that uses perennials to create low-water landscapes. Common xeriscaping plants include lavender, blue fescue, and other drought-tolerant perennials.

Manhattan's High Line garden spans 1.45 miles. Built on an old elevated train line, this perennial garden is an icon of contemporary perennial gardening.

Raised Beds

A raised bed is like a big container that warms up earlier in the spring and drains well. Planting, weeding, and harvesting are all easier in a raised bed than planting in the ground. Multiple beds create a formal garden design.

YOU WILL NEED

Wood sides: rot-resistant lumber or composite decking material

Inside supports: 4×4 stakes; place at corners and on side in beds longer than 4 feet

Hardware: galvanized or stainless-steel screws or bolts

Garden soil: ¾ topsoil and ¼ compost

1 Determine a bed location. Most vegetables and herbs require 6 to 8 hours of sun a day. Locate your raised bed in an unobstructed area. Shade-loving plants, such as ferns and hostas, can be grown in raised beds that receive less than 6 hours of sun a day. For good drainage, locate your raised bed on a level location.

2 Choose your shape. Raised garden beds can be square or retangular. You can make one or a series of them in a design. **Long rectangle(s):** For vegetables, herbs, cutting gardens, perennial borders. **Square(s):** For flower beds, small kitchen gardens, herb gardens.

3 Allow stepping space. If building multiple beds, leave space between to walk and work. Place beds no closer than 18 inches for easy access. If you plan to have grass between the beds, allow 2 feet (or the width of your lawn mower).

4 Make tall enough to suit your back. Although most raised beds should be at least 8 inches tall, you can make them taller for easier planting and harvesting. Taller beds can accommodate physical needs or design style.

▲ Before building a raised bed, level the area and improve the soil surface with a layer of compost, rotted manure, or leaf mold.

▲ Always use lumber that's rot-resistant, such as locust, cedar, cypress, or redwood. Or use composite decking material.

▲ Choose galvanized hardware to assemble your raised bed. It won't rust or break down over time.

▲ Make corner posts out of sturdy 4×4 lumber that's sunk at least 2 feet into the ground.

Plant Tags

Keep track of your crops with handmade plant tags. Ideal for container gardens, herb gardens, and when sowing seeds directly into the ground, plant tags carry on the centuries-old tradition of marking crops with Latin and common names.

YOU WILL NEED

Wooden stakes 12 inches long (wooden paint stirrers work well)

Black exterior latex paint

White paint pen

1 Select flat wooden stakes about 2 inches wide, cut to about 12 inches long.

2 Apply a coat of black latex paint to both sides of the stake. Allow to dry and apply a second coat.

3 Using a white paint pen, write the Latin or common name (or both) of the plant.

4 Insert stake in container, next to a plant in a bed or border, or at the head of a row of seeds.

WHAT'S IN A (PLANT) NAME?

All plants have internationally recognized names, in Latin, thanks to Carl Linnaeus, a Swedish botanist, who wrote *The Species of Plants (Species Plantarum)* in 1753. Linnaeus formalized the nomenclature, or the ways plants are named. For example, every gardener in the world can ask for *Thymus vulgaris* and they will get thyme because its Latin name describes the genus and species; common names, such as garden thyme, common thyme, and English thyme, are less precise. Linnaeus gave us the language to be specific about plant identification.

▲ For plant tags, always use durable exterior black paint that won't fade over time.

▲ To apply plant names to tags, use white paint or a permanent marker. Add both common and Latin names.

Biodegradable Paper Pots

Make your own biodegradable seed-starting pots using recycled paper. Grow seedlings in their own pots, then plant them directly into the ground, pot and all. The paper will dissolve under the soil.

YOU WILL NEED

Biodegradable paper, such as kraft paper or newspaper sheets

Scissors

Beverage bottle

Potting soil or seed-starting mix

Seeds

1 Cut a piece of paper to the height you would like your pot, adding about 2 to 2½ inches.
2 Roll paper around the beverage bottle. Fold the excess paper at the base of the bottle to make a pot base. Remove pot from bottle.
3 Fill pot with potting soil.
4 Plant seeds following directions on seed packets for the specific species and variety.

HARDENING OFF

When you start seeds indoors, the plants need to acclimate to outdoor conditions slowly before planting in the garden. This is called hardening off. Set seedlings in a shady and protected area outdoors for a few days before planting directly in the ground. This allows them to get used to new light levels and changing temperatures.

▲ Using kraft paper or several sheets of newspaper to create a paper pot will give it more durability and structure.

▲ For healthier seedlings, fill your paper pots with a commercial soilless seed-starting mix.

W. Atlee Burpee

IN 1876, WHEN HE WAS 18, W. ATLEE BURPEE STARTED A MAIL-ORDER CHICKEN BUSINESS. TWO YEARS LATER HE FOUNDED W. ATLEE BURPEE & COMPANY, SELLING MAINLY GARDEN SEEDS. HE WOULD BECOME THE LARGEST SEED SELLER IN THE WORLD.

▲ Burpee seed catalogs featured vegetable introductions such as 'Surehead' cabbage and 'Stringless' green pod beans. 'Iceberg' lettuce was introduced in 1894; it revolutionized the salad industry because it was the first lettuce that could be shipped long distances.

▲ W. Atlee Burpee & Company started in 1876, selling to mostly immigrant farmers.

SEEDS ARE EASIER TO MAIL THAN CHICKENS

Although W. Atlee Burpee's first love was poultry (the company kept selling livestock such as chickens, geese, and turkeys through mail order until the 1940s), he'd found that seeds were easier to mail.

Burpee was interested in finding the best flowers and vegetables, which led him on summer travels to Europe prior to World War I. He looked for new varieties and took them back home, to Fordhook Farms in Doylestown, Pennsylvania. He planted what he collected. If it did well, he'd grow it again. And again. Until he had enough to sell. In this way, his home became his test garden and laboratory as well as a place to produce seeds. Burpee was so successful that he developed some of the most iconic vegetable varieties that are still sold today: Fordhook lima beans, yellow sweet corn, iceberg lettuce.

Burpee's first seed catalog was 48 pages. By 1915, the catalog was 200 pages. He wrote all the product descriptions himself, then started using customer testimonials to tell the story of his seeds. He engaged the gardening public with cash prizes for the best advertisements and contests for home gardeners to develop new varieties, such as a white marigold. He asked his gardening public to share their growing experiences through contests such as What Burpee Seeds Have Done for Me. Burpee's marketing genius matched the quality of his seeds. In 1915, when he died, his legacy was the largest seed company in the world, with 300 employees. The company distributed 1 million catalogs that year.

HIDDEN HISTORY

George Washington Carver

George Washington Carver is known for researching and developing agricultural products from peanuts. But he was also an advocate for forward-thinking gardening practices that are trending today.

George Washington Carver was born a slave in Missouri in the 1860s and became an acclaimed agricultural scientist, researcher, and inventor who developed products from peanut, soybean, and sweet potato crops. Carver was a friend to Southern farmers because much of his research benefited farms whose soil had been depleted of nutrients by continuous cotton crops.

RESEARCHER, TEACHER, WRITER

Carver earned a master's degree in agricultural science from Iowa State University in 1896; he was the first African American student and faculty member at that university. Booker T. Washington, the first president of the Tuskegee Institute (now Tuskegee University) in Alabama, hired Carver to head its Agriculture Department. Carver

Carver promoted crop rotation, improving soil health through natural amendments, and natural food foraging.

taught, conducted research, and directed the Agricultural Experiment Station at Tuskegee Institute for 47 years.

FORWARD-THINKING IDEAS

During his time at Tuskegee Institute, Carver wrote 44 agricultural bulletins promoting innovative and forward-thinking ideas, many of which are widely accepted in mainstream gardening practices today. Carver promoted crop rotation, improving soil health through natural

amendments, and natural food foraging. He even developed recipes for cooking with the crops that he helped promote. In January 1940, he published "How to Grow the Peanut and 105 Ways of Preparing It for Human Consumption." The rationale for eating peanuts was simple: Peanuts provided a more cost-effective protein nutrient than beef. "A pound of peanuts contains a little more of the body-building nutrients than a pound of sirloin steak, while of the heat- and energy-producing nutrients it has more than twice as much." Recipes in this publication included peanut soup, mock chicken (made from peanuts, eggs, and sweet potatoes), and peanut coffee (made from roasted peanuts and cow peas).

WILD FOOD FORAGING

In his last bulletin, "Nature's Garden for Victory and Peace," Carver wrote about food foraging and the value of wild edibles. Published in 1942, it encouraged self-sufficiency, urging readers to rely on wild plants in the event that the war produced food shortages. He advocated eating dandelions, lamb's-quarters, and other weeds found in "dooryards, fields, and roadsides." Like many of today's whole-food evangelists, Carver believed that nature's bounty provides everything we need to eat and live healthfully.

▲ George Washington Carver (c. 1864–1943) was born a slave and became a world-famous American botanist and teacher. Photograph by Frances Benjamin Johnston, 1906.

Carver advocated eating dandelions, lamb's-quarters, and other weeds found in "dooryards, fields, and roadsides."

BULLETIN, FORTY-THREE

Chenopodium album—Lamb's Quarter
(After C. M. King)

BEETROOT (Beta vulgaris). Our cultivated beets belong to this group. Many housewives, dietitians do not know the leaves and stems are quite as fine as spinach when prepared in the same way. They improve the flavor of other greens when mixed with them and cooked like turnip greens. They also make an appetizing salad when steamed or boiled until tender, drained and served with mayonnaise, French or any other dressing you wish. A little shredded onion, a spring of parsley, chow-chow or mixed pickle of any kind aid much in the preparation of this versatile food stuff.

I think you will like the many combinations better than spinach. The pickled leaf stems are especially fine when served with cold meats. The entire spinach family are especially rich in iron and other mineral salts.

THE MUSTARD FAMILY (Brassicaceae)

Just a few of this large and outstanding group of edible and medicinal plants will be mentioned here.

PEPPER-GRASS (Lepidium species). There are several varieties of this common dooryard and garden plant. It belongs to the mustard family and can be cooked in the same way. It is delicious when prepared as an uncooked salad, the same as recommended for dandelion.

—9—

◀ "Nature's Garden for Victory and Peace" was published in March 1942 and was one of the gardening tracts penned by Carver to help home gardeners and farmers in the South.

▲ George Washington Carver developed hundreds of products using the peanut, helping develop a market for Southern farmers.

A MOMENT IN TIME

Victory Gardens

The U.S. Government enlisted civilian gardeners to plant Victory Gardens during times of war, rationing, and fiscal belt-tightening. Produce grown in backyards, parks, and vacant lots fed the people.

Victory Gardens made growing tomatoes and potatoes a patriotic act. Promoted by the government during both world wars, home gardeners were urged to dig up plots of lawn, schoolyards, parks, and vacant lots to help raise food for the war effort. During World War I (1914–1918) and World War II (1939–1945), more than one million Americans grew food.

FROM WAR GARDENS TO VICTORY GARDENS
Originally called "war gardens" or "food

gardens for defense," the name was changed by Charles Lathrop Pack, head of the National War Garden Commission, at the end of World War I; he coined the term "Victory Garden", which had more of a more positive, patriotic spin. Besides supporting the war effort by providing fresh vegetables and fruits to supplement rationed food, Victory Gardens were also a way to boost morale by helping regular folks with front-yard gardens help those on the frontlines. The initiative worked. In May 1943, civilian-grown Victory Gardens supplied 40 percent of the produce in America. At the same time, home canning reached its peak during the years of World War II.

PLANTING THE SEEDS OF PATRIOTISM
During World War I , seed companies got into the act with catalog covers featuring patriotic imagery. The J. Bolgiano & Son seed catalog in 1918 featured an illustration of a red-white-and-blue-suited Uncle Sam and a message from President Wilson on the cover: "Every one who cultivates a garden helps greatly to solve the

◀ "The seeds of victory insure the fruits of peace" was messaging from the National War Garden Commission during World War I. Seed companies also got into the act of promoting patriotism by growing food.

▲ Seed companies often featured patriotic images on their covers.

problem of feeding the nations." The message was clear: Growing vegetables and fruits became synonymous with being patriotic.

VICTORY GARDENERS IN FACT AND FICTION

With World War II in full swing, Victory Gardens helped supplement American diets when food was being rationed. In 1943, First Lady Eleanor Roosevelt planted a Victory Garden on the White House's front lawn. The same year, DC Comics featured Batman, Robin, and Superman harvesting cabbages in a Victory Garden. And the cover girl for the September 27, 1943, issue of *Life* magazine featured a smiling young member of the Women's Land Army (WLA) with an armful of corn. First Lady Michelle Obama brought back the tradition of the Victory Garden to the White House in 2009.

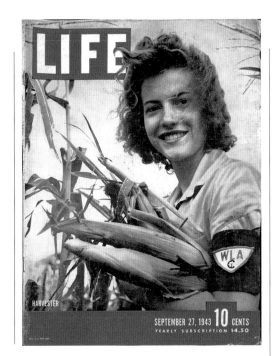

◀ Growing food for success! The September 27, 1943, issue of *Life* magazine featured a fresh-faced member of the Women's Land Army (WLA) with an armful of harvested corn.

VISIT A VICTORY GARDEN

There are two remaining official Victory Gardens in the U.S. that have lasted since the 1940s:

Dowling Community Garden in the Longfellow neighborhood of Minneapolis, Minnesota, and the Fenway Victory Gardens (renamed Richard D. Parker Memorial Victory Gardens) in Boston, Massachusetts. The Smithsonian has a Victory Garden outside of the National Museum of American History that features vegetable and flower species that were grown by Victory gardeners during World War II.

Victory Gardens supplied 40 percent of the produce in America in May 1943.

◀ During World War II, public spaces, such as the Boston Common, were plowed and planted for the Victory Garden Program. Victory Gardens supplied 40 percent of the produce in America in May 1943.

EVERYTHING OLD IS NEW AGAIN

Growing Your Own

Today's home gardeners choose to raise tomatoes, greens, and other vegetables and fruits at home, simply to enjoy fresh, flavorful food as part of a healthful lifestyle.

WHERE FOOD CAME FROM

If you were a settler in 18th-century America, you planted vegetables, fruits, and herbs in your home garden or purchased them from a local source. The concept of the modern grocery store (where you select the items you want from shelves) didn't exist in America until 1916, when the Piggly Wiggly in Memphis, Tennessee, offered self-serve grocery shopping. Through the 1940s, food came primarily from small, local farms. As food production and distribution methods improved, fresh fruits and vegetables came from farther away. By the 1960s, chain stores and supermarkets offered more vegetable and fruit choices, but also greatly increased the distance between the growers of food and the consumers of food.

LOCAL IS BACK

Edible gardens are popping up nearly everywhere: backyards and front yards, parking strips, vacant lots, rooftops, and containers. So why do some people choose to grow their own or buy from small, local growers? Local and homegrown food offer superior freshness. Food can be harvested at peak, and the time between harvest and consumption is days, not weeks. Local food production reduces transportation costs. Why eat a tomato grown thousands of miles away when you can pluck it from your backyard? Growing some of your own produce gives you a sense of self-sufficiency and control. You can raise or purchase vegetables, fruits, and herbs that are grown without pesticides or other chemicals. As an added benefit, gardening is a physical activity: pulling weeds, planting, and digging can burn up to 400 calories per hour. Plus, there is great satisfaction in growing, harvesting, and eating your food moments after it was harvested. (Oh, and it's fun, too.)

▲ Strawberries are perennial fruits, meaning that they bear year after year. While they do best in raised beds, even small-space gardeners can grow them in deck or patio planters.

▶ You can grow tastier tomato varieties at home, which often don't fit the mold of commercially produced varieties that need a long shelf life or consistent shape for easy packaging.

▼ Kids who grow or help shop for fresh fruits and vegetables develop a relationship with where their food comes from and how it is grown.

Cool-weather crops, such as lettuce and spinach, are ideal for home gardeners because they germinate quickly and are ready to eat in just weeks.

Vertical Gardening: Rustic Tepee

Settlers used materials at hand for gardening—you can, too. Use fresh-cut willow or birch canes to make a tepee on which to grow vining vegetables or flowers. The structure makes an ideal focal point for a garden. Rustic and natural, this handmade structure looks beautiful in cottage, country, and farmhouse gardens.

YOU WILL NEED

6-foot-long willow or birch canes

Nylon garden twine

Vining vegetable plants, such as pole beans and peas

OR

Vining flowers, such as sweet peas and morning glory

1 Position the canes on the ground or inside a container in a tepee formation.

2 Bind the tops with twine.

3 Plant vining plants at the base of each of the stakes.

4 Twine tendrils gently onto the sticks to help them climb.

THREE SISTERS: GROWING PARTNERS

Early settlers learned important gardening advice from Native Americans, such as the Iroquois, who were already experts at growing food crops. The Three Sisters combination of corn, squash, and beans capitalized on the growing characteristics of each plant to support the other. Corn grew tall and served as a support for beans. Beans added nitrogen to the soil to help the corn and squash. The squash spread across the ground, shading out weeds, preserving soil moisture, and repelling hungry raccoons.

▲ Choose tall, limber branches for your tepee. Willow, birch, and bamboo all work well.

▲ Tie your tepee together with nylon twine, which won't rot as the season progresses

▲ Plant a climbing vegetable or flower at the base of each branch of the tepee.

Cold Frame

Extend the season on each end of summer. Cold frames are like little greenhouses that protect tender seedlings and cold-hardy crops.

YOU WILL NEED

2×6 boards

Barn sash or old window

Potting soil

Gravel

Cool-weather seedlings

Propping stick

1 Measure the dimensions of the window and build a base using 2×6 boards so that the window can sit on top of the structure to protect seedlings from freezing temperatures or snow.

2 If you are using the cold frame as a planter, fill it with potting soil that is 6 to 8 inches deep. If you are using the cold frame as a place to harden off plants (to help them acclimate to cooler weather before planting them in the ground), add a layer of gravel for the pots to sit on; this facilitates drainage after watering.

▲ Young seedlings can dry out quickly in a cold frame. Check daily to keep them hydrated.

3 Plant seedlings in the soil. Or set potted plants inside the cold frame.

4 Using a stick, prop open the cold frame on warm days to allow heat to escape. On cold days or after the sun goes down, position the glass top over the seedlings to protect them from cold snaps.

COLD-WEATHER CROPS

Cold frames keep cool-weather crops protected even in freezing temperatures or under a layer of snow. Cold crops include greens such as spinach, arugula, cabbage, Brussels sprouts, broccoli, cauliflower, and kale.

Greens and Herb Garden

This two-tier hanging garden of fresh herbs and greens is both practical and decorative.
Herbs prefer well-drained soil; the colander containers allow water to drain through.

YOU WILL NEED

2 colanders, one larger than the other

Potting soil

Rope

Salad greens of your choice, such as lettuce, arugula, and red lettuce

Herbs of your choice such as basil, sage, rosemary, oregano, thyme, chives, parsley, and mint

1 Fill both colanders with potting soil.
2 Remove the herbs and salad greens from their growing pots and arrange them in the colanders.
3 Add potting soil to fill in around the plantings, making sure no roots are exposed.
4 String the containers together with the rope. Tie into a knot at the top. Hang in a sunny spot.
5 Water the containers.
6 Clip herbs and greens for meals. The more you clip, the more the plants grow.

USING HERBS

The flavor of herbs is at its peak if you clip and use leaves before the plant flowers. You can eat most herb flowers also, and they look beautiful sprinkled onto salads or grilled flatbreads.

HERBAL BLENDS

Classic herb blends include herbes de Provence (savory, thyme, oregano, rosemary, marjoram, and sometimes lavender), fines herbes (parsley, chives, tarragon, and chervil), and bouquet garni (thyme, bay leaf, and parsley).

▲ Always use a commercial potting mix in containers. Never use soil taken directly from your garden.

▲ Wet, soil-filled containers can be quite heavy, so use a strong support system to prevent accidents.

Rachel Carson

RACHEL CARSON'S BOOK *SILENT SPRING* HELPED TURN THE TIDE AGAINST THE USE OF THE PESTICIDE DDT. HER WORK OUTLINED THE ENVIRONMENTAL CONSEQUENCES OF INSECTICIDE OVERUSE. SHE HELPED START THE TREND OF GARDENING WITHOUT HERBICIDES AND PESTICIDES.

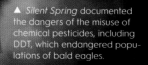

75¢

CREST BOOK t681

Silent Spring

THE EXPLOSIVE BESTSELLER THE WHOLE WORLD IS TALKING ABOUT

RACHEL CARSON

Author of THE SEA AROUND US

▲ *Silent Spring* documented the dangers of the misuse of chemical pesticides, including DDT, which endangered populations of bald eagles.

Vegetables, grains, and fruits can be certified USDA organic if they are grown in soil with no prohibited substances (chemical pesticides) applied for three years prior to harvest.

◀ Rachel Carson (1907-1964) was a nature writer and marine scientist who studied and wrote books about sea ecosystems. She ultimately became best known for her book *Silent Spring*.

MOTHER OF THE ENVIRONMENTAL MOVEMENT

Rachel Carson was a scientist and naturalist. Her book, *Silent Spring*, published in 1962, detailed the effects of the pesticide DDT on the environment. Introduced after World War II, DDT was one of the first widespread pesticides used to control mosquitoes. In *Silent Spring*, she illustrated how DDT was responsible for declines in bird populations, specifically bald eagles. The danger of DDT is that it persists in the environment and becomes concentrated in animals who sit at the top of the food chain.

After the publication of her book, Carson testified before Congress. Based on her testimony, the Environmental Protection Agency was formed. One of the EPA's first acts was to ban DDT.

In *Silent Spring*, she argued, "How could intelligent beings seek to control a few unwanted species by a method that contaminated the entire environment and brought the threat of disease and death even to their own kind?"

Carson is often credited for birthing the environmental movement.

HIDDEN HISTORY

Backyards

Peacetime, prosperity, and the postwar baby boom brought about an American invention: the backyard. Lawns became an icon of the suburban middle class.

LAWNS REDEFINE THE LANDSCAPE

Lush swaths of grass filled the suburbs. They were green, orderly, and required lots of chemicals and water to stay that way. And lawns changed the landscape.

Frederick Law Olmsted, the landscape architect who designed New York City's Central Park, is credited for popularizing turfgrass lawns for newly created suburban homes. Olmsted's landscape design for Riverside, a Chicago suburb, in 1869, included a lawn for each home. The invention of the lawn mower in 1830 made turf maintenance possible for individual homeowners.

Olmsted's Riverside landscape design required that homes be 30 feet from the street and that two trees should be planted between the sidewalk and the house. The lawn then became a permanent part of the landscape. According to Ted Steinberg, author of *American Green: The Obsessive Quest for the Perfect Lawn*, "The rise of the lawn to dominance in suburbia represents one of the most profound transformations of the landscape in American history."

Life in the suburbs in the 20th century included backyard activities such as barbecuing and entertaining outdoors.

THE BIRTH OF THE SUBURBS

The concept of the backyard is relatively new. An American invention, backyard spaces, and many of the activities that happened there, such as entertaining on the patio, grilling burgers, taking a dip in the pool, and gardening, happened in the post–World War II housing boom. As transportation improved, so did the infrastructure outside of cities. Starting with the eastern cities of New York and Boston, people began to move out to what came to be known as the suburbs. The term "suburb" comes from the Latin word *suburbium,* which means the "outlying part of a city." After World War II, affordable transportation offered middle-class Americans the option of living farther away from city centers. The first mass-produced suburb was Levittown, New York, built between 1947 and 1951. Other suburbs followed. The promise for the new suburban living was private green space, peace, and tranquility.

LET'S MEET IN THE BACKYARD

Midcentury suburban homes offered backyards that became an extension of the house. This "outdoor room" offered a place for family members to relax, play, and entertain. Patios were equipped with outdoor furniture that was made with new materials at the time: plastic and aluminum. Backyard grills made it possible to cook and eat outdoors. And pools became luxuries that many families could afford.

▲ The 'Peace' rose, a hybrid tea variety, became immensely popular after the end of World War II. In the nine years that followed the war, 30 million 'Peace' rose bushes were sold.

Nine years after the end of World War II, over 30 million 'Peace' roses bloomed worldwide.

▲ Wide swaths of lawn were the status symbol of suburban neighborhoods. Turfgrass is a crop that requires frequent care, such as watering, fertilizing, and mowing, so these became suburban activities.

▶ After World War II, backyard pools took off in popularity. In 2019, the Association of Pool & Spa Professionals (APSP) estimated that there were 10.4 million residential swimming pools in the United States.

A MOMENT IN TIME

Organic Gardening

The organic movement took hold in the early 20th century in response to the rise of chemicals used in farming. Raising plants without the aid of synthetic fertilizers or pest controls is the goal of organic gardening.

Organic gardening is gardening naturally, without synthetic chemicals. When you buy organic food in the grocery store, it is labeled "organic" by rules established by the USDA. Home gardeners can raise organic food at home using organic gardening practices, which include soil testing, adding natural soil amendments, protecting topsoil with mulch or cover crops, and rotating crops. Use of chemical pesticides and fertilizers is also discouraged.

BUILDING HEALTHY SOIL

One of the tenets of organic gardening is to start from the ground up by building healthy, nutrient-rich soil. Simply put, healthy clean soil grows healthy clean food.

Adding composted plant material helps revive poor soils by filling them with beneficial living microbes. Additionally, plants do best in soils that hold moisture but that also drain well, so adding natural materials, such as sharp sand to clay soils, improves soil drainage and makes it a more hospitable growing environment. Mulching with grass clippings, leaves, or straw also helps build soil fertility.

AMENDING SOIL NUTRIENTS

The three main types of nutrients for plant growth are nitrogen (N), phosphorus (P), and potassium (K). There are organic additives for each one of these nutrients that can be mixed into the soil. For example, natural nitrogen amendments include compost and animal manures and growing cover crops that can be tilled back into the soil; this is also called green manure.

NATURAL DISEASE CONTROL

Fungal diseases may be controlled through organic gardening techniques rather than chemicals. For example, increasing the airflow between plants, watering at ground level,

◀ Composting recycles green litter, such as food waste and grass clippings, into a valuable soil amendment.

▲ Ladybugs are beneficial insects that feed on aphids and other insects that kill plants by sucking sap. A single ladybug may consume up to 5,000 aphids in its lifetime.

▶ Organic gardening begins with healthy soil. Adding compost as a natural soil amendment improves soil quality by increasing organic materials and micronutrients.

mulching, planting in raised beds to facilitate drainage, rotating crops, and planting fungus-resistant varieties all help discourage fungal diseases in a natural way.

ORGANIC PEST MANAGEMENT

Garden pests are defined as plant pests (such as weeds), insect pests (such as aphids), and predator pests (such as birds and mammals who think your garden is as delicious as you do). Weeds can be controlled by hand removal, hoeing, mulching, and black plastic. Organic methods for insect predators include handpicking and organic insecticidal soap. Biological methods such as *Bacillus thuringiensis* (Bt), which is a natural soil-borne species of bacteria, are used for insect control. And there are larval and adult forms of beneficial insects, such as green lacewings and ladybugs, which consume harmful insects and insect eggs. And keeping mammals such as deer out of the garden can be done through tall fencing. Netting and row covers can keep fruit crops safe from birds.

▲ Rodale was an early advocate of sustainable agriculture and organic farming in America.

Building soil health with natural amendments is the basis of organic gardening.

J.I. RODALE

The term "organic gardening" was popularized by J.I. Rodale, whose Rodale Press publications promoted chemical-free gardening methods to home gardeners. While Rodale wasn't the first to introduce the concept of organic gardening, he was responsible for advocating it through his publications. In 1942, Rodale started *Organic Farming and Gardening* magazine, whose mission was to teach home gardeners and farmers how to grow food using organic techniques. In 1950, Rodale published *Prevention* magazine, which had an editorial mission to explore the connection between agriculture and health.

The concept of the bio-
dynamic French intensive
method of vegetable
gardening was brought to
the United States by Alan
Chadwick in the late 1960s.
He is credited for inspiring
the "California Cuisine"
movement.

"There is one rule in the garden that is above all others. You must give to nature more than you take. Obey it, and the earth will provide you in glorious abundance."

— Alan Chadwick

EVERYTHING OLD IS NEW AGAIN

Houseplants

Indoor gardening was popular in the '70s (both the 1870s and the 1970s!), so it's been a trend for a long time. But thanks to millennials, it's now one of the fastest-growing gardening segments.

PLANTS MOVE INDOORS

Houseplants have been part of home interiors almost since the beginning of human culture. There's evidence that ancient Romans and Greeks raised potted plants indoors. But the houseplant trend of today traces itself to 17th-century England, when Sir Hugh Plat wrote the first book on growing plants indoors: *The Garden of Eden*, published in 1653. In the mid-1800s, plant hunters scoured the jungles and brought exotic tropical species to England where enthusiastic gardeners and plant aficionados grew them in hot houses and conservatories.

GROWING UNDER GLASS

Terrariums and Wardian cases are glass enclosures that allow plant enthusiasts to grow little jungles inside a home. The glass helps trap humidity around the plants, which keeps tropical plants healthier. (Most houseplants are indigenous to the tropics or areas around the equator.) Growing under glass on a larger scale also became popular: Greenhouses and conservatories became part of people's homes and yards.

◀ Most houseplants are indigenous to the tropics or areas around the equator.

▼ Houseplants offer indoor gardeners many different options, regardless of space limits or types of light.

Plants infuse a home with nature, the ideal antidote for urban living. Many species, such as the snake plant, grow successfully in low light, making them ideal for homes and offices.

Hanging Succulent Terrarium

A garden under glass, a terrarium allows you to create a tiny jungle or a desert landscape in miniature. Planting with succulents, which require little water, makes this high-flying container garden as easy-care as it is beautiful.

YOU WILL NEED

Glass globe
hanging container

Sand

Potting soil
or compost

Small succulent plants,
such as sedum, hens-
and-chicks, and string
of pearls

Stones or gravel

1 Add a base layer of sand to the bottom of the container.
2 Add a layer of potting soil or compost on top of the sand.
3 Remove plants from plastic containers and snug them gently into the soil inside the globe.
4 Plant as many succulents as will fit in the globe.
5 Sprinkle a layer of stones or gravel over the soil for decoration.
NOTE The sand, soil, and gravel will make attractive stratified layers.

6 Suspend the hanging terrarium in a sunny window.

THE SELF-WATERING MAGIC OF A CLOSED TERRARIUM

Terrariums with tops require little care because they are almost self-watering. The plants release water vapor that collects on the glass walls, trickling back into the soil.

Even with open-top terrariums, you will need much less water than for other types of containers. And since terrariums don't have drain holes, it's important to not overwater.

▲ Succulents thrive in well-drained soil, so adding sand to your potting mix will improve drainage and plant health.

▲ Use a pencil, stick, or other narrow object to gently manipulate succulents and stones into place.

Fountain in a Planter

Fountains have been used as garden focal points for hundreds of years. The music made by moving water adds a dimension to the beauty and relaxation of a garden. A water source in the garden or landscape is also a wildlife attractant.

YOU WILL NEED

Plastic flowerpot

Scissors

Copper pipe (same width as the bubbler pump)

Concrete

Duct tape

Rubber stopper with cord hole (to fit the hole in the bottom of the large planting container)

4 large nails

Submersible recirculating bubbler pump

Waterproof caulk

Flexible tubing (to fit bubbler pump)

Large planting container

1 Cut a notch out of the plastic flowerpot to accommodate the copper pipe for the bubbler. Ask your local hardware store to bend the copper pipe 90 degrees.

2 Mix concrete according to manufacturer's directions. Position the copper pipe so it goes through the flowerpot's drainage hole and out the notch. Tape the rest of the notch to keep concrete from flowing out.

3 Fill with concrete, leaving enough head space for the rubber stopper and bubbler cord once it's placed in the large planting container. Push about 4 large nails through the sides of the flowerpot to keep the concrete from sliding out once it's turned upside down. Allow concrete to dry.

4 Tip the large container to one side, position the bubbler at the base, and run the cord through the drainage hole in the bottom.

5 Run the cord through the stopper hole and push the stopper into the hole of the large planting container, making sure it fits tight.

6 Squeeze caulking material around the stopper and press it into the hole. Allow the caulking material to dry.

7 Place the flowerpot with concrete and copper pipe upside down in the large planting container. Connect the bubbler to the copper pipe with the flexible tubing.

8 Fill the large container partway with water. Check for leaks. Fill to the top with water. You may need to cut off the top of the copper pipe to be at, or just below, the water surface.

9 Plug the bubbler into a power source.

NOTE Make sure to use a GFCI outdoor outlet.

THE GARDEN URN

In the 19th century, containers were decorative features in formal Italianate-style gardens throughout Europe. American gardeners replicated the European tradition by adding urns and decorative pots as focal points to their gardens.

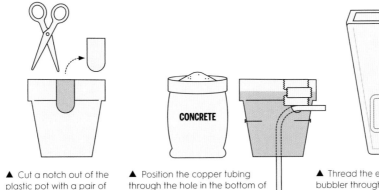

▲ Cut a notch out of the plastic pot with a pair of scissors.

▲ Position the copper tubing through the hole in the bottom of the pot. Place tape over remainder of notch. Fill the plastic pot with concrete and allow to dry.

▲ Thread the electrical cord from the bubbler through the bottom of the pot and secure with a stopper and caulk to make the container watertight. Connect the bubbler to the copper pipe with flexible tubing.

Butterfly Window Box

Pollinators, such as monarch and swallowtail butterflies, are an important part of our eco-system because they help distribute pollen, enabling seed production. Planting both food for larvae and nectar for adults creates a habitat for the stages of life for these winged wonders.

YOU WILL NEED

Window box at least 8 inches deep

Potting soil

Trowel

NECTAR-PRODUCING PLANTS

Lantana

Zinnia

Verbena

Marigold

Heliotrope

Salvia

LARVAL HOST PLANTS

Parsley

Dill

Fennel

Milkweed

1 Fill the window box to the top with potting soil. Make sure to use potting soil, not garden soil, which is too heavy and doesn't hold moisture as well as formulated potting soil.
2 Plant the taller plants, such as verbena, at the back of the window box.
3 Plant the shorter plants, such as parsley, at the front edge of the container.
4 Water plants well.
5 Avoid use of herbicides and pesticides to keep plants safe for butterflies and larvae.

NECTAR PLANTS AND HOST PLANTS
Each species of butterfly requires specific host plants. This means, for example, the black swallowtail butterfly will only lay eggs on dill, fennel, and parsley. Monarch butterflies will only lay eggs on milkweed (*Asclepias speciosa*). When the eggs hatch, the larvae eat the leaves of the plant. Choose nectar and host plants for your containers based on the type of butterflies you want to attract.

▲ To attract migrating monarch butterflies, grow fall-blooming asters and mums, which bloom when the insects pass through.

▲ Plant extra dill, fennel, or parsley in the garden so you have enough to share with black swallowtail larvae.

"If the bee disappeared off the surface of the globe, then man would have only four years of life left. No more bees, no more pollination, no more plants, no more animals, no more man."
— Albert Einstein

Planting a pollinator garden helps feed bees and other pollinators. Grow host plants for larvae and a wide variety of nectar-producing flowers to attract the most species of bees, butterflies, moths, and other insects.

Renee Shepherd

AMERICAN GARDENS SPROUTED NEW FLAVORS WHEN RENEE
SHEPHERD INTRODUCED SEEDS FROM AROUND THE WORLD. KITCHEN
GARDENERS WERE HUNGRY FOR NEW AND UNUSUAL VARIETIES. SHE HELPED
PIONEER FLAVORFUL AND COLORFUL NEW VEGETABLES AND HERBS.

▼ The Tri-Color Bean seed mix offers an ornamental and delicious selection of green, purple, and yellow beans.

▲ Custom-blended seed mixes allow gardeners to plant three different colors of beets from one seed packet.

INTERNATIONAL FLAVORS

Renee Shepherd had a good eye for beautiful crops and a discerning palate for new flavors. In 1985, she started Shepherd's Garden Seeds, a mail-order company that introduced gardeners to vegetable and herb varieties from around the world. She sold the company in 1996, then started Renee's Garden two years later. Located in Santa Cruz, Shepherd contributed to the sustainable food movement in Northern California, selling vegetable and herb seeds that connected the garden to the kitchen, a precursor to the garden-to-plate movement.

She traveled to Europe and Asia to source vegetable and herb seeds that appealed to American gardeners' interest in varieties that were beautiful, delicious, healthful—and different from what was available in the grocery. She created seed collections, such as Cut and Come Again Mesclun mix (colorful loose-leaf lettuces) and Tri-Color Bean (yellow, purple, and green pole beans). Her popular tri-color collections made it easy for gardeners to see which seeds were which; the seeds were dyed the color of the vegetable they sprouted into. These collections of vegetables and herbs inspired gardeners to cook and cooks to garden. To help connect the garden to the kitchen, Shepherd wrote three cookbooks to illustrate creative uses of the new varieties of herbs and vegetables that she supplied. Her first cookbook, *Recipes from a Kitchen Garden*, was published in 1993.

A MOMENT IN TIME

Edible Landscaping

Edible landscaping is a gardening concept in which traditional plants, such as turfgrass, trees, and shrubs, are replaced with plants that produce food, such as greens, herbs, and berry and fruiting shrubs and trees.

The practice of growing vegetables with flowers has been around for a long time. French parterre gardens from the 1800s featured vegetables growing inside primly cut boxwood hedges. But in America by mid-20th century, most vegetable gardens were relegated to the backyard or side yard, planted in rows with military precision. In the early 1980s, the concept of edible landscaping was popularized by Rosalind Creasy's book *The Complete Book of Edible Landscaping*. Vegetable-loving homeowners discovered how to replace traditional landscape plantings with equally beautiful, food-producing options.

PRETTY AND DELICIOUS
By mixing herbs, leafy and fruiting vegetables, and fruit-bearing trees into the landscape, you not only add color

Edible landscaping is also known as foodscaping, micro-homesteading, and front yard farming.

and texture to traditional garden design ways, but you do it with an edible twist. Greens such as spinach and arugula make beautiful bed or path edgers that can be planted in cool weather, harvested throughout the later spring, then replanted in the fall for a second crop. Dwarf varieties of peppers and tomatoes stay small and shrubby, intermixing with annual and perennial flowers in garden beds or containers. Their ripening fruit adds pops of color. Edible

▲ Mixing colorful vegetable crops, such as tomatoes and squash, into flower and land-scape borders allows you grow edibles in unexpected places.

▶ Choose varieties that are especially showy, such as 'Bright Lights' Swiss chard, whose leaves and stalks are as delicious as they are beautiful.

▼ Apple trees, as well as other fruit trees, provide shade and structure in a landscape as well as flowers in spring and colorful fruit in summer and autumn.

groundcovers include strawberries (which produce both red and white fruits) as well as low-growing or prostrate-form herbs, such as thyme and rosemary. Fruit-producing shrubs, such as blueberries, make attractive foundation plantings that also produce berries in summer. Fruit trees, such as apples, pears, and citrus, come in several sizes, making them scalable to any lot size; some can even be grown in large containers. Fruits, such as apples, can be trained to grow flat against a building or fence in a centuries-old pruning method called espalier. Asian pear trees have a columnar growth habit and can fit in a small yard, producing large, round, crisp fruits.

BEAUTIFUL VEGETABLES

Old and new vegetable varieties offer color and texture to gardens and landscapes. Rainbow Swiss chard features striking red, yellow, and orange stems topped with glossy green leaves; both stems and leaves are edible. Cabbage and kale varieties come in many colors—red, burgundy, white, and pink—and look as beautiful as flowers in garden beds. Herbs, such as variegated sage, standard rosemary trees, and purple basil, make beautiful and edible additions in containers and window boxes. Perennial herbs, such as chives and borage, provide flowers that can be sprinkled into salads and soups, adding color and flavor.

PLANT DIVERSITY AND SEASONAL APPEAL

By interplanting edible plants amid your other landscape plantings, you create biodiversity in your yard. The more species of plants you have in your yard, the more pollinators you will attract. Plus, many food-bearing species also offer seasonal interest to the landscape. For example, serviceberry *(Amelanchier alnifolia)* is an understory tree that offers white flowers in spring, purple berries in summer (get them before the birds do), and golden foliage in autumn.

▲ Use purple basil in beds, borders, and containers as a plant with beautiful, bold foliage that's also edible. Leaves have a spicy, clovelike flavor and scent.

Vegetables and fruits raised as close as your front yard get high marks from supporters of the locavore movement.

The front yard of edible landscaping expert Rosalind Creasy is a colorful mix of flowers, vegetables, and herbs.

A MOMENT IN TIME

Seed Sharers

Thanks to avid seed collectors, sharers, and preservers, rare and underplanted heirloom plants are collected and stored so that generations to come can savor the flavors of produce from the past.

Plants, just like animals, can become endangered and go extinct. Although most folks are aware of animals on the endangered species list, few are aware that plants can also become extinct. In fact many varieties of vegetables, flowers, and fruits that are no longer sold have silently slipped into oblivion because no one produces seeds or plants them anymore.

WHY SOME PLANTS AREN'T AVAILABLE ANYMORE

There are many reasons that plant variety seeds sold in seed catalogs for decades are no longer available. Like all inventions, some seeds were made obsolete by newer, better versions. In the latter part of the 20th century, hybrid plants were developed by commercial plant breeders, and many of those varieties replaced older nonhybrid seed varieties. (Seeds from hybrid plants can be sterile and will not produce duplicates of their parent plants, so farmers needed to buy new seeds every year.) But some varieties just went out of fashion, like hats or shoes. So by a series of improvements and lack of interest, some varieties simply became extinct.

PLANT EXTINCTION

It's a worldwide problem. Nearly 600 varieties of plants around the world have gone extinct since the 1750s. According to an article by Charles Siebert in the July 2011 *National Geographic*, "Food varieties extinction is happening all over the world—and it's happening fast. In the United States an estimated 90 percent of our historic fruit and vegetable varieties have vanished. Of the 7,000 apple varieties that were grown in the 1800s, fewer than a hundred remain." Unfortunately, food diversity is limited by

▲ 'Grandpa Ott' morning glory was one of the first seeds saved by the Seed Savers Exchange in Decorah, Iowa.

◄ Saving seeds helps keep unusual native species, such as *Echinacea paradoxa* (yellow coneflower) in cultivation.

grocery store space where only a few varieties, rather than hundreds, can be sold.

HOW SEED SHARERS HELP

Seed collectors and sharers have helped to preserve some of the home garden varieties that may have otherwise gone extinct. Seed libraries and exchanges allow home gardeners to share seeds, thereby helping preserve certain gardening traditions as well as keeping biodiversity among certain types of plants strong. Seed banks are storehouses of genetic diversity that may help provide plant options that preserve our heritage and feed increasing populations and may also help us face future gardening challenges due to changing climate conditions, such as droughts.

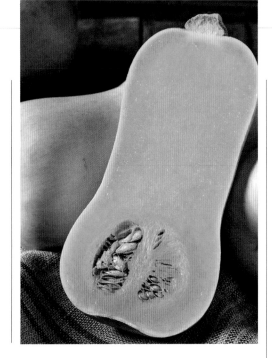

◄ Home gardeners can save seeds from fruits and vegetables, such as melons and squash, to plant in next year's garden.

SEED SAVERS EXCHANGE

The Seed Savers Exchange in Decorah, Iowa, has helped conserve and promote many endangered garden and food crops. This nonprofit group is one of the largest nongovernmental seed banks in the United States. It helps link and create a community of gardeners who collect, grow, and share heirloom seeds. Seed Savers was started in 1975 by Diane and Kent Whealy with two heirloom seeds from Diane's great-grandfather, who brought seeds to America from Bavaria in 1884. A purple and rose morning glory called 'Grandpa Ott' and a beefsteak-type tomato called 'German Pink' were the first seeds in the Seed Savers Exchange, which is now the world's largest seed exchange.

"We can only preserve heirloom seeds through active stewardship. If we don't use them, if we don't allow them to grow again, they become lost." —*Diane Ott Whealy*

◄ Saving and sharing seeds helps gardeners save money but also helps ensure species diversity and quality.

EVERYTHING OLD IS NEW AGAIN

Heirlooms

Heirloom fruits, vegetables, and flowers are like family heirlooms; they've been around for a while and are lovingly handed down for generations. Heirloom varieties offer flavors, shapes, and colors not found in commercially grown produce.

WHAT IS AN HEIRLOOM?

Heirlooms are old varieties, yet "old" is up for debate. Some folks say that heirloom varieties must be at least 50 years old. Others say 100 years old. Others say they simply need to predate World War II, after which hybrids started coming into vogue. The one thing that everyone agrees on is that heirlooms are open-pollinated (which means they are naturally pollinated by wind or insects) and that they grow true from seed. Hybrid varieties can't be grown true from seed because they are crossbred and may not look or produce like their parent plant; some seeds collected from hybrid plants can actually be sterile.

HEIRLOOM BENEFITS

For the home gardener, heirloom varieties represent an opportunity to grow unique food that may not appear in grocery stores. Lack of uniformity, short shelf life, and inconsistent appearance are why varieties of heirloom fruits and vegetables aren't mass produced. Heirlooms are also a link to the past and a walk down memory lane to flavor. Heirlooms also solve some regional gardening problems. For example, the Southern-bred 'Arkansas Traveler' tomato has crack-resistant skin, an important characteristic for hot, humid, and dry Southern summers. Heirlooms also help create biodiversity in our food supply. The more varieties of vegetables, the less likely it will be that an event like the potato famine in Ireland will recur. The famine occurred because the one variety of potato grown was susceptible to the potato blight disease, producing catastrophic crop failure.

▲ Heirloom carrots come in all shapes, sizes, and colors. Heirlooms are open-pollinated, meaning they grow true from seed.

▶ Soil, climate, and region help dictate what variety of heirloom potatoes you can grow in your garden.

Heirloom tomatoes represent a diverse category that ranges from tiny cherry tomatoes to hefty beefsteak types, such as 'Pink Brandywine', a tomato that dates back to 1885. Tomato aficionados say that heirlooms have the best flavor.

Hanging Tomato Basket

Go vertical with your tomato garden. A deep hanging planter allows you to enjoy harvests of cherry tomatoes on your deck or patio. Tomatoes need at least 6 to 8 hours of sun a day, so hang them in a sunny spot.

YOU WILL NEED

Hanging basket

Potting soil

Trowel

Cherry tomato plants, such as heirloom 'Black Cherry' or hybrid 'Super Sweet 100'

Tumbling cherry tomato plants, such as 'Rambling Gold Stripe' or 'Tumbling Tom'

1 Make sure your hanging basket has drain holes in the bottom. Then fill the basket with potting soil.

2 Pop the tomato plants from their growing pots. Dig a small hole in the potting mixture with a trowel or your hand and insert the plant into the hole. Use one plant per basket.

3 Water plants well. Continue to water daily, keeping the soil moist but not wet. Tomatoes like consistent moisture. **Note:** Hanging planters need to be watered more often than gardens planted in the ground.

4 Harvest tomatoes when they are the appropriate color for their variety.

HOW TOMATOES PRODUCE

Tomatoes come in two types based on how they produce fruit. Indeterminate varieties set fruit and continue to produce all summer until frost. Determinate varieties produce fruit all at once, then stop fruiting. Most cherry tomatoes are vining, indeterminate varieties.

▲ Choose trailing tomato varieties that are developed for growing in containers.

Heirloom Potatoes in a Bag

You don't need garden space to grow spuds. You can garden in a bag on your deck or patio. Pick a sunny spot and grow small colorful heirloom species that are fun to harvest and so tasty when eaten fresh from the garden.

YOU WILL NEED

Growing bag with drainage holes

Potting soil and compost

Small fingerling seed potatoes, such as 'Russian Banana,' 'Austrian Crescent,' 'Purple Peruvian,' 'Rose Finn Apple,' and 'Purple Majesty'

1 Roll down the top of the bag to about one-third. Fill 4 inches deep with a mix of potting soil and compost.

2 Cut seed potatoes into pieces, making sure each one has an "eye." If potatoes are small, plant the entire potato. Set seed potatoes into the bag on top of the soil.

3 Add 3 inches of soil on top of the potatoes.

4 Water the bag. Keep soil moist, not wet.

5 When potato foliage has grown about 8 inches tall, add 4 more inches of soil. Potatoes will grow along the buried stems. Repeat until the entire bag is filled with soil.

6 When the leaves turn yellow at the end of the season, dump the bag into a wheelbarrow and remove the potatoes.

POTATOES IN AMERICA

Potatoes are indigenous to South America and have been grown there for 10,000 years. Potatoes were introduced to America through many sources and became a crop for colonists because they were easy to grow and were high in calories and nutrients.

▲ Use seed potatoes, not potatoes from the grocery store. Seed potatoes are certified disease-free and don't have sprout growth inhibitors.

▲ Plant potatoes several inches from the top of the bag. Keep adding more soil and compost as they grow.

▲ Keep potatoes watered during the growing season. But don't overwater; the tubers will rot in too-wet soil.

Saving Bean Seeds

Beans produce large seeds that are easy to collect, store, and replant. Choose heirloom varieties, which grow true to seed (unlike hybrid seed). Saving seeds from your garden allows you to plant the best producers—plus, it's free seed.

YOU WILL NEED

Dried seeds in shells

Pruners

Envelopes

Pen

1 Allow the pods to completely dry on the plant. (Choose a couple of plants for seed saving and harvest the others for eating.)
2 Remove the pods from the plant.
3 Allow them to dry in a cool spot for 2 weeks.
4 Remove the beans from the pods.
5 Place bean seeds in an envelope marked with the name, variety, and year.
6 Store seeds in a cool, dry place. Replant the following spring.
NOTE Bean seeds are generally viable up to 4 years.

HEIRLOOM BEAN SEEDS

Growing heirloom beans allows you to taste the flavors of the world from time-tested varieties that taste delicious (that's why gardeners keep harvesting and replanting seed for generations).

Heirloom bean varieties are as colorful as they are diverse. Try black-and-white vaquero, brown speckled Anasazi, and purple-tinged borlotti (cranberry) beans.

▲ Slit open the pod and run your thumb down the length to remove the seeds.

▲ Store bean seeds in envelopes marked with their variety name and the date harvested.

"My special cause, the one that alerts my interest and quickens the pace of my life, is to preserve the wildflowers and native plants that define the regions of our land—to encourage and promote their use in appropriate areas and thus help pass on to generations in waiting the quiet joys and satisfactions I have known since my childhood."

— Lady Bird Johnson

Native plants are indigenous to a specific region. Gardeners find these plants easy to grow because they evolved to exist in a specific environment.

This colorful bioswale was designed by Claudia West for North Creek Nurseries outside Landenberg, Pennsylvania.

Contemporaries

The future of landscaping will become wilder and more ecologically conscious. Gardeners who feature a mixture of plants in planting communities will reflect what Mother Nature had in mind all along.

▲ Thomas Rainer at Phyto Studio is a landscape architect, teacher, and author living in Arlington, Virginia. His ecological landscape designs appear throughout the country.

Inspired by the way nature organizes the landscape, Thomas Rainer, a landscape architect and partner in Phyto Studio in Washington, D.C., designs gardens that are wilder and rangier than the gardens that have graced homes in the past century, reflecting a trend toward a more natural approach. Rainer has worked on large landscape projects on the U.S. Capitol grounds, the Martin Luther King, Jr. Memorial, and in the New York Botanical Garden.

FOLLOWING NATURE'S LEAD

City and suburban areas have been tamed into swaths of lawns and orderly gardens. It is Rainer's goal to bring back some of nature's wildness to cities and neighborhoods, making gardens and landscapes more diverse, more rambunctious, and more natural. Phyto Studio's landscape design philosophy is to follow what Mother Nature does so well throughout the world. All landscapes, from dense forests to open grasslands, are

> # "The big shift in horticulture in the next decade will be a shift from thinking about plants as individual objects to communities of interrelated species."
>
> *— Thomas Rainer*

comprised of plants that fill their space naturally; tall plants intermix with low-growing plants to create an ecosystem. The species that occupy the same space are natural plant communities that support each other. This is the new garden design: one part wildness, one part ecology, one part beauty.

NATURE FILLS A VOID

In the wild parts of the world, nature fills a void. "Think about seeing plants in the wild: There is almost never bare soil. With the exceptions of deserts or other extreme environments, bare soil is a temporary condition. Yet in our gardens and landscapes, bare ground is everywhere," Rainer says in his book, *Planting in a Post-Wild World*, published in 2015 and co-authored with horticulturalist and partner, Claudia West. His design philosophy follows the same path as nature, filling space with plants that work together. This natural method of gardening is also low-maintenance, because weeds have a hard time gaining a roothold in densely planted areas.

NATURAL HORTICULTURE

With so little actual wild nature left in the world, Rainer's gardening design philosophy helps add wildness back into the world. His book reveals how home gardeners can incorporate gardening rules made by nature in their own yards, thereby creating natural-looking landscapes that are ecologically appropriate, aesthetically beautiful, and, consequently, low-maintenance. Phyto Studio's design philosophy bridges nature with traditional horticulture.

▲ Massed plants in a Rainer perennial border

SOCIABILITY MODEL

Rainer recommends massing plants using a sociability model. Low socializers are generally tall, so plant these in small clumps of 3 to 10. More-social plants, such as groundcovers, can be planted in larger groups.

◀ In a Phyto Studio design by Claudia West, a series of bioretention facilities in Lancaster, Pennsylvania, uses more than 20 plant species to create a dense and beautiful border.

Credits

CRAFTS

14 (UP RT), Berents/Shutterstock; 14 (LO LE), Gift of Herbert Waide Hemphill, Jr. and museum purchase made possible by Ralph Cross Johnson/Smithsonian American Art Museum; 14–15 (LO CTR), Library of Congress, Prints & Photographs Division LC-USZ62-98906/Underwood & Underwood; 15 (UP RT), Princeton University Posters Collection, 1906-1950, Archives Center/National Museum of American History; 16 (UP LE), Strakovskaya/Shutterstock; 16–17 (LO), Iwanami Photos/Shutterstock; 17 (UP RT), Unknown/National Air and Space Museum Archives; 18 (UP RT), Hekla/Shutterstock; 18 (LO LE), Everett Historical/Shutterstock; 18–19 (LO RT), Michael Warwick/Shutterstock; 20 (LO LE), Courtesy Quilters Hall of Fame; 20 (LO CTR), Public Domain; 20 (LO RT), Public Domain/Wikimedia Commons; 21 (LO LE), Webster Collection, Gift of Rosalind Webster Perry, 2014.108/Indianapolis Museum of Art at Newfields; 21 (LO RT), Public Domain; 22 (UP LE), Pitkin Studio/Art Resource, NY; 22–23 (UP LE), Pitkin Studio/Art Resource, NY; 22 (LO LE), Pitkin Studio/Art Resource, NY; 22–23 (LO LE), Pitkin Studio/Art Resource, NY; 22–23 (LO RT), Pitkin Studio/Art Resource, NY; 23 (UP RT), Public Domain/Wikimedia Commons; 24 (LO LE), Archives Center/Cooper Hewitt, Smithsonian Design Museum; 24 (LO RT), Gift of Mrs. Margaret Seamans Birch/National Museum of American History; 25 (CTR), Tara Faughnan; 26 (UP LE), Gift of Miss Olive E. Hurlburt/National Museum of American History; 26 (LO CTR), Gift of Mr. and Mrs. Thomas J. White/National Museum of American History; 26–27 (CTR), Gift of Eugene A. Teter and Martha Brown Teter/National Museum of American History; 26 (LO LE), Museum purchase through the Barbara Coffey Quilt Endowment/Smithsonian American Art Museum; 26 (LO CTR), Gift of Mr. and Mrs. H. M. Heckman/National Museum of American History; 26–27 (LO RT), Gift of Mary Dickson Shrycock/National Museum of American History; 27 (UP RT), Gift of the Misses Lorraine J. and Norma O. Soher./National Museum of American History; 27 (UP RT), Gift of Mrs. Mary Harding Renshaw/ National Museum of American History; 27 (LO CTR), Gift of Mr. Stewart Dickson/National Museum of American History; 27 (LO RT), Gift of Dr. Carrie Harrison/National Museum of American History; 28 (UP LE), Waterbury Publications Inc.; 28 (UP RT), Waterbury Publications Inc.; 28 (LO LE), Waterbury Publications Inc.; 29 (CTR), Waterbury Publications Inc.; 31 (CTR), Waterbury Publications, inc.; 32 (CTR), Roman Samborskyi/Shutterstock; 34 (UP RT), Gift of Gerald G. Stiebel and Penelope Hunter-Stiebel/Cooper Hewitt, Smithsonian Design Museum; 34–35 (LO), donatas1205/Shutterstock; 34 (LO LE), Gift of Donna Limerick/Smithsonian National Museum of African American History and Culture; 35 (UP RT), Isaac M. Singer/National Museum of American History; 36 (LO LE), Bequest of Richard Cranch Greenleaf in memory of his mother, Adeline Emma Greenleaf/Cooper Hewitt, Smithsonian Design Museum; 36 (LO CTR), Gift of Mary Walker Phillips/Cooper Hewitt, Smithsonian Design Museum; 36 (LO RT), Rianne Aarts, Teddy and Wool; 37 (CTR), Rianne Aarts; 38 (UP RT), George Rinhart/Getty; 38 (LO LE), Archives Center/National Museum of American History; 38–39 (LO RT), Public Domain/National Archives Catalog; 39 (UP RT), Public Domain/National Archives Catalog; 40 (UP CTR RT), Waterbury Publications, Inc.; 40 (UP CTR LE), Waterbury Publications, Inc.; 40 (LO CTR RT), Waterbury Publications, Inc.; 40 (LO CTR LE), Waterbury Publications, Inc.; 40 (UP LE), Waterbury Publications, Inc.; 40 (UP RT), Waterbury Publications, Inc.; 40 (LO LE), Waterbury Publications, Inc.; 40 (LO RT), Waterbury Publications, Inc.; 41 (CTR), Waterbury Publications, Inc.; 42 (CTR), Waterbury Publications, Inc.; 44 (UP LE), Waterbury Publications, Inc.; 44 (UP CTR RT), Waterbury Publications, Inc.; 44 (UP RT), Waterbury Publications, Inc.; 44 (CTR LE), Waterbury Publications, Inc.; 44 (CTR), Waterbury Publications, Inc.; 44 (CTR RT), Waterbury Publications, Inc.; 44 (LO LE), Waterbury Publications, Inc.; 45 (UP LE), Waterbury Publications, Inc.; 45 (UP CTR), Waterbury Publications, Inc.; 45 (UP RT), Waterbury Publications, Inc.; 45 (LO LE), Waterbury Publications, Inc.; 45 (LO RT), Waterbury Publications, Inc.; 46 (LO LE), Debbie Patterson; 46 (LO RT), Debbie Patterson; 46–47 (LO RT), Debbie Patterson; 47 (UP RT), Debbie Patterson; 48 (LO CTR), Chris Hellier/Alamy; 49 (UP RT), Museum purchase through the Samuel and Blanche Koffler Acquisition Fund/Smithsonian American Art Museum; 49 (LO LE), US Department of the Interior/Smithsonian Institute; 49 (LO CTR), Gift of Orren and Marilyn Bradley and Kohler Foundation, Inc./Smithsonian American Art Museum; 49 (LO RT), Imagno/Getty; 50 (UP CTR), The Josef and Anni Albers Foundation/Artists Rights Society (ARS), New York Photo: Tim Nighswander/Artist Rights Society; 50 (LO CTR), The Josef and Anni Albers Foundation/Artists Rights Society (ARS), New York Photo: Tim Nighswander/Artist Rights Society; 51 (UP LE), The Josef and Anni Albers Foundation/Artists Rights Society (ARS), New York Photo: Tim Nighswander/Artist Rights Society; 51 (UP RT), Courtesy of the Josef and Ani Albers Foundation; 51 (LO LE), The Josef and Anni Albers Foundation/Artists Rights Society (ARS), New York Photo: Tim Nighswander/Artist Rights Society; 52 (LO LE), Gift of Laura Dreyfus Barney and Natalie Clifford Barney in memory of the mother, Alice Pike Barney/Smithsonian American Art Museum; 52 (LO CTR), Gift of Myra and William H. Mathers/Cooper Hewitt, Smithsonian Design Museum; 52 (LO RT), Bequest of Gertrude M. Oppenheimer/Cooper Hewitt, Smithsonian Design Museum; 53 (CTR), Vika Levkina with Anne Mills/Shutterstock; 55 (CTR), Waterbury Publications Inc.; 56 (CTR), Waterbury Publication, Inc.; 58 (CTR RT), Courtesy the Harrison-Small Special Collections Library, University of Virginia, and 'Mark Twain In His Times: An Electronic Archive; 58 (LO LE), Courtesy the Harrison-Small Special Collections Library, University of Virginia, and 'Mark Twain In His Times: An Electronic Archive; 58 (LO RT), Everett Historical/Shutterstock; 59 (RT), Courtesy the Harrison-Small Special Collections Library, University of Virginia, and 'Mark Twain In His Times: An Electronic Archive; 59 (LO), Courtesy the Harrison-Small Special Collections Library, University of Virginia, and 'Mark Twain In His Times: An Electronic Archive; 60 (UP LE), Archives Center/National Museum of American History; 60 (UP RT), Archives Center/National Museum of American History; 60–61 (UP RT), Archives Division/National Air and Space Museum Archives; 60 (CTR LE), Archives Center/National Museum of American History; 60 (CTR), Archives of American Art/Smithsonian Institute; 60 (LO LE), Smithsonian Institute/National Air and Space Museum Archives; 60–61 (LO RT), Archives of American Art/Smithsonian Institute; 61 (UP CTR), Archives Center/National Museum of American History; 61 (UP RT), Mr. Yamada/National Air and Space Museum Archives; 61 (LO LE), Gift of Dr. Julie Silver/National Museum of American History; 61 (LO RT), Archives of American Art/ Smithsonian Institute; 62 (UP RT), Mostovyi Sergii Igorevich/Shutterstock; 62 (LO LE), Archives Center/ National Museum of American History; 62–63 (LO RT), Archives Center/National Museum of American History; 64–65 (LE), KingaPhoto/Shutterstock; 64 (LO LE), Binney and Smith/National Museum of American History; 64 (LO LE), Keith Homan/Shutterstock; 64 (LO CTR), Lambert/Getty; 65 (UP RT), Unknown; 66 (LO LE), Gift of Ira Blount/Anacostia Community Museum; 66 (LO RT), Gift of Ira Blount/ Anacostia Community Museum; 67 (CTR), Hiromi Moneyhun; 68–69 (CTR), Michael Loccisano/Getty for The Michaels Companies; 70 (LO LE), Bonchan/Shutterstock; 70 (LO CTR), Bonchan/Shutterstock; 70 (LO RT), Jessica Marquez; 71 (CTR), Jessica Marquez; 73 (CTR), Jessica Marquez; 74 (CTR), Waterbury Publications, Inc.; 77 (CTR), Waterbury Publications Inc.; 78 (LE), Gift of Patricia L. Harris/ Cooper Hewitt, Smithsonian Design Museum; 78–79 (LE), Gift of Patricia L. Harris/Cooper Hewitt, Smithsonian Design Museum; 78 (CTR LE), Gift of Patricia L. Harris/Cooper Hewitt, Smithsonian Design Museum; 78–79 (CTR), Patpitchaya/Shutterstock; 78 (CTR), Gift of Patricia L. Harris/Cooper Hewitt, Smithsonian Design Museum; 78 (CTR RT), Gift of Patricia L. Harris/Cooper Hewitt, Smithsonian Design Museum; 78–79 (RT), Gift of Patricia L. Harris/Cooper Hewitt, Smithsonian Design Museum; 79 (CTR LE), Gift of Patricia L. Harris/Cooper Hewitt, Smithsonian Design Museum; 79 (CTR), Gift of Patricia L. Harris/Cooper Hewitt, Smithsonian Design Museum; 79 (CTR RT), Gift of Patricia L. Harris/ Cooper Hewitt, Smithsonian Design Museum; 79 (RT), Gift of Patricia L. Harris/Cooper Hewitt, Smithsonian Design Museum; 80–81 (UP LE), The Modern Quilt Guild; 80 (LO LE), The Modern Quilt Guild; 81 (UP RT), The Modern Quilt Guild; 81 (LO LE), The Modern Quilt Guild

COOKING & FOOD

84 (UP), Everett Historical/Shutterstock; 84 (LO LE), Lagui/Shutterstock; 85 (UP RT), Jeffrey B. Banke/Shutterstock; 85 (LO LE), L.E. Leininger/National Museum of American History; 86 (LO LE), GraphicaArtis/Getty; 86 (LO RT), ZUMA Press, Inc./Alamy; 87 (CTR), Brad Barket/Stringer/Getty; 89 (CTR), Waterbury Publication, Inc.; 90–91 (LE), Michael Snell/Alamy; 90 (LO LE), North Wind Picture Archives/Alamy; 92 (CTR), Waterbury Publication, Inc.; 94 (LO LE), Waterbury Publication, Inc.; 94 (LO RT), Waterbury Publication, Inc.; 95 (CTR), Waterbury Publication, Inc.; 96 (LE), Waterbury Publication, Inc.; 96 (CTR LE), Waterbury Publication, Inc.; 96 (CTR RT), Waterbury Publication, Inc.; 96 (RT), Waterbury Publication, Inc.; 97 (CTR), Waterbury Publication, Inc.; 98 (CTR), Waterbury Publication, Inc.; 99 (LO LE), Waterbury Publication, Inc.; 101 (CTR), Waterbury Publication, Inc.; 102 (CTR), Waterbury Publication, Inc.; 104 (UP RT), United States Library of Congress's Prints and Photographs; 104 (LO LE), Archives Center/National Museum of American History; 105 (CTR), lidante/ Shutterstock; 106 (LO LE), Waterbury Publication, Inc.; 106 (LO CTR), Waterbury Publication, Inc.; 106 (LO RT), Waterbury Publication, Inc.; 107 (CTR), Waterbury Publication, Inc.; 108 (LE), Waterbury Publication, Inc.; 108 (CTR LE), Waterbury Publication, Inc.; 108 (CTR RT), Waterbury Publication, Inc.; 108 (RT), Waterbury Publication, Inc.; 109 (CTR), Waterbury Publication, Inc.; 111 (CTR), Zagor Inna/ Shutterstock; 113 (CTR), Waterbury Publication, Inc.; 114 (CTR), Waterbury Publication, Inc.; 117 (CTR), Waterbury Publication, Inc.; 118 (UP RT), American Stock Archive/Getty; 118 (LO LE), National Archives and Records Administration; 118–119 (LO RT), Everett Historical/Shutterstock; 120 (CTR), Waterbury Publication, Inc.; 123 (CTR), Waterbury Publication, Inc.; 124–125 (CTR), Alina Yudina/Shutterstock; 124 (LO LE), Bettmann/Getty; 124 (LO RT), Public Domain; 126 (LO LE), Chronicle/Alamy; 126 (LO RT), kcline/Getty; 127 (LO CTR), William Gottlieb/Getty; 128 (CTR), Waterbury Publication, Inc.; 130 (LO RT), Gorodenkoff/Shutterstock; 131 (LO), Courtesy Thermo King; 133 (CTR), Waterbury Publication, Inc.; 134 (CTR), Waterbury Publication, Inc.; 135 (LO LE), Waterbury Publication, Inc.; 135 (LO CTR),

Index